Abstracts of the
TESTAMENTARY PROCEEDINGS
of the
PREROGATIVE COURT OF MARYLAND

Volume VII: 1693–1697

Libers: 15B, 15C, 16

by
V. L. Skinner, Jr.

CLEARFIELD

Printed for
Clearfield Company, Inc., by
Genealogical Publishing Co., Inc.
Baltimore, Maryland
2006

International Standard Book Number: 0-8063-5311-2

Made in the United States of America

INTRODUCTION

Purpose of the Prerogative Court.

The Prerogative Court was the central point for probate for Provincial Maryland. It was mirrored after the Prerogative Court of Canterbury. There was a judge as well as clerk(s) of the court. Initially, all probate was brought directly to the Prerogative Court, located in the Provincial Capital. As the Province became more populous, all documents were still to be filed with the Prerogative Court; however, administration of probate was delegated to the various county courts. Even so, there are documents only in the Prerogative Court and not in the appropriate county, and vice versa.

Documents filed in the Prerogative Court.

The following documents were filed in the Prerogative Court: administration bond, will, inventory, administration accounts, and final balances. The testamentary proceedings contain the administration bond and the docket for the court. If the administrator is lax in filing documents, then a summons is also recorded.

Equity Court

The Prerogative Court was also the court for equity cases--resolution of disputes over the settlement and distribution of an estate. The case was brought before the judge and could take several years to resolve. Often depositions were taken and recorded in the minutes.

Notes on the Abstraction.

1. The left hand column contains the liber/folio number. The folio numbers are presented just as they appear in the actual document, e.g., 32a, 78½.

2. The right hand column contains the abstraction text.

3. Various libers specify a particular session for the Prerogative Court, e.g., 1678; or, September Court 1742. This information is presented as "Court Session:" followed by the

appropriate session. Should no session have been specified, then the phrase "no date" is used.

4. An ellipsis (...) is used to indicate a continuation of the previous information, but no relevant genealogical information is present.

5. The following symbols are used in the abstraction:

?   difficult to read.
\#   pounds of tobacco.
!   [sic].

Abbreviations.

The following abbreviations have been used throughout this abstraction:

AA - Anne Arundel Co.
ACC - Accomac Co.
BA - Baltimore Co.
CE - Cecil Co.
CH - Charles Co.
CR - Caroline Co.
CV - Calvert Co.
dbn - de bonis non
DE - Delaware
DO - Dorchester Co.
ENG - England
FR - Frederick Co.
g - gentleman
HA - Harford Co.
IRE - Ireland
KE - Kent Co. MD
KEDE - Kent Co. DE
LaC - letters ad colligendum (for temporary collection & preservation of assets)
LoA - letters of administration
MA - Massachusetts
MD - Maryland
MO - Montgomery Co.
NE - New England
NEI - "non est inventar" (not found)
NY - New York
NYC - New York City
p - planter
PA - Pennsylvania
PG - Prince George's Co.
PoA - power of attorney
QA - Queen Anne's Co.
SM - St. Mary's Co.
SMC - St. Mary's City
SO - Somerset Co.
TA - Talbot Co.
VA - Virginia
WA - Washington Co.
WO - Worcester Co.

This volume is a continuation of the series, covering 1693 to 1697. After the Glorious Revolution, the official in charge of the Orphan's Court in each of the various counties became the Deputy Commissary for that county. With this designation begins the delegation of authority for processing general probate to the county courts. Numerous outstanding equity cases are tried. Liber 16 has various Calvert Co. probate proceedings.

15B:1   **14 September.** Mr. John Bearecroft (SM) exhibited oath of Thomas Carvile & Edward Tipton, appraisers of John Tyrling (SM), sworn 4 July 1692.

Anne Medley wife of William Medley (SM) vs. estate of George Reynolds (SM). Caveat exhibited.

3 October. Elias King (KE) exhibited that Hester Benton widow of Mark Benton (KI) was granted administration on his estate. Appraisers: Lewis Meradith, John Doynes. Date: 15 September 1692 at Yarmouth.

7 October. Garrat Murry & his wife Susanna only surviving issue of William Brockhus (CE) vs. Edward Jones (CE). Summons to answer libel.

20 October. Ebenezar Blakiston (sheriff, CE) exhibited above as "Non est inventor".

22 October. Exhibited will of Fobby Roberts (supposed dead, absent for about 20 years), proved. Thomas Courtney (SM) & his wife Eleanor (one of co-heirs) were granted administration.

John Hynson (KE) one of executors of Joseph Wicks (KE) petitioned for new LoA. Mentions: other surviving executor is Robert Burman.

15B:2   **29 October.** Thomas Tench, Esq. (AA) was granted administration on estate of George Hawes (CV), as principle creditor. Appraisers: MM Thomas Tasker, Thomas Greenfeild. Thomas Brooke, Esq. to administer oath.

Mr. Robert Burman one of executors of Joseph Wicks vs. Mr. John Hynson other executor of said Wicks. Said Hynson summoned.

31 October. Col. Edward Pye (g) administrator of Col. Benjamin Rozer was summoned to render accounts.

Mordecai Moore & his wife Ursula
executrix of Col. William Burges
executor of Nicholas Painter who married
Judith Parker (alias Judith Cumber)
executrix of John Cumber was summoned to
answer complaint of John Cumber
grandchild of said Cumber.

10 November. William Serjeant & his
wife Damoras executrix of John Ward were
summoned to answer complaint of Edward
Millstead & his wife Elisabeth one of
daughters of said Ward.

Edward Pye (g, CH) was summoned to
answer complaint of Roger Brooke & his
wife Mary executrix of Winifred Mullet.

24 November. Sheriff (SM) to summon:
- Edward Morgan executor of John
  Evans.
- John Bullock executor of Lionell
  Oakley.
- James Swann administrator of
- Thomas Orman & his wife Penelope
  executrix of John Tong.
- Kath. OBryan administratrix of Bryan
  OBryan.
- Elisabeth Brimmer administratrix of
  James Brimmer.
- John VanReswick & his wife Frances
  executrix of Christopher Goodson.
- Michael Curtis & his wife Sarah
  executrix of Jus. Gerard.
- Thomas Gwither administrator of
  Morgan Prance.
- James Cullen executor of Nicholas
  White.
- Elisabeth Portwood administratrix of
  John Portwood.
- Francis Greene & Thomas Clark
  executors of Leonard Greene.
- James Browne & his wife
  administratrix of Thomas Pue.
- Thomas Griffin administrator of
  Thomas Griffin.
- Edward Morgan executor of John
  Evans.
- Philip Lynes administrator of
  William Haughton.
- Thomas Waughob administrator of
  Robert Graham.

15B:3 Sheriff (CH) to summon:
- Philip Hoskins & his wife administratrix of Margaret Lemaire.
- John Godshall administrator of Mary Weyman.
- Robert Thompson, Jr. administrator of Thomas Elwes.
- Anne Burford executrix of Thomas Burford.
- John Bracher administrator of Hugh Thomas.
- Robert Benson administrator of John Francis.
- Richard Isles administrator of Domindigo Agambra.
- William Moss administrator of John Clark.
- Anne Slade administratrix of George Gore.

Sheriff (CV) to summon:
-
- John Holloway & his wife executrix of John Vines.
- Hugh Montgomery & his wife executrix of George Parker.
- George Plowden administrator of Robert Thompson.
- Sarah Winfen administratrix of James Winfen.
- Benjamin Evans & his wife Sarah administratrix of William Rout.
- Francis Collier & his wife Sarah administratrix of John Evans.
- Rebecca Finch administratrix of guy Finch.
- Margaret Moore administratrix of William Moore.
- Sarah Waring et. al. executors of Basil Waring.
- Henry Mitchell administrator of Charles Parvy.
- Richard Leake & his wife executrix of Daniel Bloyd.
- Nicholas Sewall executor of Martha Pinnock.
- Darby Sullivan executor of John Dew.
- Thomas Johnson & his wife administratrix of Roger Baker.
- Margaret Isaacks executrix of Joseph Isaacks.
- Francis Billingsley & John Leach

administrators of Francis Davis.
- Elias Lowry administrator of Henry Lowry.
- Daniel Sheridin administrator of William Keepe.
- Symon Nichols administrator of William Smith.
- William Meads executor of John Cobreth.
- Joseph Edloe administrator of Peter Pheppard.
- William Howes administrator of William Edwards.
- George Hawes administrator of William Shaw & his wife.
- Katharine Lloyd administratrix of Hugh Lloyd.
- Andrew Tanyhill & Elisha Hall executors of John Muffet.
- Anne Greene executrix of Thomas Greene.

Sheriff (AA) to summon:
- Edward & John Dorsey executors of Joshua Dorsey.
- John Marriorty executor of John Acton.
- Christian Wheeler administratrix of John Wheeler.
- Eleanor Chiney administratrix of Richard Chiney.
- Mary Giles administratrix of John Giles.
- John Howard & his wife executrix of John Macubin.
- Thomas Tench administrator of William Marshall.
- John Pettybone administrator of Thomas Pettybone.
- Jane Fergason administratrix of William Fergason.
- Edward Selby, John Cross, & John Haggot executors of Edward Selby.
- Nicholas Nicholson administrator of John Baker.
- Elisabeth Vassine administratrix of Francis Vassine.
- Walter Phelps administrator of George Benson.
- Susanna Sewick executrix of John Sewick.
- Joanna Longman administratrix of

John Longman.
- Rachall Stimpson executrix of John Stimpson.
- William Foreman administrator of Thomas Bowles.
- Esther Nicholson administratrix of Nicholas Nicholson.
- Samuel Thomas administrator of Sarah Thomas.
- Jos. Chew & his wife Margaret administratrix of Francis Holland.
- Honor Durdan administratrix of John Durdan.
- Jane Pattison executrix of Thomas Pattison.
- Samuell Yong & his wife administratrix of Thomas Francis.
- Richard Baily administrator of Mark Johnson.
- Patrick Murphy & his wife administratrix of John Gray.

Sheriff (BA) to summon:
- William Kane administrator of John Dyemond.
- William Cole administrator of David Adams.
- Elisabeth Edmonds executrix of Richard Edmonds.
- Mary Pottell administratrix of Francis Pottel.
- Jenkin Griffith administrator of James Collier.
- Michael Hastings administrator of Francis Petit.
- Mary Reeves executrix of Edward Reeves.
- Richard Askue administrator of John Hammond.
- Said Askue administrator of Samuell Brands.

15B:4 Sheriff (SO) to summon:
- Thomas Morris administrator of John Murfue.
- Mary Dixon executrix of Ambrose Dixon.
- William Whittington & his wife Elisabeth executrix of Thomas Osborne.
- Cornelius Ward administrator of Nathaniell Daugherty.

- Donnough Dennis executor of Roger Ocane.
- Thomas Pile administrator of John Steery.
- Mary Cottingham administratrix of Thomas Cottingham.
- Elisabeth Wilson executrix of Robert Wilson.
- Elisabeth Roberts administratrix of John Roberts.
- Elisabeth Lampin administratrix of Thomas Lampin.
- Alice Willin executrix of Thomas Willin.
- John Davis administrator of Samuell Jackson.
- Ann Addison administratrix of Alexander Adison.
- Thomas Gordon administrator of Jenkin Morris.
- John Vigorous administrator of Ann Smith.
- Kath. Heathley administratrix of William Heathley.
- William Jenkinson administrator of Amos Cooke.
- Mary Carroll administratrix of Thomas Carrol, Sr.
- Thomas Bramley & his wife executrix of Thomas Osbourn.
- Rhoda Francis executrix of John Cropper.
- William Elgate administrator of William Elgate.
- William Jones executor of Cornel. Johnson.

Sheriff (TA) to summon:
- William Barton administrator of Thomas Yong.
- James Sedgewick administrator of Thomas Collins.
- Elisabeth Carman administratrix of Thomas Carman.
- Charles Hemsley administrator of Richard Hedger.
- Frances Kennimount executrix of John Kennemon.
- Ann Mitchell executrix of John Mitchell.
- Thomas Mason administrator of Robert Wild.

- Michael Leads administrator of William Leads.
- Thomas Thomas administrator of Christopher Thomas.
- Margaret Dunderdale executrix of William Dunderdale.
- Thomas Bruff & his wife executrix of James Earle.
- Ann Smith (alias Ann Bonham) administratrix of William Bonham.
- Edmond ODwyer administrator of John Stuard.
- William Welch executor of John Yonger.
- Margaret Layfield executrix of Bartholomew Ramsey.

Sheriff (CE) to summon:
- Sarah Meeks executrix of Walter Meeks.
- Thomas Bostick executor of Thomas Bostick.
- Martha Gibson executrix of William ODarry.
- Mary Howell executrix of Nathaniell Howell.
- Olley Ollison administrator of Peter Ollison.
- James Wilson administrator of William Jones.
- Thomas Webb administrator of Nicholas Jones.
- Philip Kennard administrator of Thomas Willham.
- Elisabeth Yerbery executrix of Thomas Yerberry.
- Thomas Christian administrator of Lawr. Christian.

Sheriff (KE) to summon:
- Thomas Parker administrator of James Parker.
- William Harris & John Hynson administrators of Henry Kennet.
- Samuell Wheeler administrator of John Boucher.
- Kath. Playne (alias Kath. Inglish) executrix of William Inglish.
- Said Playne administratrix of Edward Inglish.
- Edward Cox et. al. executors of Charles Stuard.

- William Harris administrator of Charles Turnor.
- Cornelius Comegys & his wife executrix of John Cambell.
- Edward Sweatnam administrator of John Abrams.

Sheriff (DO) to summon:
- John Ford administrator of Edward Creek.
- Thomas Wall administrator of John Walker.
- Walter Cambell & his wife Susanna executrix of John Edwards & executrix of Phineas Blackwood.
- Mary, Thomas, William, & Joseph Ennalls executors of Barth. Ennalls.
- Joan Bassey executrix of Michael Bassey.
- Roger Trotton administrator of Thomas Scott.
- Ann Thompson administratrix of Joseph Thompson.

LAC of estate of Robert Arbuckle (merchant, SM) committed to MM Richard Clouds & Gilbert Clark.

15B:5 Daniel Moy son & heir of Richard Moy vs. Robert Carvile (g) executor of said Richard. Said Carvile summoned to answer libel.

1 December. Col. Humphry Warren (high sheriff, CH) exhibited that he delivered summons to:
- Col. Edward Pye administrator of Col. Benjamin Rozer.
- Said Pye to answer complaint of Roger Brooke & his wife Mary executrix of Winifred Mullet.
- William Serjeant & his wife Damaras executrix of John Ward to answer complaint of Edward Milstead & his wife Elisabeth daughter of said Ward.

Mr. John Bearecroft (SM) exhibited oath of William Rosewell & Thomas Clark, appraisers of Mr. Joseph Pile (g), sworn 10 November 1692.

Court Session: 1692

Robert Mason (sheriff, SM) exhibited citations delivered:
- Thomas Orman & his wife.
- John VanReswick & his wife.
- Philip Lynes.
- Thomas Waughob
- James Browne & his wife.
- Thomas Griffin
- James Cullen
- Thomas Gwyther
- Edward Morgan.

Sheriff (SM) to summon:
- John Bullock executor of Lionel Oakley.
- James Swann administrator of William Ningfinger.
- Thomas Orman & his wife executrix of John Tong.
- Kath. Obryan administratrix of Bryan Obryan.
- Elisabeth Brimmer administratrix of James Brimmer.
- John VanReswick & his wife administratrix of Christopher Goodson.
- Michael Curtis & his wife Sarah executrix of Justinian Gerard.
- Thomas Gwither administrator of Morgan Prance.
- Elisabeth Portwood administratrix of John Portwood.
- Francis Green & Thomas Clark executors of Leonard Greene.
- James Browne & his wife administratrix of Thomas Pue.

15B:6   Sheriff (TA) to summon:
- William Barton administrator of Thomas Yong.
- James Sedgewick administrator of Thomas Collins.
- Elisabeth Carman administratrix of Thomas Carman.
- Charles Hemsley administrator of Richard Hedger.
- Frances Kennimon executrix of John Kennimon.
- Anne Mitchell executrix of John Mitchell.
- Thomas Mason administrator of Robert Wild.

Court Session: 1692

- Michael Leads administrator of William Leads.
- Thomas Thomas administrator of Christopher Thomas.
- Margaret Dunderdale administratrix of William Dunderdale.
- Thomas Bruff & his wife executrix of James Earle.
- Anne Smith (alias Anne Bonham) administratrix of William Bonham.
- Edmond ODwyer administrator of John Steward.
- William Welch executor of John Younger.
- Margaret Layfield administratrix of Bartholomew Ramsey.

Sheriff (SO) to summon:
- Thomas Morris administrator of John Murfue.
- Mary Dixon executrix of Ambrose Dixon.
- William Whittington & his wife executrix of Thomas Osborn.
- Cornelius Ward administrator of Nathaniel Daugherty.
- Donnaugh Dennis executor of Roger Ocane.
- Thomas Piles administrator of John Steery.
- Mary Cottingham administratrix of Thomas Cottingham.
- Elisabeth Wilson executrix of Robert Wilson.
- Elisabeth Roberts administratrix of John Roberts.
- Elisabeth Lampin administratrix of Thomas Lampin.
- Alice Willin executrix of Thomas Willin.
- John Davis administrator of Samuell Jackson.
- Ann Addison administratrix of Alexander Addison.
- Thomas Gordon administrator of Jenkin Norris.
- John Vigorous administrator of Ann Smith.
- Katharine Heathley administratrix of William Heathley.
- William Jenkinson administrator of Amos Cooke.

Court Session: 1692

- Mary Carroll administratrix of Thomas Carrol.
- Thomas Bramley & his wife executrix of Thomas Osbourne
- Rhoda Fraucit executrix of John Cropper.
- William Elgate administrator of William Elgate.
- William Jones executor of Cornelius Johnson.

Sheriff (DO) to summon:
- John Ford administrator of Edward Creek.
- Thomas Wall administrator of John Walker.
- Mary, Thomas, William, & Jos. Ennalls executors of Bartholomew Ennalls.
- Walter Cambell & his wife executrix of John Edwards & executrix of Phineas Blackwood.
- Joan Bassey executrix of Michael Bassey.
- Roger Trotton administratrix of Thomas Scot.
- Ann Thompson administratrix of Joseph Thompson.

3 December. Philip Cox & his wife vs. Thomas Courtney & his wife Eleanor administrators of Fobbe Roberts. Said Courtneys summoned to show cause why administration should not be granted to said Cox.

Daniel Moy son & heir of Richard Moy vs. Robert Carvile executor of Richard Moy. Said Carvile summoned to answer libel.

Thomas Waughob administrator of Robert Graham summoned to render accounts. John Watson & Philip Clark summoned.

Philip Lynes administrator of James Yore vs. Robert Cooper (SM) & his wife Patience. Defendants summoned
15B:7 to answer complaint.

John Bowlds & his wife sister to Cuthbert Scot (dec'd) vs. John Baptista Carbury Said Carbury summoned to show

Page 11

cause by administration of estate of said Scot should not be granted to said Bowlds.

Sheriff (TA) to summon William Dixon & his wife Elisabeth & William Sharp executors of Winlock Christison to answer complaint of Murty Horney & his wife Elisabeth.

Col. Edward Pye administrator of Col. Benjamin Rozer (CH) summoned to render accounts.

Col. Edward Pye summoned to answer complaint of Roger Brooke & his wife Mary executrix of Winifred Mullet.

Coroner (CH) to summon Col. Humphry Warren (sheriff) executor of Robert Thompson to render accounts.

Sheriff (AA) to summon:
- Edward & John Dorsey executors of Joshua Dorsey.
- John Marriarty executor of John Acton.
- Christian Wheeler administratrix of John Wheeler.
- Eleanor Chiney administratrix of Richard Chiney.
- Mary Giles administratrix of John Giles.
- John Howard & his wife executrix of John Macubin.
- Thomas Tench, Esq. administrator of William Marshall.
- John Pettibone administrator of Thomas Pettibone.
- Jane Ferguson administratrix of William Ferguson.
- Edward Selby, John Cross, & John Haggot executors of Edward Selby.
- Nicholas Nicholson administrator of John Baker.
- Elisabeth Vasine administratrix of Francis Vasine.
- Walter Felps administrator of George Benson.
- Susanna Seawick executrix of John Seawick.
- Joanna Longman administratrix of

John Longman.
- Rachel Stimpson executrix of John Stimpson.
- William Forman administrator of Thomas Bowls.
- Esther Nicholson administratrix of Nicholas Nicholson.
- Samuel Thomas administrator of Sarah Thomas.
- Joseph Chew & his wife Margaret administratrix of Francis Holland.
- Honor Durdan administratrix of John Durdan.
- Jane Pattison executrix of Thomas Pattison.
- Samuell Younger & his wife administratrix of Thomas Francis.
- Richard Baily administrator of Mark Johnson.
- Patrick Murphy & his wife administrator of John Gray.

Sheriff (BA) to summon:

15B:8 ...
- William Kane administrator of John Dimond.
- William Cole administrator of David Adams.
- Elisabeth Edmonds executrix of Richard Edmonds.
- Mary Pottell administratrix of Francis Pottell. Jenkin Griffith administrator of James Collier.
- Michael Hastings administrator of Francis Pettit.
- Mary Reeves executrix of Edward Reeves.
- Richard Askue administrator of John Hammond.
- Said Askue administrator of Samuel Brands.

Court Session: 1693

15C:0 Commission to Kenelm Cheseldyne. Date: 3 October 1693.

15C:1 Prepared by George Plater (Attorney General).

15C:2 2 October. Benjamin Scrivner (sheriff, AA) exhibited summons to Mordecai Moore & his wife Ursula executrix of Col.

William Burges executor of Nicholas
Painter who married Judith Parker (alias
Judith Cumber) executrix of John Cumber
to answer complaint of John Cumber
grandchild of said Cumber.

John Hall (sheriff, AA) exhibited
summons to render accounts to: Elisabeth
Edmunds, Mary Reeves, Richard Askue.

Said sheriff exhibited summons to Martha
Goldsmith & Mary Beedle (alias Mary
Utie) to answer regarding estate of
James Fendall. Said persons are
administratrices of Edward Beedle
executor of James Fendall.

Said sheriff exhibited summons to
Margaret Walston administratrix of John
Walston regarding estate of James
Fendall & estate of her husband John
Walston.

Charles Tilden (sheriff, KE) exhibited
summons to render accounts.

Exhibited inventory of Jonathon Grafton
(KE), by appraisers Edward Blay & Morgan
Jones. Also exhibited bond of John
Hurson administrator. Security: Charles
Tilden.

Exhibited inventory of John Cole (KE),
by appraisers John Bowles & Sutton
Quinney.
15C:3   Also exhibited bond of William Woodland
administrator. Security: Thomas Piner.

Exhibited inventory of Joseph Wicks
(KE), by appraisers Hans Hanson &
Francis Smith.

4 October. Exhibited will of Lionel
Copley, Esq. (Governor). Ruling: will
is null & void. Mr. Lionel Copley (son
& heir) appeared. He is the rightful
administrator; however he is a minor.
He chose as the administrator: Col.
Nehemiah Blakiston, Thomas Tench, Esq.
Said Blakiston & Tench were granted
administration, on behalf of said Lionel
& other children. Securities: George

Plater, Esq., Mr. Benjamin Scrivener,
Mr. Philip Lynes, Mr. John Edmondson.

6 October. Appraisers (said estate):
Mr. John Cornish (merchant), Mr. John
West, Mr. Edward Greene.

15C:4 24 October. A. Neale & Thomas Turner
administrators of Capt. Jos. Pile were
granted continuance.

31 October. Samuel Fendall (g, BA)
exhibited PoA from John Fendall
(mariner, Topsham, Devon), only brother
& heir of James Fendall (BA, dec'd), to
his cousin said Samuel. Date: 4 October
1692. Witnesses: Walter Lyle, Roger
West. Notary: Thomas Perriman.
15C:5 Thomas Stephens & Edward Manning deposed
that John Fendall (mariner, sometimes of
BrightHelmstone, Sussex) & now of Topham
is only & elder brother of James Fendall
(BA, MD, dec'd). Also, Elisabeth the
widow of said James & his only child are
since dec'd; they died in Cork, IRE
about a year ago. Also, that Elisabeth
Fendall mother of said James & John is
also dec'd. Also, James Fendall son of
said John is abroad at sea & has not
been heard from for a long time & is
supposed to be dead. So said John is
heir-at-law to said James. Date: 4
October 1692. Before: Thomas Perriman
(notary).

Samuel Fendall vs. John Hall & his wife
Martha & George Uty & his wife Mary &
William Osbourne & his wife Margaret.
Summons to defendants. Said Martha &
Mary are daughters & administratrices of
Edward Beedle. Said Margaret is
executrix of John Walston. Said Beedle
& Walston were administrators of James
Fendall (dec'd).

4 November. Sheriff (SM) to summon
Philip Lynes (g, SM) administrator of
James Yore to render accounts.

6 November. Joshua Guibert (SM)
exhibited
15C:6 LoA granted to him on estate of Luke

Barber, & that a will exists in the possession of Luke Barber, Jr. Said Luke summoned.

8 November. At the request of Sir Thomas Dawmer (SM), sheriff (SM) to summon Charles Seager (merchant) to take administration for widow of Nicholas Honey on his estate, or to renounce administration & LoA to be given to said Dawmer, as greatest creditor. Said Honey died about 1 week ago. Richard Clouds deposed that the widow lives in Barbadoes & his very poor.

John Llewellin was appointed Registrar.

15C:7 10 November. Exhibited inventory of William Lyle (CV), by appraisers Ninian Beal & John Chitten, sworn on 21 May 1589. Amount: £197.7.0. Also exhibited bond of Priscilla Lyle administratrix. Sureties: William Johnson, Timothy Seawell.

13 November. Jane Skipper relict of John Skipper (SM) was granted administration on his estate. Appraisers: Thomas Attoway, John Bullock. Sureties: Robert Carse, Mary Poulter. Richard Clouds (g) to administer oath.

William Rosewell (SM) vs. estate of Nicholas Hungford (SM). Caveat exhibited.

15C:8 Sheriff (SM) to summon Elisabeth Talbot (SM) administratrix of Charles Cox (clerk, SM) to render inventory.

15 November. Thomas Tench, Esq. surviving administrator of Lionel Copley, Esq. exhibited that Mr. John Cornish, Mr. John West, & Mr. Edward Greene are appraisers. Col. Nehemiah Blakiston the other administrator is dec'd. Philip Lynes (g, SMC) & Henry Denton (g, SMC) to appraise in SMC belongings in land of Col. William Digges (SMC).

Court Session: 1693

16 November. Philip Lynes & Henry Denton exhibited inventory of Lionel Copley.

18 November. Robert Mason (sheriff, SM) exhibited summons to Elisabeth Talbott administratrix of Charles Cox to render inventory & accounts.

Also summons to Edward Barber.

Said sheriff also exhibited summons to Charles Segar at suit of Thomas Dawmer.

15C:9   19 November. Thomas Tench, Esq. administrator of Lionel Copley, Esq. vs. Miles Burroughs & his wife Elisabeth, William Harpam, Benjamin Juncan, & Elisabeth Talbott. Summons to defendants.

25 November. Charles Segar (merchant, SM) was granted administration on estate of Nicholas Honey (SM), on behalf of Ann relict. Security: John Taunt. Appraisers (SM): Charles Gough, John Jarbo. Also exhibited inventory.

2 December. Benjamin Hunt (g, DO) was appointed Deputy Commissary for DO.

William Rosewell (g, SM) was granted administration on estate of Benjamin Hobson (SM), on behalf of relict. Sureties: William Nutthead, John Newman. Appraisers: Capt. Thomas Attoway, John Bullock. Richard Clouds (g) to administer oath.

15C:10   8 December. Exhibited inventory of Mr. Andrew Abington (CV), by appraisers Charles Carrol & Richard Keene, sworn 12 June 1692.

Exhibited inventory of John Edwards (g, CV), by appraisers William Haines & Richard Keene, sworn 7 December 1693.

9 December. Commission to Mr. Benjamin Hunt (DO) as Deputy Commissary is withdrawn as he "keeps an Ordinary" which by law incapacitates him, per

Page 17

Capt. Ennals. Mr. John Haslewood (DO)
is appointed in his stead. Signed:
Kenelm Cheseldyne.

11 December. Dr. John Harrison (CH)
was granted administration on estate of
Alexander Fullerton (CH), as principle
creditor. Appraisers: Anthony Neale,
Randolph Brandt. Robert Yates (g) to
administer oath.

15C:11 Mr. Collier for Thomas Brooke, Esq. (CV)
& Thomas Greenfeild (g, CV) petitioned
that Mr. Richard Charlett (merchant)
came to Mr. John White on 5th instant
in the freshes of Petuxant & was found
dead there the next morning. He has
considerable estate, but no kindred nor
near relations in the country. He has
divers very near kindred & relations in
ENG. Date: 7 December 1693.

15C:12 LaC issued to said Brooke & Greenfeild.
Thomas Tasker (g, CV) to administer
oath.

15C:13 ...

15C:14 Edward Randolph, Esq. vs. Madam
Elisabeth Blakiston widow of Col.
Nehemiah Blakiston. She is to take LoA
on his estate or show cause why not.

Sheriff (SM) to summon Philip Lynes
administrator of James Yore (SM) to
render accounts.

20 December. Sheriff (CV) to summon
Joseph Edloe administrator of Ed. Martin
to answer complaint of Richard Keene.

22 December. Samuel Manthorpe attorney
for Christopher Harris (g, London), as
principle creditor of Robert Burman
(dec'd), petitioned for sheriff (KE) to
summon Ann Burman widow of said Robert
to take LoA on his estate or to show
cause why not.

30 December. John Edmondson (TA)
petitioned for LoA on estate of William
Johnson (mariner, London).

15C:15 Mentions: bill of Mr. Philip Lynes.
Thomas Donellan was granted

administration on said estate.
Securities: John Edmondson, William
Taylard. Appraisers: Daniel Walker,
George Herlock. Mr. Edward Mann to
administer oath.

Said John Edmondson vs. Daniell
Donnavan & his wife Mary administratrix
of James Derumple. Caveat exhibited.

15C:16 LAC returned per Mr. Thomas Collier on
estate of Richard Charlett (CV). Also
letter from Mr. Thomas Greenfeild.
15C:17 Thomas Tasker petitioned that Mr.
Brookes & his family are dangerously
sick & that he, Tasker, knows Charlet's
sisters in London.

15C:18 2 January. Sheriff (CV) to summon
Samuell Watkins & his wife Ann
administratrix of John Baine to render
accounts.

Sheriff (CV) to summon Franc. Collier &
wife to answer complaint of James Baker
& to render accounts on estate of John
Evans.

15C:19 4 January. Dr. Benjamin Arnold deposed
concerning the estate of late Governor
Col. Copley. Mentions: said Governor's
daughter Ann Copley, gift to Barbara
Gold.

Sheriff (SM) to summon Thomas Barron &
Thomas Towell to testify in suit between
George Short & John Bean.

13 January. Thomas Hopkins (sheriff,
SO) exhibited:
• bond of Samuel Johnson administrator
of Jahne Wollis. Securities: Robert
Peirce, Thomas Smith. Date: 10
August 1693. Inventory, by
appraisers Richard Chambers &
William Low.
• bond of John King & Thomas Jones
administrators of Stephen Luffe
(SO). Securities: Stephen Horsey,
Randall Revell. Inventory, by
appraisers William Fasitt & Robert
Nearn.

15C:20   Exhibited was bond of Christopher Jones administrator of Christopher Chipindale (SO). Securities: John Lane, William Robinson. Also exhibited was inventory, by appraisers William Coulborn & Benjamin.

20 January. Thomas Tasker petitioned regarding estate of Richard Charlett. That he has been met with significant losses & family sickness. Also Mr. Greenfeild & his wife lie dangerously sick.

15C:21   Said Tasker & Greenfeild refuse administration on said estate. Henry Lowe (g, CV) & Thomas Collier (g, CV) were granted administration. Mr. James Keetch to administer oath.

24 January. Sheriff (SM) to summon Jane relict of Michaell Radiagh & now wife of Manuell Pitcher to take LoA on his estate.

26 January. Henry Lowe & Thomas Collier vs. Thomas Greenfeild. Sheriff (CV) to summon Thomas Greenfeild (g) to answer complaint. Sheriff (CV) also to summon said Lowe & Collier.

Sheriff (CV) to summon Eleanor relict of Thomas Parslow to prove her husband's will.

Sheriff (CV) to summon Ann relict of Samuell Bourne to prove her husband's will.

15C:22   Mrs. Ann Brent relict of Henry Brent (CV) was granted administration on his estate. Mr. James Ketch to administer oath.

30 January. LoA were granted to Henry Lowe (g, CV) & Thomas Collier (g, CV) on 20 January on the estate of Richard Charlett (CV). Thomas Greenfeild (g, CV) petitioned for said Lowe & Collier to show cause why said LoA should not be revoked. Neither party is kindred nor creditor. Each had equal right. Mentions: letter from Mr. Thomas Tasker

15C:23 (CV) who twice refused administration. Ruling: LoA to said Lowe & Collier were approved. Mentions: ship Mary of London & Thomas Wythinton (commander), servants of said Charlett.

15C:24 John Bouge appointed Registrar of Court.

3 February. Summons to Thomas Tench, Esq. one of administrators of Lionel Copley, Esq. to render inventory.

6 February. Katherine relict of William Bevens exhibited his will, constituting her executrix, proved by James Stevenson & Robert Smith (2 of witnesses). Said Katherine was granted administration. Appraisers: Robert Smith, James Thomson.

Emanuell Pitcher who married Jane relict of Michaell Radiagh (SM) was granted administration on his estate. Securities: John Watson, Elisabeth Baker. Appraisers: Richard Atwood, William Herbert. Mr. John Wattson to administer oath.

15C:25 William Brabant (CV) exhibited will of John Hambleton (CV), constituting him executor, proved by Richard Shirley & Lewis Botty (2 of witnesses). Administration had been granted by John Bigger (Deputy Commissary, CV) to John Mackdowell, as principle creditor. Said Mackdowell is summoned to show cause why LoA should not be revoked. Said Mackdowell appeared. Ruling: award to said Brabant. Appraisers: Thomas Burnell, William Moston. Capt. Benjamin Mitchell to administer oath.

John Wheatly (SM) brother of Andrew Wheatly (SM) exhibited his will, constituting him executor, proved by 4 witnesses. Said John was granted administration. Appraisers: Thomas Samon, Thomas Notingham. John Bouye to administer oath.

Exhibited was will of Abraham Clarke (CV), proved by 3 witnesses before Capt. John Bigger. Executor: Abraham Clarke (son).

15C:26 Exhibited was inventory of Col. Lionel Copley, Esq., by appraisers John Cornish, John West, & Edward Green. Thomas Tench, Esq. one of administrators was granted continuance.

Exhibited was will of James Mackall (CV), proved before Capt. John Bigger. Executrix: Mary Mackall (widow).

Capt. John Bigger exhibited:
* bond of John Mackdowell administrator of John Hambleton. Security: William Marston.
* bond of Richard Marsham administrator of James Minney. Security: William Barton.
* bond of Michaell Higgins administrator of John Guyat. Security: Ed. Barracraft.
* bond of Geremagh Eldridge administrator of Roger Cooper. Security: William Head.

Exhibited was inventory of Robert Freeland (CV), by appraisers John Leach, Jr., James Heigh.

15C:27 Henry Bonner (AA) exhibited:
* will of James Ellis, proved by Richard Purnell & Mathew Bellamy (2 of witnesses). Executrix: Mary (widow).
* will of Hugh Gill, proved. Executrix: Margarett (widow).
* bond of Allix Archer administratrix of Henry Archer. Security: William Groves.
* bond of Anne Dryfeild administratrix of Thomas Dryfeild. Securities: Thomas Tench, Esq., James Stoddert.
* bond of George Burges administrator of William Walker. Security: John Larkins.
* inventory of Henry Archer, by appraisers Richard Deavour & William Powell.
* inventory of James Ellys, by appraisers James Sanders & Samuell Young.

- inventory of John Atkins, by
  appraisers Robert Lockwood & William
  Elviss.

15C:28 Col. Henry Darnall son of Mary Darnall
(CV) was granted administration on her
estate. Thomas Brookes, Esq. to
administer oath.

Thomas Clarke (SM) was granted
administration on estate of William
Heather (SM). Appraisers: Thomas
Barber, Thomas Carville. Mr. Philip
Brisco to administer oath.

7 February. Arthur Wheately (DO)
husband of Sarah Wheatley (DO) was
granted administration on her estate, on
behalf of her children. John Haselwood
(DO) to administer oath.

15C:29 Thomas Baron deposed regarding will of
William Lange. Said Lange bequeathed
all to George Short.

Thomas Towell deposed the same & that
Capt. John Dent refused to prove the
verbal will.

Said George Short vs. Mr. John Bean.
Said Bean summoned to show cause.

17 February. Exhibited bond of Dr.
John Harrison administrator of Alexander
Fulerton (CH). Security: Ralph Smith.

James Ketch (g, CV) exhibited oath of
Edward Cole & Robert Clarke, appraisers
of Richard Charlett. Also exhibited was
bond of Henry Lowe & Thomas Collier,
administrators of said Charlett.
Securities: Henry Jowles, Richard
Fenwick.

15C:30 Mr. Cleborne Lomax (CH) exhibited:
- oath of Henry Hawkins (g, CH)
  administrator of Hugh Moore (CH),
  sworn 15 December last. Security:
  John Hawkins. Inventory, by
  appraisers William Barton & Thomas
  Smoote.
- will of Winifred Mullett (CH),

proved.
- will of Roger Brooks, constituting his widow Mrs. Margaret Brooks executrix, proved.
- oath of Nicholas Cooper (CH) administrator of Robert Downes (CH), sworn 17 January. Security: Michaell Martin.
- will of Ed. Ford, constituting no executor, proved on 19 January by 3 witnesses. Elisabeth Ford relict was granted administration. Security: Thomas Austin.

15C:31 23 February. Exhibited was bond of Ann Brent relict & administratrix of Henry Brent (CV). Securities: Richard Marsham, Baker Brooks.

Margery Gardiner relict & executrix of Richard Gardiner (CV) was granted administration on his estate. James Ketch (g, CV) to prove said will & administer oath.

28 February. Exhibited was inventory of Andrew Wheatly (SM), by appraisers Thomas Salmon & Thomas Nottingham.

Exhibited was inventory of James Mackall (CV), by appraisers John Soot & Fran. Freeman.

1 March. Robert Yates & his wife executrix of Laurence Hoskins (CH) exhibited additional accounts, proved before Cleborne Lomax.

Henry Hawkins & his wife executrix of Allexander Smith (CH) exhibited accounts.

15C:32 William Sergeant & his wife administratrix of Charles Shepherd (CH) were granted continuance.

James Swann administrator of William Ningfinger (SM) was granted continuance.

James Browne who married relict & administratrix of Thomas Pue (CV) exhibited accounts. Continuance was granted.

Robert Mason (sheriff, SM) exhibited summons to several persons.

Ninian Beall (sheriff, CV) exhibited summons to several persons.

Humphry Warren (sheriff, CH) exhibited summons to several persons.

Benjamin Scrivener (sheriff, AA) exhibited summons to several persons.

Philip Cox (CV) vs. Thomas Courtney (SM). Said Courtney appeared. Continuance was granted.

15C:33 Cleborne Lomax (CH) exhibited:
- will of Joseph Cornell, constituting William Herbert executor, proved by 2 witnesses. Inventory by appraisers Robert Yates & John Wilder.
- will of John Lambert (CH), constituting Thomas Mitchell & Mr. William Dent executors, proved by 2 witnesses. Said Mitchell & Dent were granted administration.
- bond of Susanna Thomas administratrix of George Barton (CH). Security: William Dent.

At the request of Mr. Gilbert Clarke, John Ryley (SM) deposed that Robert Arbuckle disposed of chattel to Mr. Richard Clouds.

15C:34 Arthur Wheatley (DO) husband & administrator of Sarah Wheatley & Charles Wheeler (DO) & his wife Mary were granted administration on estate of William Worgan (DO), unadministered by Dr. John Brookes (TA, dec'd). Said Sarah & Mary are daughters of said William. John Haselwood (g, DO) to administer oath.

Michaell Curtis & his wife Sarah executrix of Justinian Gerrard (SM) exhibited accounts. Continuance was granted.

Philip Briscoe (g, SM) exhibited oath of
Thomas Clarke administrator of William
Heather (SM). Also exhibited oath of
Thomas Barber & Thomas Carville,
appraisers. Securities: Richard Clouds,
Clement Haly. Also exhibited inventory.

Philip Cox & his wife Sarah
administratrix of John Johnson (SM) vs.
Thomas Courtney & his wife Eleanor.
Exceptions exhibited.

8 March. John Browne (SM) was granted
administration dbn on estate of Thomas
Pue (CV), in right of orphan,
unadministered by Ann Browne late Ann
Pue widow & administratrix. Securities:
Charles Caroll, Thomas Grunwing.

Mary Aud (SM) widow of Thomas Aud
exhibited her renunciation of
administration of his estate. John
Graves (SM) was granted administration
on said estate, as principle creditor.
Securities: Henry Poulter, Charles
Watts.

15 March. Francis Freeman (g, CV) to
prove will of Thomas Parslow (CV) & to
administer oath to Eleoner relict &
executrix. Appraisers: John Holland,
Nathaniell Deare.

15C:36 20 March. Jane Lidyatt (CV) widow of
Edward Hurlock & widow of John Lidyate
was granted administration on both
estates. Appraisers: Daniel Palmer,
William Read. John Read (g, CV) to
administer oath.

Exhibited will of Anne Assiter (SM),
constituting her daughter Mary Payne
executrix. Will was proved by Henry
Wriothesly, Richard Vowles, & John
Reyley. Said Payne was granted
administration. Appraisers: Richard
Vowles, John Reyley. Mr. Joseph
Guybert to administer oath.

23 March. Thomas Tench, Esq. one of
administrators of Col. Lionel Copley
exhibited that the dec'd desired his

clothes to be distributed to his
attendants: William Harpen, (N) Hinman,
& William Bleden.

Court Session: 1694

15C:37 26 March. Samuell Hopkins (SO)
exhibited:
- will of Robert Houston (SO),
  constituting William Smith & John
  Taylour executors, proved by John
  Taylour & William Benston (2 of
  witnesses). Said Smith & Taylour
  renounced administration. Grace
  Houlston relict was granted
  administration on said estate.
  Securities: Francis Thorowgood, John
  Williams. Inventory, by appraisers
  John Cornish & John Henderson.
- Martha Poole relict of John Poole
  (SO) was granted administration on
  his estate. Security: John
  Windsmillaine. Inventory, by
  appraisers Richard Chambers & George
  Land.
- James Dunkin was granted
  administration on estate of William
  Pattent (taylor, SO). Security:
  John Steel. Inventory, by
  appraisers David Miller & John
  Steel.

15C:38 Ephraim William (sheriff, SO) exhibited
summons to several persons.

27 March. Philip Lynes (g, SM)
petitioned for LoA on estate of John
Tompson (SM), in case the widow refuses
administration. Sheriff (DO) to summon
widow of said John Thompson to
administer the estate or show cause why
not.

Richard Williams & his wife vs.
Alexander Moore & his wife Sarah
executrix of John Coppin. Said Moore
summoned to answer libel.

John Dawson (g, TA) on behalf of his
wife Sarah & his brother Ralph Dawson &
his wife Mary were granted
administration on estate of Mary Omely

relict of Bryon Omaley. The dec'd is the mother of said Sarah & Mary. Mr. Edward Mann to administer oath.

Ralph Dawson & his wife Mary & John Dawson & his wife Sarah vs. Ralph Fishborne, Abraham Morgan, John Edmondson, William Dixon, & William Sharpe. Defendants summoned to answer libel. Said Mary & Sarah are surviving children of Bryon Omaley & his wife Mary.

15C:39   Robert Carville executor of Elisabeth Moy executrix of Richard Moy (SM) exhibited further accounts. Continuance was granted.

Exhibited was inventory of Joshua Welsteed (CV), by appraisers Fredrick Grimshaw & Josh. Cecell. Capt. John Bigger (CV) had granted administration to Mary Welsteed relict.

28 March. Edward Mann (g, TA) exhibited:
- bond of Thomas Donellon administrator of William Johnson (mariner, London) on behalf of John Edmondson. Securities: said Edmondson, James Edmondson. Also oath of Daniell Walker & George Hurlock, appraisers.
- bond of John Tolye administrator of Joseph Thornbery (Bullenbrooke, TA). Securities: William Care, Jesse Holton. Also inventory, by appraisers John Hinson & William Morison.

15C:40   ...
- bond of Sarah Coppin administratrix of John Coppin (TA). Securities: Alexander Moore, Philip Massy. Also inventory, by appraisers John Tibbals & John Morgan.

3 April. Thomas Burton administrator of Thomas Young (TA) exhibited accounts.

Exhibited was inventory of William Beavens (SM), by appraisers James Thompson & Robert Smith.

Richard Winsett administrator of Bryan Obryan was granted continuance. Said Winsett married relict & administratrix of said Obryan some years past.
15C:41 Mentions: Mr. Clement Hill, Col. Blakiston. Mr. Llewellin delivered papers from amongst effects of Col. Blakiston, an account allowed by Mr. Clement Hill. Date: 25 July 1690.

Philip Cox vs. Thomas Courtney. Their attorneys did not appear. Continuance was granted.

Daniell Moy vs. Robert Carvile. Mr. Carvile is absent. Continuance was granted.

15C:42 Exhibited bond of Edward Day (SO) who married executrix of Capt. Thomas Walker. Security: William Stevens (Pocomoke). Date: 7 September 1685. Mentions: children of said Walker. Witnesses: Sa. Cooper, Stephen Luff, Edm. Beauchamp.

15C:43 Jane Lidyatt relict of John Lidyatt (CV) was granted continuance.

6 April. Exhibited was inventory of Capt. Richard Gardiner (CV), by appraisers Charles Ashcom & Luke Gardiner.

12 April. Edward Mann (g, TA) petitioned for LoA on estate of Nicholas Northover (TA). Joseph Rogers also petitioned for LoA, as principle creditor. He is a Quaker & not qualified to take oath of administration. Said Rogers summoned to show cause why administration should not be granted to said Mann.

Robert Carvile procurator for Samuell Fendall administrator of James Fendall (BA) vs. (N) Hall & his wife & (N) Utie & his wife & (N) Osborne & his wife. Libel exhibited.

15C:44 Edward Mann (TA) exhibited:
• will of John Londey (TA),

constituting Henryetta Lloyd
executrix, proved. Also exhibited
inventory, by appraisers James Scott
& Richard Bennett.

- will of Thomas Browne (TA),
constituting James Bishop executor,
proved. Also exhibited bond of John
Bishop administrator of said Browne.
Securities: John Clift, William
Gwin. Also inventory, by appraisers
Thomas Robins & Samuell Abbott.

- bond of Thomas Hopkins administrator
of Clement Hopkins (TA).
Securities: John Graves, Kalibb
Izgate. Also inventory, by
appraisers Michaell Turbatt & John
Valliant.

- bond of Thomas Hobkins administrator
of Jacob Abrahams (TA). Securities:
Richard Fiddeman, Henry Frith. Also
inventory, by appraisers Michaell
Turbatt & John Valliant.

15C:45 ...

- bond of Phillip Hemsley
administrator of John Rice (TA).
Securities: William Scott, John
Ross. Also inventory, by appraisers
John Ross & William Mathews.

Henry Bonner (AA) exhibited:
- will of Faith Gongo (AA),
constituting Anne Gonge & Faith
Gongo executors, proved by 4
witnesses. Said Anne & Faith were
granted administration.

- will of Robert Hawkins (AA),
constituting his widow Mary
executrix, proved by 2 witnesses.

- will of Robert Owens (AA),
constituting John Cross executor,
proved by 2 witnesses.

14 April. Capt. John Bigger (CV)
exhibited:
- will of Thomas Watters (CV),
constituting John Davis executor,
proved by 3 witnesses.

- will of John Stone (CV),
constituting his widow Mary
executrix, proved by 3 witnesses.

15C:46 ...

- will of Petter Lemare (CV), which

named no executor, proved by 4
witnesses. Distribution to: widow
Francis & 3 daughters Anne, Mary, &
Margaret & John Davis (trustee) &
Joseph Edwards (trustee).

- will of Henry Dakes (CV),
  constituting his widow Persillia
  executrix, proved by 4 witnesses.
- verbal will of Robert Kemp (CV),
  which named no executor, proved by 6
  witnesses. All is left to Capt.
  Richard Bright for benefit of his
  son Richard (under age).
- will of Thomas Cornwell (CV),
  constituting Thomas Wharton & John
  Turner executors, proved by 2
  witnesses. They are to give
  accounting to Anthony Cornwall
  (merchant, London, brother to
  dec'd).
- bond of Martha relict &
  administratrix of Robert Freesland.
  Security: Benjamin Ball.
- bond of Alice Watkins administratrix
  of William Barnett. Security: James
  Mackboy.
- bond of Walter Smith administrator
  of Henry Taylor. Security: Hugh
  Montgomery.
- bond of Thomas Hillery administrator
  of Baruck Williams. Security:
  William.
- bond of George Young administrator
  of Thomasin Viney. Security:
  William Williams.

15C:47 20 April. Samuel Hopkins (SO)
exhibited:
- will of Nicholas Carpenter (SO),
  constituting Maj. Robert King &
  Capt. John King executors, proved
  by 2 witnesses. Security: John
  Macknitt. Also inventory, by
  appraisers Nathaniell Horsey & John
  West.
- bond of Hanah Maynard executrix of
  James Maynard. Securities: Mathew
  Scarbrough, Peter Bodkin. Also
  inventory, by appraisers Peter
  Bodkin & William Round.
- bond of Thomas Cross administrator
  of John Wood. Security: John

Painter. Also inventory, by
appraisers Thomas Willson & John
Richins.

21 April. Exhibited inventory of Joseph
Stanaway (DO), by appraisers William
Shainton & James Pearle. Arthur Whitley
administrator exhibited accounts.

15C:48 John Haselwood (DO) exhibited:
- will of William Winslow (DO),
  constituting his widow Mary
  executrix, proved by 3 witnesses.
- will of Edward Newton (DO),
  constituting his widow Margarett
  executrix, proved by 3 witnesses.
- will of Robert Winsmore (DO),
  constituting his widow Mary
  executrix, proved by 4 witnesses.
- will of Andrew Gray (DO),
  constituting his widow Philadelphia
  executrix, proved by 3 witnesses.
- bond of Jane Bosswell administratrix
  of Robert Bosswell (DO).
  Securities: Gournay Crowe, Benjamin
  Hunt. Also inventory, by appraisers
  Thomas Wall & Obadiah Hayman.

28 July. Thomas Hussey (CH) exhibited
will of William Langworth (SM),
constituting him executor. Said Hussey
was granted administration. Richard
Clouds (g) to prove said will &
administer oath.

15C:49 1 May. John Watson (g, SM) exhibited
oath of Richard Atwood & William
Herbert, appraisers of Michaell Radiagh
(SM), sworn 6 February last.

Exhibited inventory of John Lambeth
(CH), by appraisers Richard Harrison &
John Booker.

Elisabeth Hopewell relict of Hugh
Hopewell (CV) exhibited his will,
constituting her executrix. Said
Elisabeth was granted administration.
George Plater, Esq. to prove said will &
administer oath.

Court Session: 1694

Exhibited inventory of Abraham Clarke (CV), by appraisers James Heigh & John Leach.

John Booker & his wife executrix of Richard Price (CH) exhibited LoA granted in county court. Appraisers: Mr. William Dent, Francis Harrisson. Mr. John Stone to administer oath.

15C:50   John Holsworth (CV) was granted administration dbn on estate of George Abbott, unadministered by Isabella relict & executrix & late wife of said Holsworth. Securities: Thomas Spencer, Robert Hobs.

Exhibited inventory of Ed. Ford (CH), by appraisers John Cornish & Thomas Austin.

Exhibited bond of Jane Lidyatt administratrix of Edward Hurlock (CV). Securities: Robert Carville, James Moore.

Exhibited bond of Jane Lidyatt administratrix of John Lidyatt (CV). Securities: Robert Carville, James Moore.

James Phillips (BA) administrator of John Bird (BA) exhibited accounts.

Said Phillips administrator of Adam Burchell (BA) exhibited accounts.

Said Phillips executor of his father James Phillips exhibited accounts.

15C:51   Edward Boothby (BA) exhibited:
- bond of Samuell Fendall administrator of James Fendall (BA). Securities: Samuell Bren, Thomas Browne. Also inventory, by appraisers John Kemble & Roger Mathews.
- will of George Goldsmith (BA), constituting his widow Martha executrix, proved by 2 witnesses before Thomas Smith. Petition of John Hall who married said Martha.
- inventory of Andrew Hykae (BA), by

appraisers Thomas Greenfeild & Henry Hazelewood.

- bond of Elisabeth Gibson administratrix of Miles Gibson (BA). Securities: James Phillips, Edward Boothby.
- bond of Elisabeth Deyson (alias Elisabeth Voghea) relict & administratrix of William Deyson. Securities: James Maxwell, Richard Adams. Also inventory, by appraisers Richard Adams & Robert Doulas.
- bond of James Phillips administrator of Adam Burchell (BA). Securities: Simeon Jackson, George Smith. Also inventory, by appraisers George Smith & Simeon Jackson.

15C:52 ...

- will of Anthony Demondidier (BA), constituting his widow Martha executrix, proved by 4 witnesses before Thomas Staly. Also inventory, by appraisers John Thomas & Nicholas Corbin.
- inventory of John Bird (BA), by appraisers William Ebden & William Richardson.
- inventory of James Phillips, Sr. (BA), by appraisers John Hall & William Osborne, dated 4 June 1689.

2 May. John Holsworth (CV) administrator of George Abbott exhibited accounts.

John Stone (g, CH) exhibited bond of Robert Thompson, Jr. attorney for George Elwes (merchant, London) administrator of Thomas Elwes (merchant). Securities: Cleborne Lomax, William Thompson.

Anne Bourne relict of Capt. Samuell Bourne (CV) was granted administration on his estate.

15C:53 Exhibited inventory of John Woodward (DO), by appraisers Thomas Wickers & Andrew Parker. Dr. Jacob Lockerman on behalf of relict & executrix Martha exhibited judgements from DO County court. Discharge was granted.

Court Session: 1694

Philip Clarke procurator for Franc. Miles vs. Phillip Lynes administrator of Thomas Yearsly. Libel exhibited.

John Hall & his wife Sarah executrix of George Hooper (BA) exhibited additional accounts.

Exhibited inventory of Thomas Tonnard (TA), by appraisers Thomas Dorman & Haniball Wells. Andrew Tonnard administrator exhibited accounts.

15C:54 Dr. Jacob Lockerman (DO) exhibited:
- will of Thomas Cooke (DO), constituting his widow Anne executrix, proved by 4 witnesses. Securities: Thomas Ennall, Thomas Hickes.
- will of William Hill (DO), constituting Edward Pindar & Hugh Eccleston executors, proved by 2 witnesses. Said Pindar is dec'd. Said Eccleston was granted administration. Securities: Benjamin Hunt, Charles Powell. Also inventory, by appraisers Edward White & John Flowers.
- will of John Smith (DO), constituting his widow Mary executrix, proved by 2 witnesses. Securities: John Lyon, John Draper. Also inventory, by appraisers James Canon & Thomas Lewes.
- bond of Mary Heather administratrix of Thomas Gillmin (DO). Securities: John Davis, John Wade. Also inventory, by appraisers John Nicolls & Andrew Gray.

15C:55 ...
- bond of Mary Heather administratrix of William Heather (DO). Securities: John Davis, John Wade. Also inventory, by appraisers Andrew Gray & John Nicolls.
- will of John Steevens (DO), constituting his widow Dorathy executrix, proved by 3 witnesses.
- will of John Braday (DO), constituting John Nicholls executor, proved by 2 witnesses. Also bond of John Nicolls administrator.

Securities: Roger Woolford, Phillip
Tall. Also inventory, by appraisers
Thomas Butler & Andrew Gary.

- bond of Sarah Pindar administratrix
of Edward Pindar (DO). Securities:
John Edmondson, William Sharp. Also
inventory, by appraisers Thomas
Taylor & Phillip Pitts.
- bond of Arthur Whitley administrator
of Joseph Stanaway (DO).
Securities: John Kirke, William
Douse.

15C:56 ...

- will of Nicholas Masey (DO), proved
by 3 witnesses. Also bond of
Nicholas Masey (son) administrator.
Securities: Edward Brannock Sr.,
John Brannock. Also inventory of
said Nicholas Massey, by appraisers
William Toope & Anthony Thompson.

Edward Mann (TA) exhibited:

- bond of John Longe administrator of
William Dale (TA). Securities:
Thomas Clements, Jessy Halton. Also
inventory, by appraisers Thomas
Delahay & James Saywell.
- bond of William Carr administrator
of Joseph Wigget (TA). Securities:
Thomas Clements, John Millar. Also
inventory of said Joseph Wiggett, by
appraisers Thomas Robins & Samuell
Abbot.
- bond of Jesse Holton administrator
of Marye Mulraine (TA). Securities:
John Edmondson, William Anderson.
Also inventory of said Mary
Mulraigne, by appraisers Samuell
Abbott & Franc. Chaplin.

15C:57 ...

- bond of John Millar administrator of
William Ashlye (TA). Securities:
Edward Williams, Charles Harbour.
Also inventory, by appraisers Thomas
Clements & William Carr.

Joseph Rogers exhibited that Nicholas
Northover (TA) died in house of said
Rogers. Said Rogers is principle
creditor to said Northover. But, for
conscience sake, said Rogers cannot take
oath. John Paine (TA) was granted

administration, on behalf of said
Rogers. Securities: said Joseph Rogers,
John Edmondson.

William Parker (g, CV) exhibited oath of
Thomas Sedgwick & Edward Coudry,
appraisers of John Stone (CV). Also
exhibited inventory.

Mary Sempill executrix of Joseph Sempill
(SM) was granted continuance. William
Johnson summoned to give evidence on her
behalf.

15C:58 3 May. Henry Bonner (AA) exhibited:
- will of Luke Gregory (AA),
  constituting John Willson executor,
  proved by 2 witnesses. Said Willson
  could not take oath for conscience
  sake. Elisabeth Willson wife of
  said John was granted
  administration. Security: her
  husband.
- bond of Katherine Keely
  administratrix of John Keely (AA).
  Security: George Eager.
- inventory of Robert Hawkins (AA), by
  appraisers William Powell & Edward
  Masson.

John Hinson & William Harris
administrators of Henry Kennett (KE)
exhibited accounts.

4 May. Samuell Browne one of executors
of Daniel Peverell (BA) vs. George
Smith. Caveat exhibited.

15C:59 Thomas Thomas administrator of
Christopher Thomas (TA) exhibited
accounts.

Robert Robinson who married Margarett
relict & administratrix of William
Dunderdale (TA) exhibited accounts.

Exhibited inventory of Capt. James
Fendall (BA), by appraisers William
Osborn & Roger Mathews

Madam Brent petitioned for appraisers
for estate of her husband Henry Brent.

5 May. Sarah Moore (alias Sarah Coppin, TA) deposed, regarding the burning of the will of her husband John Coppin, that the will was burned on advice of Humphry Hubbart & that said Hubbart was advised by a gentleman. Sheriff (DO) to summon said Hubbart.

15C:60 Henry Rosse to Henry Poulter. Mentions: said Poulter's letter dated 10 November & received on 25th. Mr. Hobson is dec'd. Said Rosse will not be executor of estate of Mr. Joseph Hanniford. Chief purpose of his will was to ship tobacco for ENG on account of Mr. Gabbs (dec'd), as he was a trustee with Mr. Simeon Robins. Date: 20 December 1693 Yeocomico.

Said Poulter exhibited that said Joseph Hanniford died at his house, having no relation in this country. Said Poulter was granted administration. Mr. Richard Clouds to administer oath.

Exhibited bond of Hans Hanson administrator of John Ottridge (KE). Security: Charles Tilden.

15C:61 Cleborne Lomax (CH) exhibited:
- bond of Jane Bould administratrix of John Bould (CH). Securities: Thomas Dixon, James Cox.
- bond of Hester Speakman widow & administratrix of William Speakman (CH). Security: Francis Meakes.
- will of Elisabeth Bullett (CH), constituting Peter Mackmillian executor, proved by 3 witnesses. Security: Capt. Phillip Hoskins.
- bond of Penolope Land administratrix of Richard Land (CH). Security: John Theobalds.
- inventory of Robert Downes (CH), by appraisers John Smith & James Aisbrooke.

Exhibited inventory of John Guyatt (CV), by appraisers John Turner & John Hollaway.

Exhibited inventory of John Hambleton (CV), by appraisers Thomas Purnell & William Marston.

15C:62 Richard Clouds (g, SM) exhibited will of William Langworth (SM), constituting Thomas Hussey (CH) executor, proved by 4 witnesses. Said Hussey was granted administration. Security: William Rosewell. Also inventory, by appraisers William Roswell & Charles Carles.

Exhibited bond of John & Rebeccah Newman administrators of John Bercraft (SM). Securities: Timothy Mahome, Thomas Sympson.

Charles Carroll procurator for Ralph & John Dawson who married Mary & Sarah Omealy surviving children of Bryon Omealy & his wife Mary (TA) vs. Robert Gouldborough procurator for Ralph Fishborne, Abraham Morgan, John Edmondson, William Dixon, & William Sharp executors of said Bryon & said Mary. Libel exhibited. Continuance was granted.

15C:62½ Charles James (CE) exhibited:
- bond of Ann Whitton administratrix of Richard Whitton (CE). Securities: Caspares Herman, George Stevens. Date: 19 April 1693. Also inventory, by appraisers George Stevens & Thomas Simpers.
- will of Josias Crouch (CE), constituting his son John Crouch executor, proved by 3 witnesses. Said John was granted administration. Also inventory, by appraisers Edward Skidmore & George Sturton.
- will of Henry Higgs, constituting his widow Ann Higgs executrix, proved by 3 witnesses. Also inventory, by appraisers Francis Childe & Robert Drury.
- will of John Faulke (CE), constituting Jane Faulke executrix, proved by 2 witnesses. Also inventory, by appraisers Samson George & Thomas Parsons.

- will of Michaell Skidmore,
constituting his mother Alice
Stockett & his brother Samuell
Skidmore executors, for his child
Joseph Skidmore, proved by 2
witnesses. Also inventory, by
appraisers Edward Skidmore, George
Sturton.

15C:63 7 May. Silbella Barber relict of Edward
Barber (SM) exhibited his will,
constituting her executrix. Philipp
Briscoe (g) to prove said will.
Appraisers: Thomas Turner, Samuell
Williams. Said Briscoe to administer
oath.

Elias King (KE) exhibited oath of John
Wells administrator of William Richards
(KE). Securities: Franc. Stevens,
Mathew Erreakson. Also inventory, by
appraisers Mathew Eareckson & John
Downes.

Exhibited inventory of Henry Taylor
(CV), by appraisers James Gamlin &
Jeremiah Eldridge. Continuance was
granted.

George Ashman (g, BA) & John Thorn (g,
BA) deposed that Samuell Fendall had
summoned John Hall & his wife Martha &
George Utie & his wife Mary & William
Osborne & his wife Martha to answer his
complaint.

15C:63½ 3 May. John Hinson (KE) who married
Anne relict & administratrix of Jonathon
Grafton (KE) exhibited accounts.

Exhibited inventory of John Otridge
(KE), by appraisers Abraham Taylor &
Charles Hynson. Hans Hanson
administrator of said John Ottridge
exhibited accounts.

Thomas Tench administrator of Gov.
Lyonell Copley petitioned for John Lowe
& Edward Hilliard to appraiser said
estate. Robert Masson to administer
oath & Joseph Edloe & James Harper
appraisers.

Court Session: 1694

Elisabeth Gibson (BA) formerly Elisabeth Hazelewood executrix of John Collett (BA) exhibited that she exhibited accounts in 1673. She exhibited:
- additional accounts of John Collett.
- accounts of Henry Hazelewood.
- accounts of Richard Edmonds. Continuance was granted.
- accounts of Miles Gibson. Continuance was granted.

15C:64 8 May. Joane Bassey (DO) widow of Michaell Bassey exhibited accounts, proved before John Hazelwood (DO).

John Scott & his wife Sarah executrix of Thomas Sterling (CV) exhibited additional accounts.

Exhibited inventory of Hans Peterson (CE), by appraisers John Waggott & Mathew Hendrickson. James Watkins (CE) exhibited accounts for John Petterson who is incapable of taking an oath "being defective in his intellect".

14 May. Philip Clarke procurator for Col. Charles Hutchins, Col. David Browne, Capt. John Addison, & rest of the Justices of the Provincial Court vs. Thomas Tench, Esq. administrator of Gov. Lionell Copley, Esq. Caveat exhibited.

Col. David Browne executor of Archibald Ereskin was granted continuance.

15C:65 15 May. John Hall & his wife Martha & George Utie & his wife Mary administratrices of Edward Beadle & William Osborne & his wife Margarett executrix of John Walston who were executors of Capt. James Fendall (BA) exhibited accounts on estate of said Fendall.

George Smith & his wife Hanna executrix of Daniel Peverell (BA) & Samuell Browne executor of said Peverell exhibited accounts. Also exhibited inventory attested by Thomas Hedge (clerk, BA), by appraisers Lawrence Taylor & William Osborne.

Page 41

Exhibited inventory of John Boone (CV),
by appraisers Franc. Freeman & William
Deremple. Date: 25 July 1689.

15C:66 Francis Freeman (CV) exhibited will of
Thomas Parslow (CV), constituting his
widow Ellen Parslow executrix, proved by
3 witnesses. Also exhibited oath of
Nathaniell Deare & John Holland,
appraisers.

Edward Boothby (BA) exhibited:
- bill of Mr. Philip Lynes (merchant)
  to Mr. James Fendall (merchant,
  BA). Date: 15 April 1689.
- bill of Mr. Lynes to Abraham Blagg.
  Date: 4 July 1687, assigned on 22
  April 1689.
- account of Abraham Blaggs of said
  bill. Date: 25 February 1687/8.
Said documents were in hands of Edward
Beedle & John Walston overseers of James
Fendall (dec'd).
15C:67 Witnesses: P. Deyzar, Daniell Langhorne.
15C:68 Exhibited copy of bill to Mr. Thomas
Stork (merchant, Towre St., London). At
request of Mr. Samuell Groome
(merchant, London) by Paul Porten
(notary), protest exhibited, dated 14
May 1688.
15C:69 Also exhibited assignment of Abraham
Blagg to Mr. James Fendall. Date: 25
February 1687/8. Witnesses: Robert
Slye, Thomas Orrell.

15C:70 John Hall (g, BA) exhibited that on 5
May at the house of Mr. Philip Lynes in
the presence of Madam Elisabeth
Blackiston, he inquired of the papers of
estate of Mr. James Fendall (BA).
Mentions: wife of said Lynes.
15C:71 Mr. Phillip Lynes deposed that he knew
nothing of any papers of said Fendall.

Robert Carvile procurator for Samuell
Fendall vs. Charles Carroll procurator
for John Hall & his wife Martha & George
Utie & his wife Mary administratrices of
Edward Beedle & William Osborne & his
wife Margarett executrix of John Walston
executors of James Fendall. Said
Carroll exhibited papers. Mentions:

estate unadministered by Edward Beedle &
John Walston, debt by Mr. Lynes, Col.
Blackiston, Abraham Blagg will to
management of

15C:72 Mr. Miles Gibson who died soon
afterwards. Several legatees of will of
said Fendall died in ENG & John Fendall
only brother is heir, sent PoA to said
Samuell.

15C:73 Ruling: suit to force an accounting,
15C:74 defendants dismissed.

16 May. Samuell Watkins one of
executors of John Edwards (CV)
petitioned for copy of will to be sent
to ENG.

William Dent attorney for William
Anderson (ACC) exhibited that said
Anderson is attorney for John Plaissed
(NE) & Elisabeth Plaised executrix of
Elisha Plaised. Said Dent was granted
administration on said estate, for the
executrix. Mr. Samuell Hopkins (SO) to
administer oath. LoA from NE & PoA
exhibited:

15C:75 ...

- Date: 4 May 1693 Portsmouth,
  Newhamshire. Elisabeth Plaisted is
  sole executrix of Mr. Lisha
  Plaisted (mariner). Said Lisha made
  will, dated 26 October 1690,
  bequeathing all to said Elisabeth.
  Said Elisabeth gave PoA to her
  brother-in-law Mr. John Plaisted
  (merchant, Portsmouth), dated 25
  April 1691, to collect debts, etc.,
  from Barbadoes, VA, or MD. Signed:
  John Hinckes (President).
- John Plaisted (Newhamshire) was
  engaged with Licia Plaisted to Mr.
  Samuell Massey for a bill of
  exchange drawn by John Edmondson
  (MD) on Joshua Buddno (London).

15C:76 ...

Date of bill: 4 June 1684. Samuell
Massey PoA to Ralph Burdant. Said
Plaisted PoA to William Aderson
(ACC, VA) to recover from John
Edmondson. Date: 4 August 1692.
Witnesses: Beriah Higgens, Robert
Smart, John Rowe.

15C:77 ...

Sworn before John Brandhurst & Edm.
Custis. Date: 10 October 1692.
- William Anderson PoA to William
Dent. Date: 10 May 1694.
Witnesses: William Bladen, William
Harpam.

17 May. Exhibited inventory of Michaell
Radiagh (St. Gerome's), by appraisers
Richard Atwood & William Harbert.

Jane relict & executrix of Emanuell
Pitcher (SM) exhibited his will, proved
by 3 witnesses. Said Jane was granted
administration. Appraisers: John Low,
John Doxy. Mr. John Watson to
administer oath.

15C:77½ William Smoote vs. Robert Yates. At
Court at SM. Came Thomas Smoote (p, CH)
by his procurator William Dent & Robert
Yates & his wife Rebeccah executrix of
James Tyre executor of John Bowles who
married Margery Battin executrix of
William Battin by their procurator
Robert Carvile. Said Battin made will
on 29 May 1662, disposing of the residue
as: ½ to said Margery, other ½: 4 parts:
(1) plaintiff William Smoote. Will
constituted said Margery as executrix &
overseers: Capt. Jonas Fendall, Robert
Henly, Thomas Smoote (plaintiff's
father). Said Margery possessed herself
of the entire estate & married John
Bowles (g, CH) in 1663.

15C:78 Soon thereafter said Margery died
intestate. Said John administered
estate as Margery Bowles & possessed
himself of said estate. Some short time
thereafter, said John died. Said James
Tyre possessed himself of the estate.
Said James died, leaving his estate to
his wife Rebecca who married Robert
Yates (merchant, London). The plaintiff
was of full age in 1682.

15C:79 Defendants found a receipt amongst
papers of said Tyre for legacy to Newman
Smoote & their children. Mentions: (N)
Webb (NE).

15C:80 ...
- Elinor Beane deposed that she heard

Thomas Smoote (plaintiff's father) say he sold his part of the estate to Capt. Fendall.

- Humphry Warren deposed that he heard Capt. Fendall paid Thomas Smoote some part of his legacy & that Capt. Fendall cheated said Smoote.
- Lydia Manners deposed that Thomas Smoote (plaintiff's father) received some items. Mentions: her late husband George Newman.
- James Witcherly deposed. Mentions: Mr. Rowland & his wife. Mrs. Rowland is the plaintiff's mother.

15C:81 ...
- Thomas Stowe deposed that he heard (N) Newman say he was satisfied with his portion.
- William Burnham deposed that Capt. Fendall employed Mr. Thomas Lomax in keeping the accounts of said Battin's estate.
- Mary Browne deposed that she heard (N) Rowland, who had married mother of said William Smoote, say that when William Smoote came of age he had #10,000 to pay him which was left of his uncle Battin. Mentions: Mr. Thomas Lomax, William Burnham.

Ruling: said William Smoote to recover his legacy; defendants to be discharged. But said William was underage at the time of the payment.

15C:82 Defendants were dismissed.

Elias King (KE) on behalf of Catharine Nicholson administratrix of Edward Inglish (CE) & executrix of William Inglish (CE) exhibited accounts on both estates. Estates are overpaid. Quietus est was granted.

21 May. Elisabeth Warren relict of William Warren (SM) was granted administration on his estate. Securities: James Greenwell, Henry Taylor.

22 May. Exhibited will of James Bowling (SM), constituting Mary Bowling executrix, proved before John Beane (g). Said Mary was granted administration.

Edward Randolph, Esq. (Surveyor General) on behalf of their Majesties exhibited account as caveat vs. estate of Col. Nehemiah Blackiston.

15C:83 Mentions: Patrick Meene, Esq., ship Thomas Lanyon bound for NE & ship Mayflower Joseph Hawley (master) bound for Mountsuratt, sloop of John Lambert bound for Salemm NE, ship Margarett William Burnett (master),

15C:84 John Winslow (merchant), Gustavus Hambleton.

23 May. Exhibited inventory of Edward Hurlock (CV), by appraisers William Reade & Daniel Palmer.

Exhibited inventory of John Lidyett (CV), by appraisers William Reade & Daniel Palmer.

30 May. Sarah Raylon relict of William Raylon (SM) was granted administration on his estate. Securities: Owen Guyther, John Langley. Appraisers: Anthony Edwards, William Twesden. Capt. Greenhalgh to administer oath.

15C:85 4 June. Mary Thompson relict of John Thompson (SM) was granted administration on his estate. Security: Thomas Courtney. Appraisers: Abraham Rhodes, William Asquith.

5 June. Court at SM. Philip Cox vs. Thomas Courtney. Trial set for next court.

Daniel Moy vs. Robert Carvile. Trial set for next court.

John Watson vs. Philip Clarke. Trial set for next court.

Ralph & John Dawson vs. Ralph Fishbourne et.al. executors of Bryon Omealy. Trial set for next court.

Robert Carvile procurator for Humphry Hubbart (DO) petitioned for copy of libel by widow Coppin. No libel found.

Daniel Moy vs. Robert Carvile. Answer exhibited.

15C:86 9 June. Sheriff (CH) exhibited summons to Thomas Hussey.

Exhibited inventory of John Bould (CH), by appraisers Randolph Brandt & Robert Gates.

Philip Brisco (g, SM) exhibited will of Edward Barber (SM), proved. Also exhibited bond of Cibilla relict & administratrix. Securities: Thomas Turner, Samuell Williamson. Appraisers: said Turner, said Williamson.

11 June. Thomas Husey (CH) petitioned for sheriff (SM) to summon Anne Langworth, James Martin, & Agnes Druet.

Exhibited inventory of Capt. Henry Johnson (BA). Edward Boothby who married Elisabeth relict & administratrix of said Johnson exhibited accounts & additional accounts.

15C:87 15 June. William Dent procurator for Edward Milstead & his wife one of daughters of John Ward (CH) exhibited that William Sargeant & his wife Damares administratrix of Charles Sheppard & relict & executrix of said John Ward have not answered libel. Ruling: attachment to said William & Damares.

16 June. Edward Parish (AA) who married daughter of Andrew Roberts (AA) vs. Dr. Wolfran Hunt administrator of said Roberts. Summons to said Hunt.

15C:88 Exhibited inventory of William Raylon (SM), by appraisers Anthony Evans & William Twesden.

19 June. John Beecher & his wife Edith relict & executrix of Joseph John Williams (BA) was granted continuance. Appraisers Maj. John Thomas & Mr. John Ferry to appraise plantation in Suffrax. Mr. Thomas Richardson to administer oath.

21 June. Francis Hutchings (g, CV)
exhibited oath of Mr. William Parker &
Richard Durham, appraisers of William
Barnett (CV). Also exhibited inventory.

Exhibited inventory of Richard Price
(CH), by appraisers William Dent &
Francis Harrison.

Exhibited inventory of Thomas Aude (SM),
by appraisers Capt. Thomas Ataway &
Francis Sweales.

15C:89 22 June. Anne Burman (KE) relict &
executrix of Robert Burman (KE)
exhibited her renunciation. Samuell
Manthrop (g, taylor, KE) attorney for
Christopher Harrison (scrivener, London)
was granted administration on said
estate, as principle creditor.
Mentions: Mr. George Plater,
15C:90 PoA from said Harrison to said Manthrop.
15C:91 ...
15C:92 Witnesses: William Chamberlaine, Leend.
Oosterhaven. Date: 11 December 1691.
15C:93 William Chambers attested to PoA.
Signed: Charles Bass.
 • Leerd. Oosterhaven, age 27, deposed.
 Signed: William Markham (Lt. Gen.,
 New Castle, PA).
Mr. Elias King (KE) to administer oath.

15C:94 25 June. Exhibited inventory of
Michaell Swift (CV), by appraisers
Thomas Taney & John Dossett.

John Bigger (CV) exhibited:
 • will of Michaell Swift (CV),
 constituting Margarett Swift relict
 executrix, proved by 3 witnesses.
 Said Margarett was granted
 administration.
 • bond of Mary Wolsted administratrix
 of Josuah Wolsted (CV). Security:
 Thomas Taney.
 • bond of Sarah Robinson
 administratrix of Thomas Robinson
 (CV). Security: John Godscrose.

26 June. John Watson (g, SM) exhibited
oath of John Low & John Doxey,
appraisers of Emanuell Pitcher.

Court Session: 1694

30 June. Sheriff (DO) exhibited summons to Humphry Hubbart.

Thomas Witchell & his wife Mary relict & administratrix of Edward Sarson (AA) exhibited accounts. Accountant is Quaker. Residue to: widow (1/3rd), orphans.

15C:95 Thomas Ennalls (g, DO) exhibited accounts of Martha Woodward relict & administratrix of John Woodward.

2 July. Exhibited inventory of Ed. Barber (SM), by appraisers Thomas Turner & Samuell Williamson.

Sheriff (AA) exhibited summons to Dr. Wolfran Hunt.

3 July. John Read (CV) exhibited oath of Daniell Palmer & William Read, appraisers of Edward Hurlock & John Lidyatt.

Thomas Waughop (g, SM) exhibited oath of John Taunt & Laurence Tetershall, appraisers of William Warren (SM).

Philip Cox vs. Samuell Watkins procurator for Thomas Courtney & his wife Elioner. Answer exhibited.

Francis Miles (SM) vs. Philip Lynes administrator of Thomas Yearsley. Said Miles appeared as summons by said Lynes. Libel was by said Miles. Said Lynes did not appear to exhibit answer.

15C:96 Court at SM. George Plater procurator for Daniell Moy vs. Robert Carvile. Said Moy is son & heir of Richard Moy & Elisabeth his mother executrix of said Richard. Said Carvile is executor of said Elisabeth, with Clement Hill the other executor who renounced administration. Henry Cary the other executor died before said Elisabeth. At death of said Richard, said Daniell was a tender infant. Said Elisabeth tendered guardianship of said Daniell to defendant.

15C:97 Said Elisabeth died 2 months after the appraisal of estate of said Richard. Mentions: Philip Calvert (Judge of Court), Mr. Christopher Rousby, Mr. Robert Ridgely.

15C:98 Ruling:
15C:99 plaintiff.

George Plater procurator for Thomas Waughop (SM) administrator of Robert Graham (SM) & guardian of Robert Graham (son, a tender infant) vs. Philip Clarke & his wife Hannah one of daughters & administratrix of George Mecall unadministered by Robert Graham & his wife Anne executrix of said George & administered by John Watson & his wife Jane another daughter & administratrix of said Mecall.

15C:100 Mentions: Robert Williams (merchant, Falmouth), Philip Calvert (Judge).
15C:101 Ruling: plaintiff.

Philip Clarke procurator for John Dawson vs. Ralph Fishbourne, Abraham Morgan, John Edmondson, William Dixon, & William Sharp executors of Bryon Omealy & his wife Mary (TA). Ruling: defendants are attached.

15C:102 Anne Langworth (widow, SM) petitioned that her brother exhibited that Mr. Thomas Hussey executor of her husband had carried off chattel from said estate.

15C:103 4 July. Thomas Hussey (SM) administrator of William Langworth (SM) appeared. Ruling: said Anne to receive her 1/3rds. Mentions: Mr. Clement Hill.

5 July. Ralph & John Dawson vs. George Plater procurator for Ralph Fishbourne et. al. executors of Bryon Omealy. Ruling: attachment of contempt.

George Plater procurator for Philip Cox vs. Samuell Watkins procurator for Thomas Courtney & his wife Elenor. Answer exhibited.

Court Session: 1694

7 July. Edward Morgan executor of John Evans (SM) exhibited additional accounts.

15C:104 9 July. Edward Mann (TA) exhibited:
- will of Robert Towe (TA), constituting his wife executrix, proved by 2 witnesses. Also, bond by Hugh Dwyer administrator. Securities: John Edmondson, Thomas Delehay. Also inventory, by appraisers Robert Gough & Ed. Latham.
- will of Joseph Wiggett (TA), constituting William Carr & John Syley executors, proved by 2 witnesses. Also bond by William Kare administrator. Securities: Thomas Clements, John Millar. Also inventory.
- will of Denis Mahoney (TA), constituting Cornelius Odwyer executor, proved by 3 witnesses. Also bond of Cornelius Dwyer administrator. Securities: William Riche, Francis Harris. Also inventory, by appraisers William Wintersell & Franc. Harris.

15C:105 ...
- will of Thomas Cockx (TA), constituting Thomas Toas & John Mann executors & guardians of his son William Cocks, proved by 2 witnesses. Said Mann was granted administration. Securities: Ambroise Foard, Nathaniell Tegall. Also inventory, by appraisers Ambroise Foard & William Shanahan.
- bond of Capt. John Davis administrator of Thomas Welch (TA). Securities: Daniell Walker, Philip Masse. Also inventory, by appraisers Daniell Walker & Philip Walker.
- bond of James Smith & Andrew Hambleton administrators of James Gill (alias James Gibson, TA). Also inventory, by appraisers John Hamer & Thomas Smith.
- bond of David Rogers administrator of John Burrell (TA). Securities: Capt. John Hatfeild, John Pursell.

15C:106 ...

Also inventory, by appraisers
William Hatfeild & John Pursell.

- will of Edward Edwards (TA), proved
  by 2 witnesses. Also bond of
  William Thomas administrator.
  Securities: Richard White, John
  Price. Also inventory, by
  appraisers Richard White & John
  Price.
- bond of John Needles administrator
  of William Rooke (TA). Securities:
  Richard Dudlye, Ed. Turner. Also
  inventory, by appraisers Ed. Turner
  & Richard Dudley.
- bond of Prudence relict of Joseph
  Bell (TA). Security: Thomas Taylor.
  Also inventory, by appraisers Thomas
  Taylor & William Watts.
- oath of Ralph Dawson & his wife Mary
  & John Dawson & his wife Sarah
  administrators of Mary Omealy (TA).
  Also, oath of Dr. Benson & Daniell
  Sherwood, appraisers.
- oath of William Swelling & Richard
  Sanders, appraisers of Nicholas
  Northover (TA). Also inventory.

15C:107 10 July. Exhibited inventory of Thomas
Viney (CV), by appraisers John Jenkins &
William Williams.

Nathan Veatch administrator of James
Veatch (CV) exhibited accounts. Said
Nathan administrator of John Veatch also
exhibited accounts on his estate.

Thomas Tench, Esq. administrator of Gov.
Lionell Copley, Esq. petitioned for
appraisers of goods on the ship Anne:
John White (g, CV), Nicholas Spurne (g,
CV). Capt. Hurle & Capt. Thomas Pell
to assist. Mr. Thomas Tasker to
administer oath.

13 July. Charles Carroll procurator for
Edward Parrish (AA) & his wife Mary vs.
Dr. Wolfran Hunt & his wife Jane relict
& executrix of Andrew Roberts (AA).
Libel exhibited. Said Mary is daughter
of said Andrew. Said Wolfran summoned.

Court Session: 1694

15C:108 Ralph Dawson & his wife & John Dawson & his wife vs. Robert Goldsborough procurator for John Edmondson & other executors of Bryon Omealy (TA). Answer exhibited. Also exhibited inventory of said Omealy. Also exhibited accounting of what was delivered from estate of said Bryon to Mary Omealy. Susannah Omealy one of the daughters of said Bryon exhibited accounting of what was delivered to her. Isabella Omealy another daughter of said Bryon exhibited accounting of what was delivered to her. Exhibited inventory of Mary Omealy, & accounts by Ralph Fishbourne.

16 July. John Thompson (CE) exhibited that on 9 June he granted LoA to John Leycocke & his wife Elisabeth relict of John Talley (CE). Securities: Ed. Scidmore, Michaell Trumell. Also exhibited oath of Ebenezar Blackiston & Mich. Trumell, appraisers.

15C:109 Elias King (KE) exhibited:
- bond of Elisabeth relict & administratrix of John Murphey (KE). Security: Robert Smith. Also inventory, by appraisers Walter Kerby & Valentine Suthern.
- bond of Thomas Baxter administrator of Alexander Meconikin. Security: Roger Baxter. Also inventory, by appraisers Alexander Walters & Walter Kerby.
- bond of Mary Meconikin relict & administratrix of John Meconikin. Security: George Winson. Also inventory, by appraisers Francis Stevens & Matt. Eareckson.
- bond of Elisabeth relict & administratrix of Morriss Wollohand (KE). Security: Joseph Sudler. Also inventory, by appraisers Ed. James & Mathew Eareckson.
- bond of John Downes administrator of Paul Winbrough (KE). Security: Francis Stevens. Also inventory, by appraisers Anthony Workman & John Wells.

15C:110 19 July. Philip Clarke procurator for
Richard Keene (CV) vs. Joseph Edloe
executor of Edward Mollins (CV). Libel
exhibited.

21 July. Exhibited inventory of
Elisabeth Bullet (CH), by appraisers
John Godshall & Moses Jeary.

John Edmondson (TA) petitioned for
summons to Samuell Watkins (CV) to show
cause by he does not administer estate
of William Johnson.

Thomas Williams & his wife Elisabeth
were granted administration on estate of
Franc. Dacostha (SM). Said Decostha had
no relations, except his sister said
Elisabeth. Securities: Thomas Haddock,
John Gant. Appraisers: Salomon Jones,
Thomas Griffin.

27 July. (N) Dawson vs. John Edmondson
(TA), Abraham Morgan (TA), William Dixon
(TA), & William Sharpe (TA). Answer
exhibited, regarding estates of Bryon &
Mary Omealy (TA).

15C:111 Henry Red (SO) & his wife Bethania
relict & executrix of John Smock (SO)
exhibited accounts.

28 July. Exhibited inventory of George
Rennalls (SM), by appraisers Stephen
Gough & Thomas Kersely.

John Holdsworth administrator of George
Abbott (CV) exhibited additional
accounts. Said Holdsworth also
exhibited inventory & additional
inventory of William Martin (CV),
attested by Henry Fernly (clerk, CV), by
appraisers Thomas How & William Bartton.
Said Holdsworth married Isabella relict
& administratrix of said Martin. Also
exhibited accounts.

John Taunt administrator of John
Blomfeild (SM) exhibited accounts.

Nicholas FitzSimons who married relict
of Joseph Heathcote (BA) exhibited

accounts.

15C:112 Mr. Samuell Hopkins (SO) exhibited:
- will of Thomas Clifton (SO), constituting his wife Hannah executrix, proved by 3 witnesses. Also inventory, by appraisers John Purnell & John Pope.
- will of Thomas Purnell, Sr. (SO), constituting his 2 sons John & Thomas Purnell executors, proved by 3 witnesses. Security: Samuell Hopkins. Also inventory, by appraisers Mathew Scarborough & John Pope.
- will of John Covington (SO), constituting his brother Nehemiah Covinton & his friend Levin Denwood executors, proved by 2 witnesses. Said Denwood refused to take oath. Said Nehemiah was granted administration. Securities: John Painter, Ed. Day. Also inventory, by appraisers John Painter & William Johns.

15C:113 ...
- bond of Ann Butcher administratrix of Robert Butcher (SO). Security: Robert Holland. Also inventory, by appraisers John Purnell & Richard Holloway.
- bond of Elisabeth Kennet administratrix of William Kennet. Securities: John Franklin, William Turvile. Also inventory, by appraisers John Franklin & William Turvile.

30 July. Mr. Michaell Miller (KE) exhibited that Rebecca Comigges executrix of John Cambell & executrix of Benjamin Smith is incapable of coming to Office. Mr. Elias King to examine accounts.

Mrs. Ann Brent exhibited that former appraisers of Henry Brent are not willing to appraise said estate. New appraisers: Richard Fenwick, Ralph Haywood. Mr. James Ketch to administer oath.

15C:114 7 August. Exhibited inventory of Capt.
Samuell Bourne (CV), by appraisers John
Griggs & Samuell Holsworth.

Exhibited inventory of Roger Booger
(CV), by appraisers William Head &
George Hardestye.

Exhibited inventory of Emanuell Pitcher
(SM), by appraisers John Lowe & John
Doxie.

Exhibited inventory of James Lewis (SM),
by appraisers John Biscoe & Owen
Guyther.

8 August. Rhodia Francklin executrix of
John Cropper (SO) exhibited accounts.

15C:115 John Vigorous administrator of Ann Smith
(SO) exhibited accounts.

Edward Fowler who married Alice
executrix of Thomas Willin (SO)
exhibited accounts.

Donnough Dennis executor of Roger OKeane
(SO) exhibited accounts.

Darby Sullivane executor of John Due
(CV) exhibited accounts.

James Pindle on behalf of his mother
Eleanor Chiney administratrix of Richard
Chiney (AA) exhibited accounts. She is
old & decrepit. Estate is overpaid.

William Welsh executor of John Younger
(TA) exhibited accounts.

Thomas Mason administrator of Robert
Wild (TA) exhibited accounts.

15C:116 Elias King exhibited that:
- Samuell Manthrop administrator of
  Robert Burman.
- petition for discharge on estates of
  Edward & William Inglish. Date: 2
  August 1694 Chester River.
  Discharge granted to Catherine
  Nicholson administratrix.
- Samuell Manthrop summoned to show

cause why administration should not
be given to Capt. John Davis (g,
TA), as greatest creditor. Summons
to Nicholas Millbourne (TA), Charles
Hemsley (TA), Capt. Nicholas
Gassaway (AA).

15C:117 Exhibited additional inventory of
Francis Butler (TA), by appraisers John
Power & Richard Feeddeman. James
Murphey & Lawrence Knowles
administrators exhibited accounts.

Robert Carvile procurator for Franc.
Miles vs. Phil. Lynes. Defendant has
not replied. Attachment rendered to
said defendant.

Regarding attachments to executors of
Bryan Omealy (TA). Ralph Fishburne
exhibited accounts and was granted
continuance.

William Dent for Grisl Ponds vs.
Richard Southern & Capt. Brightwell
administrators of Mary Trueman. Summons
to render accounts.

15C:118 Robert Carvile for Robert Grundy (TA)
vs. John Sollars executor of John
Skrigley. Summons to complete accounts.
Mentions: Deborah wife of said Grundy is
sister to dec'd.

Charles Carroll procurator for Edward
Parrish (AA) vs. Dr. Wolfran Hunt. No
answer rendered. Attachment to
defendant.

Exhibited inventory of William Redd
(CV), by appraisers James Cranford &
William Turner. Samuell Fowler executor
exhibited accounts.

Exhibited inventory of John Hanniford
(SM), by appraisers John Dash & Ed.
Tipton.

Charles Garret administrator of Thomas
Patrick (CH) exhibited accounts,
attested by Cleborn Lomax (clerk, CH).

Court Session: 1694

15C:119 Cleborn Lomax (CH) exhibited will of Richard Smith (CH), constituting his wife Anne & his son Richard executors, proved by 3 witnesses. Said Anne & Richard were granted administration on 18 July last. Appraisers: Ralph Smith, Thomas Taylor.

Exhibited bond of Mary Duglas relict & administratrix of Robert Duglas (CH). Securities: John Harrison, Walter Story.

Exhibited bond of Elenor relict & administratrix of Edward Frawner (CH). Security: John Gorley.

9 August. Exhibited inventory of Henry Brent (CH), by appraisers Raphaell Haywood & Richard Fenwick.

11 August. Exhibited inventory of George Barton (CH), by appraisers Joseph Huchison & Ed. Rookwood.

Joseph Edloe administrator of Peter Phippard (CV) exhibited accounts.

15C:120 Exhibited inventory of Anne Asiter (SM), by appraisers Richard Vowles & John Reyley.

13 August. Exhibited inventory of Thomas Robinson (CV), by appraisers William Whittington & John Willymott.

15 August. Mary Thompson administratrix of John Thompson (SM) petitioned for appraisers: Abraham Rhodes, William Asquith.

20 August. John Evans (SM) vs. estate of William Pawlett. Caveat exhibited, as said Evans is one of principle creditors.

24 August. Frank Miles vs. Philip Lynes administrator of Thomas Yearsley (SM). Answer exhibited.

25 August. Philip Clarke (g, SM) vs. estate of William Pawlet. Caveat exhibited.

Court Session: 1694

27 August. John Graves administrator of Thomas Aude (SM) exhibited accounts.

15C:121 Exhibited will of William Pawlett (CV), constituting Philip Clarke & Robert Taylor executors, proved by 2 witnesses. Said Clarke & Taylor were granted administration. Appraisers: Cecell Butler, Joseph Edloe. George Plater, Esq. to administer oath. Also exhibited oath of appraisers. Also exhibited inventory.

31 August. Exhibited will of Richard Royston (TA), constituting his widow Mary Royston executrix, proved by 3 witnesses. Edward Mann to grant administration to said Mary.

3 September. Walter Taylor (p, SM) was granted administration on estate of William Jones (p, SM), who died at house of said Taylor, as principle creditor. Securities: William Taylard, William Nuthead. Appraisers: William Asquith, Roger Tolly.

15C:122 James Keech (g, CV) exhibited will of Capt. Richard Gardiner (CV), proved by Charles Carles (witness).

Justinian Tennison vs. Charles Watts administrator of Absolom Tennison. Caveat exhibited. Mention: Thomas Sikes.

4 September. William Parker (sheriff, CV) exhibited summons to Richard Southern & Capt. Brightwell.

William Holland (sheriff, AA) exhibited summons to Capt. Nicholas Gassaway & attachment to Dr. Wolfran Hunt.

Charles Carroll procurator for Ed. Parrish vs. Dr. Wolfran Hunt (AA). Answer exhibited.

Exhibited inventory of Henry Lawrence (SM), by appraisers John Miller & Thomas Medford.

15C:123 Francis Miles vs. Phillip Lynes. None
of attorneys appeared. Continuance
granted.

Philip Lynes (SM) administrator of James
Yore exhibited accounts. The relict
Patience, now wife of Robert Cooper,
summoned to answer his libel.

Said Lynes administrator of William
Hawton exhibited that accounts were
filed before Col. Blackiston.

Elias King (KE) exhibited:
- bond of Sarah Toulson administratrix
  of Andrew Toulson. Securities:
  Mathew Erreckson, John Wells. Also
  inventory.
- bond of Samuell Manthrop
  administrator of Robert Burman.
  Securities: Michaell Miller,
  Casparus Herman. Also inventory, by
  appraisers Edward Sweatnam & Simon
  Wilmer.

15C:124 Henry Read who married Perthenia relict
& administratrix of John Smock (SO)
exhibited accounts. Discharge was
granted.

Samuell Manthrop administrator of Robert
Burman (KE) vs. Capt. John Davies (TA).
Said Davis was to prove his right as
greatest creditor. Continuance was
granted.

John Bigger (CV) exhibited:
- will of Edward Isaack (CV),
  constituting his widow Jane
  executrix, proved by 3 witnesses.
- bond of Margaret Sunderland
  administratrix of John Sunderland
  (CV). Securities: William Nicholls,
  William Holland.
- bond of John Forrest administrator
  of Phillip Laurence (CV). Security:
  Murphey Ward.
- bond of Dorathy Harrington
  administratrix of Charles Harrington
  (CV). Security: Thomas Harrington.

15C:125 John Haslewood (DO) exhibited:
- will of Jermiah Davies (DO), constituting his widow Elisabeth executrix, proved by 2 witnesses.
- will of John Sutton (DO), proved by 3 witnesses. Sarah Pindar was granted administration. Securities: Charles Powell, Andrew Parker. Also inventory, by appraisers John Kirke & John Winsmore.
- bond of Hannah Charlescroft administratrix of William Prichett. Securities: Richard Owen, Jarvis Cutler. Also inventory, by appraisers John Frank, John Willis.
- inventory of Ed. Newton (DO), by appraisers Phillip Pitts & Andrew Parker.
- inventory of Andrew Gray (DO), by appraisers Simon Richardson & Henry Whitaker.
- inventory of Robert Winsmore (DO), by appraisers Phillip Pitt & John Pierson overseer.
- will of Elinor Corkerin (DO), constituting Thomas Buttler executor, proved by 3 witnesses. Said Buttler is in Barbadoes.

15C:126 6 September. Charles Carroll procurator for Evan Rice & his wife Elisabeth one of legatees of Thomas Binks (CV) vs. Nathaniell Deare executor of said Binks. Libel exhibited. Sheriff (CV) to summon said Nathaniell Dare.

8 September. Exhibited inventory of William Jones (SM), by appraisers William Asquith & Roger Tolly.

Exhibited inventory of Frank Decosta (SM), by appraisers Salomon Jones & Thomas Griffin.

Exhibited inventory of William Speakman (CH), by appraisers Ed. Ming & Francis Meeke.

10 September. Samuell Fendall administrator of James Fendall (BA) exhibited accounts.

Robert Carville & Clement Hill executors of James Bodkin (SM) exhibited 2nd accounts.

15C:127 13 September. Charles Carroll procurator for Edward Parrish (AA) vs. Dr. Wolfran Hunt. Response to answer exhibited.

Frances Lawrence (SM) widow of Henry Lawrence exhibited his will, constituting her executrix, proved by 2 witnesses: Jeremiah Jadwin, Rebeckah Orchard. Said Frances was granted administration. Appraisers: John Miller, Thomas Medford.

Exhibited inventory of John Thompson (SM), by appraisers William Asquith & Abraham Rhodes.

Charles Watts who married Elisabeth relict of Absolom Tennison (SM) was granted administration on his estate. Securities: Thomas Sickes, William Watts.

15C:128 17 September. George Plater, Esq. exhibited will of Hugh Hopwell (CV), constituting his widow Elisabeth executrix, proved by Maj. Nicholas Sewall & Nicholas Richardson. Also exhibited oath of said Elisabeth. Also oath of Joseph Edwards & John Wisman, appraisers.

John Hall (sheriff, BA) exhibited summons to Martha Caige. Also exhibited that Samuell Fendall is dec'd. Said John Hall vs. estate of Samuell Fendall. Caveat exhibited. Date: 13 September 1694.

18 September. Henry Bonner (AA) exhibited:
• will of Maren Duvall (AA), constituting his widow & rest of children executors, proved by 5 witnesses. Said widow & Robert Tyler renounced administration. John Duvall (eldest son) was granted administration.

Court Session: 1694

15C:129 ...
- will of Jacob Hollet (AA), proved by 3 witnesses. William Clarke was granted administration.
- will of Margrett Tench wife of Thomas Tench, Esq., proved by 3 witnesses.
- bond of Mary Morse administratrix of John Morse (AA). Security: Mark Richardson.
- inventory of John Keely (AA), by appraisers Allen Robinett & Josias Collins.
- inventory of John Pettibone, by appraisers Robert Eagle & Hugh Marikin.
- inventory of Thomas Drifield, by appraisers John Scott & Zachary Allein.
- inventory of Faith Gongoe, by appraisers William Powell & Augustin Hawkins.
- inventory of Luke Gregory, by appraisers Anthony Smith & James Butler.
- inventory of William Walker, by appraisers Robert Kirkland & William Goodman

15C:130 ...
- will of John Pettibon (AA), proved by 5 witnesses. Edward Chapman was granted administration. Said Chapman is guardian of the children. Security: Jos. Merikin.

20 September. Cleborne Lomax (CH) exhibited:
- will of John Smallwood (CH), constituting his brothers James & Thomas Smallwood executors, proved by 2 witnesses. Said James renounced administration. Said Thomas was granted administration. Also inventory, by appraisers Cornelius Madock & John Garner.
- Further inventory of Hugh Moore, by appraisers William Barton & Thomas Smoot.
- inventory of Edward Frawner, by appraisers John Gourbe & John Knight.
- inventory of Michaell Minock, by

Page 63

appraisers Thomas Smoote & Michaell
Martin. William Foster is former
administrator.

Exhibited inventory of William Warren
(Newton Hundred, SM), by appraisers John
Taunt & Laurence Totershill.

15C:131 Samuel Hopkins (SO) exhibited oath of
William Anderson administrator of Elisha
Plaisted (NE). Securities: Peter
Bodkin, Samuell Hopkins. No inventory.
Only a debt from John Edmondson.

John Thompson (CE) exhibited:
- Thomas Browning & his wife Anne
  relict of Darby Nolan (CE) was
  granted administration on his estate
  16 June last. Securities: William
  Boulding, John Bavington. Also
  inventory, by appraisers Richard &
  Thomas Terrey.
- will of William Burden (CE),
  constituting his widow Margrett
  executrix, proved by 2 witnesses.
  Said Margrett was granted
  administration. Appraisers: Daniell
  Smith, William Chamberlaine.

25 September. Exhibited inventory of
Henry Deikes (CV), by appraisers Ninian
Beale & John Chittam.

15C:132 Mr. Robert Carvile & William Hains to
secure assets of Jane Lidyatt (CV).

Exhibited inventory of George Goldsmith
(BA), by appraisers Lodwick Martin &
Thomas Greenfeild.

Edward Boothby (BA) exhibited:
- will of John Arden, constituting his
  widow Sarah executrix, proved by 4
  witnesses. Said Sarah was granted
  administration. Also inventory, by
  appraisers William Willkinson & John
  Hayes.
- will of William Gaine, constituting
  his widow Mary executrix, proved by
  2 witnesses. Said Mary was granted
  administration. Also inventory, by
  appraisers John Ensor & John Broade.

15C:133 ...
- will of Elisabeth Devege (BA), constituting John Devege executor, proved by 3 witnesses. Said John was granted administration.
- will of Jacob Lotton, constituting his widow Elisabeth executrix, proved by 2 witnesses. Said Elisabeth was granted administration.
- bond of Thomas Staly & Robert Owlas administrators of John Nichols (BA). Securities: James Maxwell, Richard Adams. Also inventory, by John Skilton & John Rallings.
- bond of Sarah Teal administratrix of Edward Teal (BA). Security: Philip Roper. Also inventory, by appraisers Philip Roper & William Slade.

27 September. Samuell Watkins (g, CV) vs. estate of Lohn Lidyatt. Unadministered by Jane Lidyatt (CV, now dec'd). Said Watkins is greatest creditor. Caveat exhibited.

15C:134 28 September. Samuell Watkins was granted administration on estate of John Lidyatt (CV), as greatest creditor. Said Watkins married relict of Adrew Abington & John Edwards, unadministered by Jane Lidyatt (now dec'd). Securities: Philip Lynes, William Taylard. George Plater, Esq. to administer oath. William Joseph, Esq. & Robert Carvile (g) to audit accounts.

29 September. Robert Hancok administrator of John Keely (AA) exhibited accounts.

Edw. Milstead vs. Charles Carroll procurator for William Sergeant & his wife Damaris executrix of (N) Ward (CH). Answer exhibited.

15C:135 1 October. Thomas Whitton (CE) vs. John James (CE) & his wife Anne relict of Thomas Whitton. Summons to render accounts.

Court Session: 1694

3 October. Gabriell Parrott
administrator of Daniel Longman
exhibited accounts.

5 October. Benjamin Williams (AA)
exhibited will of his brother Joseph
Williams (BA), constituting his widow
Edith executrix. Said Edith has married
John Beecher, who has absented himself
from the Province. Said Edith is dec'd
& left 4 children by said Joseph. Said
Benjamin was granted administration.
Appraisers: Leonard Wayman, John Powell.
Capt. Nicholas Gassaway to administer
oath.

15C:136 ...
  • Robert Parker, ferryman, age 36,
    deposed that on 22 September
    instant, he took John Beecher over
    the Potapsco River & that said
    Beecher told him that he was going
    to leave the Province & that he left
    all he had in possession of Richard
    Cromwell & that said Beecher did not
    have any papers of estate of Joseph
    Williams.
Date: 28 September 1694 before George
Ashman.

Exhibited inventory of Robert Dowglas
(CH), by appraisers John Harrisson &
Walter Story.

Ralph & John Dawson vs. Ralph Fishborne
et.al. executors of Bryon Omealy.
Continuance was granted.

William Turner administrator of James
Straitch (CV) exhibited additional
account.

15C:137 William Finney (TA) exhibited on 19
September 1694:
  • will of Izabella Doude (TA),
    constituting Thomas Studem & Thomas
    Mawman, Sr. executors, proved by 2
    witnesses. Said Studem & Mawman
    were granted administration.
  • will of John Brooke (TA),
    constituting his widow Judith
    executrix, proved by 3 witnesses.
    Said Judith was granted

administration.
- will of Francis Shepherd (TA), constituting Robert Norriss executor, proved by 2 witnesses Said Norriss was granted administration.
- will of Samuell Wosly (TA), constituting George Pratt & James Ridley executors, proved by 3 witnesses. Said Pratt & Ridley were granted administration.
- bond of Samuell Withers administrator of Christopher May (TA). Securities: Thomas Brufe, John Robins. Also inventory, by appraisers Edward Elliott & Richard Skeddmore.

15C:138 6 October. Court at SMC. Charles Carroll procurator for Edward Parrish vs. Dr. Wolfran Hunt. Ruling: said Hunt to exhibit accounts on estate of Andrew Roberts.

Thomas Blake who married Jane relict & administratrix of Robert Webb (CV) exhibited accounts.

John Haslewood (DO) exhibited bond of Elisabeth White administratrix of Edward White (DO). Securities: Allen Smith, John Drapper. Also inventory, by appraisers Obadiah King & Thomas Harpin.

15C:139 10 October. Charles Carroll procurator for Garrett Murrey (CE) vs. Edward Jones (CE) administrator of William Brackhurst. Libel exhibited.

13 October. Edward Jones administrator of William Brokas (CE) exhibited accounts.

John Rawlins (DO) appointed Deputy Commissary.

16 October. Edward & John Dorsey executors of Joshua Dorsey (AA) exhibited additional accounts.

Darby Heley (CE) who married Elisabeth relict & administratrix of Thomas Strickland exhibited accounts.

Dr. Jacob Loockerman was granted administration on estate of Henry Raddon (DO), as greatest creditor. Security: Elias King. Appraisers: Roger Woolford, John Kirke. William Michew (g) to administer oath.

15C:140 George Plater, Esq. exhibited oath of Mathew Lewis appraiser of John Lidyatt (CV).

17 October. Dr. John Vigorous administrator of Anne Smith (DO) was granted discharge.

18 September. Exhibited inventory of Robert Keemble (BA), by appraisers Simeon Jackson & John Jackson, sworn before Mr. Boothby.

19 September. Appointments as Deputy Commissary:
  Mr. Edward Boothby (BA). Security: Elias King.
• Elias King (KE). Security: Ed. Boothby.
• Cleborne Lomax (g, CH). Securities: Henry Wriothesly, Robert Carse.

15C:141 26 October. John Graves administrator of Thomas Aud (SM) exhibited accounts.

Exhibited inventory of John Reyley (CV), by appraisers Obadiah Evans & Edward Dikinson.

Appointment of Kenelm Cheseldyn
15C:142 as Judge or Commissary General for Probate.
15C:143 Signed: Francis Nicholson (Governor). Date: 18 October 1694.

7 November. Philip Barrett (CE) administrator of William Sincler exhibited accounts.

Nicholas Fitzsimons who married relict & administratrix of Joseph Heathcote (BA) exhibited additional accounts. Discharge was granted.

Court Session: 1694

William Barne (CV) was granted
administration on estate of John Duncon
(CV), as principle creditor. Security:
Thomas Hussey. Appraisers: John Snuggs,
John Rablin. Mr. Thomas Greenfeild to
administer oath.

15C:144 10 November. Mr. Richard Clouds for
Thomasine Dammer widow of Thomas Dammer
(SM) was granted administration on his
estate.

Exhibited inventory of Absolom Tennison
(SM), by appraisers Thomas Atway & John
Bullock.

John Paine & Joseph Rogers
administrators of Nich. Northover (TA)
exhibited accounts.

Exhibited inventory of Thomas Watters
(CV), by appraisers David Small & Ed.
Ball.

Exhibited inventory of Mrs. Mary
Darnall (CV), by appraisers Thomas
Greenfeild & Richard Marsham

Exhibited inventory of Edward Isaacks
(CV), by appraisers William Nicholls &
Thomas Hinton.

15C:145 12 November. John Haslewood (DO)
exhibited:
* will of William Norcom (DO), proved
  by 3 witnesses. Grace Cleaford was
  granted administration. Securities:
  William Spencer, John Ward. Also
  inventory, by appraisers Thomas
  Compton & John Franke.
* bond of James Foxon administrator of
  Simon Hubert (DO). Securities:
  Gwiny Crowe, Thomas Summer. Also
  inventory, by appraisers Richard
  Meekins & William Shinton.

Mary Ellis executrix of James Ellis (AA)
exhibited accounts, proved before Mr.
Samuell Young. Discharge was granted.

Alexander Moore & his wife Sarah
administratrix of John Coppin (TA)

exhibited accounts.

15C:146 Exhibited bond of Mary widow &
administratrix of Richard Beaumont (CH).
Date: 5 June 1689. Securities: Anthony
Neale, Gilbert Clarke. Also oath of
said Neale & said Clarke, appraisers,
sworn by Mr. Humphrey Warren.

Exhibited inventory of John Morse (AA),
by appraisers R. Wayman, Daniell Clarke.

Edward Mann (TA) exhibited:
- will of Henry Alexander (TA),
  constituting his widow Margarett
  executrix, proved by 2 witnesses.
  Said Margarett was granted
  administration. Security: Thimoty
  Lane. Also inventory, by appraisers
  John Mullikin & William Welsh.
- bond of Nicholas Milburne
  administrator of William Herron
  (mariner, TA). Securities: Ralph
  Jackson, Thomas Delahay. Also
  inventory, by appraisers said
  Jackson & Thomas Bennett.

15C:147 ...
- will of Edward Pollard (TA),
  constituting his widow Martha &
  Robert Grundy executors, proved by 3
  witnesses. Said executors were
  granted administration. Also
  inventory, by appraisers Michaell
  Turbott & Andrew Tonnard.
- will of Judith Brooke (TA),
  constituting Hugh Sherwood executor,
  proved by 2 witnesses. Also
  inventory, by appraisers James
  Benson & R. Gouldesborough.
- bond of Ralph Moone, Jr.
  administrator of Ralph Moone, Sr.
  (old ENG & TA). Securities: Robert
  Smith, John Edmondson. Also
  inventory, by appraisers Ra. Jackson
  & Thomas Delahay.

Ralph Dawson (TA) & John Dawson (TA) in
right of their wives were granted
administration on estate of Bryan Omeley
(TA). Securities: John Edmondson,
Lawrence Knowles.

15C:148 15 November. Court at SMC. Philip Clarke procurator for Franc. Milles (alias Francis Miles) vs. Phil. Lynes administrator of Thomas Yearsly. Said Miles & Yearsly were partners in keeping a stable in SMC.

15C:149 Ruling: plaintiff.

Robert Carvile & Charles Carroll procurators for Ralph & John Dawson vs. Robert Gouldesborough procurator for executors of Bryan & Mary Omaley. William Sharp & Abraham Morgan exhibited accounts. Mentions: John Edmondson.

15C:150 Accounts of Bryan Omaley. Date: 13 November 1694. Payments to: John Davis, James Rouglas (plasterer), William Sharp for a servant, Charles Goffe, James Ferron, Jeffrey Brofet, John Oldridge, Jeffry Horny, Franc. Moldyn, Thomas Delahay, Dr. Benson, Susanna Omaley (her legacy), Isabella Omaley (her legacy), Abraham Morgan for his wife's legacy, William Montague. Distribution to (equally): Susanna Omaley, Isabella Omaley, Mary Omaley. Further payments to: Mary Omaley her portion & 3 children (4 equal parts), Mary Omaley (her legacy), Sarah Omaley (her legacy), Ralph & John Dawson.

15C:151 Amount: £927.0.11. Further payments to: Daniel Toas, Thomas Hutchison. Mentions: brother (dec'd) to the girls, Sarah Omaley, widow Omaley, Mary Omaley.

15C:152 Notice to: Ralph Fishborne, John Edmondson, William Sharp, William Dixon, Abraham Morgan. Mentions: Ralph Dawson & his wife Mary, John Dawson & his wife Sarah. Said Mary & Sarah are surviving children of Bryan Omaley & his wife Mary. Ralph Fishborne did not appear.

15C:153 Mentions: 4 children,

15C:154 accountants are Quaker, Mary Omaley died 4 or 5 months after her husband, Bryan Omaley (son) died before payment of his legacy, Isabella & Susanna (2 daughters) had received their share, Ralph Fishborne illegally procured LoA on the estate of Mary (mother).

15C:155 Ruling: for plaintiffs, for residue of estate of Bryan Omaley,

15C:156 from said Fishborne for payments from

Court Session: 1694

estate of Mary Omaley.

15 November. Exhibited inventory of
Thomas Impey (TA).

Exhibited inventory of Capt. James
Bowling (SM), by appraisers Capt. John
Addison & Mr. William Hutchison.

(N) Randolph, Esq. vs. estate of Lyonell
Copley. Caveat exhibited to ship Anne,
for debt due said estate.

15C:157 17 November. Mr. Carvile for Richard
Hubbart (SM), in letter dated 15th
instant, was granted administration on
estate of Allexander Currey, who died at
house of said Hubbart, as greatest
creditor. Appraisers: Anthony Simes,
Gilbert Croper. Benjamin Hall to
administer oath.

20 November. Thomas Tench, Esq.
administrator of Col. Lionel Copley was
granted continuance.

Charles Carroll procurator for Edward
Parrish (AA) & his wife Mary eldest
daughter of Andrew Robert (AA, dec'd)
vs. Thomas Bland procurator for Dr.
Wolfran Hunt (AA) & his wife Jane
executrix of said Roberts.

15C:158 Said Roberts died in 1682. Mentions:
legacies to his sons. Residue
bequeathed to his wife Jane, his
daughter Mary now wife of Edward
Parrish, & his daughter Katherine, so
long as Jane remained a widow; if she
(re)marry, then she to receive 1/5th.
Short time after the inventory, said
Jane married

15C:159 said Hunt. Said Jane is now dec'd.
John Roberts (eldest son of said Andrew)
has received from estate of said Jane.

15C:160 Ruling: Said Hunt to provide accounts of
estate of said Roberts. Said Hunt's
answer was full of contradictions &
erroneous in law. Also, per the law,
the husband answers for the wife.

15C:161 Plaintiff to recover.

15C:162 Henry Bonner (AA) exhibited verbal will of John Brashas (AA), bequeathing all to Alce Bishop (servant to Capt. Hanslap), proved by 3 witnesses. No administration was granted.

15C:163 4 December. Nathan Veatch (CV) administrator of his brother John Veatch exhibited additional accounts.

Robert Carvile procurator for Nathaniell Dare (CV) was granted continuance.

6 December. Exhibited will of Edmond Dennis (CV), proved by 3 witnesses. No administration was granted.

7 December. Thomas Tench, Esq. administrator of Col. Lionell Copley exhibited accounts, delivered to Mr. Philip Clark, attorney for creditors, to examine.

6 December. David Hellein who married Susanna administratrix of William Melton (CV) exhibited accounts.

15C:164 John Turner (CV) who married Mary executrix of Robert Taylor (CV) exhibited accounts.

Hugh Montgomery (CV) exhibited that he rendered accounts on the estate of George Parker to Col. Blakiston. Continuance was granted, until Mr. John Llewellin comes from over the Bay.

Exhibited inventory of Thomas Cornwell (CV), by appraisers Thomas Johnson & John Smith.

24 December. Exhibited inventory of Thomas Parslo (CV), by appraisers John Hellins & Nathaniell Dare.

William Dent procurator for Edward Milstead (CH) vs. William Sergeant & his wife Damaris. Exceptions exhibited.

15C:165 31 December. John Bigger (CV) exhibited will of James Graves (CV), proved by 3 witnesses. Fran. Graves widow was granted administration.

Exhibited bond of Ursula Howse
administratrix of William Howse (CV).
Security: James Cranford.

Exhibited bond of Bridgett Reyley
administratrix of John Reyley (CV).
Security: Robert Blinkhorne

15 January. John Long (SM) exhibited
will of Clement Hely (SM), constituting
him executor. Said Long was granted
administration. Capt. John Bayne to
prove said will. Appraisers: Thomas
Clarke, Thomas Carvile. Said Bayne to
administer oath.

15C:166 21 January. Edward Cole (CV) was
granted administration on estate of
Samuell Smith (CV), as greatest
creditor. Mr. Henry Lowe to administer
oath.

George Carroll procurator for Evan Rice
(CV) & his wife Elisabeth vs.
Nathaniell Dare (CV). Petition for
attachment for not answering libel.

25 January. Charles Durfft (SM) was
granted administration on estate of
William Medley (SM), as greatest
creditor. Securities: John Browne,
William Stone. Appraisers: William
Husband, Thomas Kerkley.

26 January. Capt. John Bayne exhibited
will of Clement Heley (SM), proved by
both witnesses.

15C:167 Cleborne Lomax (CH) exhibited:
- will of Joshuah Graves (CH),
  constituting no executor, proved by
  3 witnesses. Dorathy Graves relict
  was granted administration.
  Security: Robert Smallpage.
- will of John Cheribub (CH),
  constituting William Herbert
  executor, proved by 3 witnesses.
  Said Herbert was granted
  administration.
- bond of Hugh Teares (CH)

administrator of Nicholas Skidmore
(CH). Security: Henry Hawkins.
- bond of David Lewis administrator of
Robert Jones (CH). Security: John
Smith.
- bond of Maj. James Smallwood who
married Mary relict & administratrix
of Robert Thompson, Jr. (CH).
Security: Samuell Luckett.
- bond of William Penn administrator
of John Lineger (CH). Security:
James Cotterell.

15C:168 1 February. Benjamin Hall (g, SM)
exhibited bond of Mr. Richard Hubbard
administrator of Alexander Currey (SM).
Securities: John Higdon, Alexander
Willson. Also oath of Anthony Simes &
Gilbert Croper, appraisers.

Henry Bonner (AA) exhibited:
- will of John Quatermus (AA),
constituting his widow Jane
executrix, proved by 3 witnesses.
Said Jane was granted
administration. Security: Humphrey
Jarvis. Also inventory, by William
Jefferis & David Makelfresh,
appraisers.
- will of Robert Wade (AA),
constituting George Westale executor
& William Bateman (his neighbor) as
assistance to his son Robert & his
daughter Jane, proved by 4
witnesses.
- bond of Mordica Moore administrator
of William Elvidge (AA). Security:
John Meriton.
- bond of Robert Emerton administrator
of William White (AA). Security:
Robert Gott.
- inventory of Jacob Hallet (AA), by
appraisers Francis Mead & Thomas
Dorsone.

15C:169 4 February. Exhibited inventory of
Maren Duvall (AA), by appraisers James
Sanders & Samuell Young.

Richard Harrisson (CV) was granted
adminiStation on estate of John
Abington (merchant, died in ENG, CV), as

greatest creditor. Mr. George Lingan (g, CV) to administer oath.

5 February. Philip Clarke for creditors of Col. Lionell Copley vs. Thomas Tench, Esq. administrator of said Copley. Exceptions to accounts exhibited.

Garrett Murrey & his wife Susanna vs. said Clarke procurator for Ed. Jones (CE). Continuance was granted.

15C:170 James Cranford (g, CV) attorney for Richard Harrisson (CV) was granted administration on estate of John Abington (merchant, CV). Mr. George Lingan to administer oath.

Evan Rice & his wife Elisabeth vs. Robert Carvile procurator for Nathaniell Dare (CV). Answer exhibited.

Evan Rice vs. estate of Thomas Binkes. Caveat exhibited.

15C:171 Samuell Cooksey (g, SM) administrator of John Winslow (merchant, Boston, NE) exhibited accounts.

7 February. Gilbert Turbervile (SM) who married relict of Thomas Pearce (SM) exhibited additional accounts.

Diana Nuthead (SM) widow of William Nuthead was granted administration on his estate. Securities: Col. John Coode, Henry Wriothesly. Appraisers: John Evans, James Cullings.

8 February. Charles Hughs who married Abigail relict & administratrix of George Carter (CV) exhibited accounts.

15C:172 11 February. Samuell Lee (SM) who married Susanna relict of Edward Baxter (St. George's) was granted administration on his estate. Securities: Richard Benton, Thomas Beale. Appraisers: John Cheverell, John Suks. Also inventory.

Court Session: 1694

18 February. John Bouge (SM) was
appointed Registrar.

William Abeston son & heir of William
Abeston (SM) vs. Richard Attwood
administrator of said Abeston. Said
Abeston exhibited that he delivered
papers to Mr. Llewellin.

15C:173 6 March. Samuell Cooksey (g, SM)
administrator of John Winslow (merchant,
Boston, NE) exhibited accounts.

18 March. George Lingan (g, CV)
exhibited oath of James Cranford
administrator of John Abbington.
Securities: William Parker, William
Holland. Also oath of William Turner &
Elisha Hall, appraisers.

Capt. Henage Robinson (merchant,
London) attorney for Margarett Harman
(London) widow of Thomas Harman was
granted administration on his estate.
Securities: John Hawkins, Robert Smith.
[Paragraph in Latin.] Mentions: George
Hooper.
15C:174 Signed: Thomas Welham. Date: 12
December 1694. Witness: Jeremiah
Jeakins (notary).
15C:174½ Mentions: Margarett Harman (Stepney,
Middlesex) relict & administratrix of
Thomas Harman, John Hawkins (p, Chester
River).
15C:175 Witness: Fra. Harbin.

16 March. John Thompson (CE) exhibited:
• bond of Christopher Mounts
    administrator of Nicholas Dorrill
    (CE). Securities: Isacc Calke,
    James Porter. Also inventory, by
    Edward Lademore & John Atkins,
    appraisers. Also renunciation of
    Mary Peterson (spinster) of
    administration of her father-in-law
    said Dorrill. Date: 6 February
    1694.
15C:176 ...
• bond of William Sparkes
    administrator of Nicholas Hodson
    (CE). Securities: Isaack Calke,
    Daniell Smith.

- bond of Ann Galoway administratrix of Joseph Galoway (CE). Securities: Gerrard Wessels, Edward Skidmore.
- bond of Mary Archer administratrix of Jonas Maddox (CE). Securities: Mathew Vanderheyden, Edward Laddemore. Also inventory, by John Atkins & Isaacke Calke, appraisers.
- bond of Mary Archer administratrix of Jacob Archer (CE). Securities: Mathew Vanderheyden, Edward Laddemore. Also inventory, by John Atkins & Isaack Calke, appraisers.
- bond of Diana Drake administratrix of William Drake (CE). Securities: Thomas Lyndsey, George Steevens. Also inventory, by John Waggott & Mathew. Hendrickson,
- Edward Laddemore executor of Robert Mony (CE) exhibited accounts.

15C:177 Ephraim Willson (sheriff, SO) exhibited summons.

Samuell Hopkins (SO) exhibited:
- bond of William Fasitt administrator & Elisabeth Whittington & Ursula Whittington administratrices of Andrew Whittington (SO). Security: Samuell Worthington. Also inventory, by appraisers Richard Chambers & William Boseman.
- bond of Wilmoth Hill administratrix of Richard Hill (SO). Security: William Wouldhave. Also inventory, by appraisers John Franklin & Henry Read.
- bond of Elisabeth Lynch administratrix of Henry Lynch (SO). Securities: John King, Peter Bodkin. Also inventory, by appraisers Peter Dent & Robert Chambers.
- Thomas Bramley administrator of Thomas Osborne (SO) exhibited accounts.

Court Session: 1695

15C:178 26 March. Capt. John Bigger (CV) exhibited:
- will of George Hardesty (CV), constituting his widow Cecily

- executrix, proved by 3 witnesses.
- will of Andrew Tenehill (CV), constituting his widow Ann Tenehill executrix. She refused administration. John Short (CV) was granted administration. Security: Joseph Hall.
- will of Joseph Fry (CV), constituting his widow Elisabeth Fry executrix, proved by William Carter (witness). Other 2 witnesses are dec'd. Said Elisabeth died soon after, constituting her son-in-law Philip Willisey executor, proved by 3 witnesses. Also bond of Phillip Willis administrator of Joseph Fry. Security: Ignatius Craycroft.
- will of William Marks (CV), constituting his widow Anne Marks executrix, proved by 3 witnesses. She renounced administration, in favor of her son John Chittam. Said Chittam was granted administration. Security: Thomas Tuker.

15C:179 ...
- will of William Graves (CV), constituting his widow Elisabeth executrix, proved by 2 witnesses. Other witness is dec'd.
- will of Francis Baxton (CV), constituting his widow Mary Baxton executrix, proved by 3 witnesses.
- bond of Mary White administratrix of John White (CV). Security: John Mackdowell.
- bond of James Bigger administrator of Richard Hill (CV). Security: William Head.
- bond of Elisabeth Peirson administratrix of Thomas Peirson. (CV). Security: Isaack Williams.
- bond of Joseph Greare administrator of Benjamin Greare. Security: Thomas Padgett.
- bond of Absolom Kent administrator of Richard Gibbs (CV). Securities: George Young, John Kent.
- bond of Elisabeth Heast administratrix of John Heast (CV). Security: Bryant Mackdannah.
- bond of Thomas Tauney administrator of Elisabeth Lethworth (CV).

Securities: James Bigger, Jeremiah Sheriden.
- bond of James Clarke administrator of Thomas Lucas. Security: Thomas Lareson.

15C:180 Mr. Henry Bonner (AA) exhibited:
- will of Thomas Ploumer. (AA), constituting his widow Elisabeth Ploumer executrix, proved by 3 witnesses.
- bond of Joseph Pettybon administrator of Isaac Pettybon (AA). Security: Richard Bagly.
- inventory of William White (AA), by appraisers John Chappell & Robert Gott.

Mr. Cleborne Lomax (CH) exhibited:
- bond of Richard Harrison & Richard Wade administrators of John Wright (CH). Security: William Dent.
- inventory of John Linegar (CH), by appraisers James Cotterell & Thomas Smith. Administrator: William Penn.
- inventory of Joshua Graves (CH), by appraisers Robert Small & Francis Frampton.
- inventory of Nicholas Skidmore (CH), by appraisers William Thompson & John Holles.
- additional inventory of John Bowld (CH), by appraisers Randolph Brandt & Robert Yates.

15C:181 Philip Cox vs. Thomas Courtney. Continuance was granted.

Charles Carroll procurator for John Scott & William Derumple vs. Robert Carvile for John Holsworth administrator of George Abbott & administrator of William Martin. Said Scott to file libel. Said Scott petitioned for summons to: Capt. Henry Mitchell, William Barton, John Mackdowell, Thomas How.

Charles Carroll procurator for Evan Rice vs. Nathaniell Dare. Continuance was granted.

15C:182 Sarah Raylon, now wife of Arthur Neale, administratrix of William Raylon (SM) exhibited accounts.

Thomas Williams & his wife Elisabeth administratrix of Francis Decosta (SM) exhibited accounts.

William Holms who married Sibilla relict & executrix of Edward Baker (SM) exhibited accounts. Continuance was granted.

Charles Watts & his wife Elisabeth administratrix of Absolom Tennison (SM) exhibited accounts. Continuance was granted.

Walter Taylor administrator of William Jones (SM) exhibited accounts.

15C:183 Jane Skipper administratrix of John Skipper (SM) exhibited accounts.

Nicholas Cooper administrator of Robert Downes (CH) exhibited accounts.

John Davies executor of Thomas Watters (CV) exhibited accounts.

Abraham Clarke executor of his father Abraham Clarke (CV) exhibited accounts.

27 March. LAC were granted to Samuell Cooksey (g, SM) on estate of Capt. John Winslow (merchant, Boston, NE). Nathaniell Cary (merchant, NE) exhibited PoA from Abigall Winslow relict & administratrix of said John. Said Cary was granted LoA on estate of said John, for said Abigall. Securities: Philip Clarke, Roger Hensley. LAC to said Cooksey were revoked.

15C:184 Said PoA granted to Mr. Nathaniell Cary (Charles Town). Date: 15 March 1694/5. Witnesses: Robert Starkey, Nathaniell Cary.

Henry Lewis & his wife Abigall executrix of Robert Thomas (SM) exhibited additional accounts.

15C:185 28 March. LoA were formerly granted to John Edmondson (TA) on estate of William Johnson (mariner, London). Samuell Watkins (g, CV) was granted for LoA dbn on said estate. George Plater, Esq. to administer oath.

29 March. Henry Hawkins (g, CH) administrator of Hugh Moore (CH) exhibited accounts. James Knox (g, Glasgow, Scotland) exhibited PoA from Cilias Moore relict & administratrix of said Moore. Said Knox was granted administration. Securities: Cleborne Lomax, William Cooper.

15C:186 1 April. Richard Keene for Mary Edwards exhibited will of Joseph Edwards (CV), constituting his widow Mary executrix, bequeathing her all. Said Mary is very sick & unable to travel to Office. Said Keene was granted administration, for said Mary. John Griggs (g) to administer oath.

2 April. Exhibited inventory of William Nuthead (SM), by appraisers John Evans & James Cullins.

15 April. Fortue Seemes executrix of Marmaduke Seemes exhibited accounts.

William Bladen (clerk, SM) transmitted proceedings kept during the late Revolution.

15C:187 Garrett Murrey vs. Philip Clarke procurator for Edward Jones (g, CE). Answer exhibited.

Philip Clarke & his wife Hanah administratrix of George Mekall (SM) exhibited accounts.

LAC were formerly granted on the estate of Richard Charlett (merchant, CV). James Bigger for self & Thomas Greenfeild (CV) exhibited that said Bigger & Greenfeild are attorneys for Richard Kings (merchant, London) executor of said Charlett. LoA were granted to said Bigger & Greenfeild.

15C:188 Maj. John Bigger to administer oath.
• letter from William Ashhurst knight,
Lord Mayor & alderman of London.
William Smith (g, London), age 30,
deposed at the request of Richard
Kings (tailor & merchant, London)
executor of Richard Charlett
(Swanson's Creek, CV) that he saw
said Kings give PoA to MM Thomas
Greenfeild (g, CV) & James Bigger
(p, CV).

15C:189 ...
Date: 15 October 1694. Signed: (N)
Goodfellow.
• [Paragraph in Latin.]

15C:190 ...
Mentions: Thomas Welham. Signed:
William Smith. Date: 16 October
1694.
• PoA from said Kings to said
Greenfeild & Bigger.

15C:191-192 ...
Witnesses: James Goulton, William
Lightman, William Smith.

22 April. Exhibited inventory of Philip
Larrance (CV), by appraisers Charles
Bevan & George Naylor.

15C:193 Charles Carroll procurator for William
Chew (g, AA) vs. estate of his mother
Mrs. Anne Chew (AA). Caveat exhibited.
Date: 18 April 1695.

29 April. Frances Lawrence
administratrix of her husband Henry
Lawrence (SM) exhibited accounts.

Mary Stone administratrix of John Stone
(CV) exhibited accounts.

Thomas Clarke (SM) administrator of
William Heather (SM) exhibited accounts.

15C:194 Marke Smith (CV) administrator of
Richard Wheeler (CV) exhibited accounts.

30 April. Madam Anne Brent (CV)
administratrix of Henry Brent (CV)
exhibited accounts. Continuance was
granted.

Court Session: 1695

Anne Hopewell executrix of Hugh
Hopewell, Sr. (CV) exhibited accounts.

Edward Cole administrator of Samuell
Smith (CV) exhibited accounts.

Exhibited inventory of Clement Hely
(SM), by appraisers Thomas Clarke &
Thomas Carville.

Exhibited inventory of Samuell Smith
(CV), by appraisers Richard Fenwicke &
John Fenwicke.

15C:195 Mr. John Griggs (CV) exhibited verbal
will of Joseph Edwards (CV), bequeathing
all to his wife (also sick). Mentions:
his sister in ENG. Will was made on 2
March last. Date: 2 April 1695.
Witnesses: Elisabeth Hewell, Elisabeth
Hopewell. Mary relict was granted
administration, but refused to enter
bond. Appraisers (sworn 1 April last):
Richard Keene, Richard Shirly. Also
exhibited inventory.

15C:196 1 May. Charles Darffe & his wife Anne
(alias Anne Medley) administratrix of
her brother George Renolls (SM)
exhibited accounts. Also exhibited
inventory of William Medley (SM).

Richard Clouds (g, SM) exhibited oath of
Thomasine Dammer administratrix of
Thomas Dammer (SM). Security: John
Smith. Also inventory of said Thomas
Damer, by appraisers John Smith & Thomas
Aunis.

Thomas Warren (SM) & his wife Rebecka
executrix of Robert Cole (SM) exhibited
accounts.

15C:197 James Pattison (SM) administrator of
Edward Ward (SM) & administrator of
James Watkins (SM) exhibited accounts
for both estates.

Cox vs. Courtney. Continuance was
granted.

Page 84

Court Session: 1695

Ignatius Warren (SM) administrator of
John Warren (SM) exhibited accounts.

William Roswell administrator of Thomas
Hobson was granted continuance.

Andrew Neale & Thomas Turner executors
of Joseph Piles (SM) exhibited accounts.

15C:198 Kenelm Cheseldyn exhibited from AA
County Court of 4 March 1694/5.
- oath of Henry Wriothesly as clerk.
- Mrs. Mary Duvall widow of Marren
  Duvall (AA) exhibited LoA granted to
  John Duvall (eldest son) on said
  estate by Mr. Henry Bonner. Said
  Mary was named executrix. Said John
  was summoned. Mentions: orphans.
15C:199 ...
- At the request of John Duvall, Henry
  Hanslap (AA), age 59, deposed that
  last August he was at the house of
  Marren Duvall when Mr. Henry Bonner
  brought the witnesses to prove said
  will. Said Mary expressed her
  desire to renounce said will.
  Witnesses: Nicholas Gasaway, Samuell
  Young.
15C:200 ...
- At the request of Mary Duvall,
  William Richardson deposed that on
  13 August last, he was at the house
  of Mary Duvall with Capt. Hanslap,
  James Sanders, Samuell Young, et.al.
  & Henry Bonner to prove the will of
  Marren Duvall, Sr.
- Robert Tyler, one of the executors
  of his father-in-law Marren Duvall,
15C:201 ...
  renounced administration. Date: 18
  August 1694. Witnesses: Samuell
  Young, John Elsey, Henry Bonner.
- Exhibited renunciation of Mary
  Duvall relict of Marren Duvall.
  Date: 13 August 1694. Witnesses:
  Samuell Young, James Sanders,
  Clement Davis.
  Ruling: widow's renunciation is void.
15C:202 Said Mary was granted administration.
Securities: Capt. Richard Hill, Mr.
Samuell Young. Appraisers: Maj. Henry
Ridgly, Mr. James Sanders.

Court Session: 1695

Ralph & John Dawson exhibited that they
had served Ralph Fishborne with the
sentence & that he refused to give
obedience. Date: 28 February 1694.
Thomas Smithson deposed that said John
had delivered the sentence to said
Fishborne & William Dixon who also
refused obedience.

Court Session: Calvert Co. Court 1689

16:1 21 January. Present: Col. Henry
Jowles, Capt. Samuell Bourn, Mr.
Francis Collier, Mr. James Keetch, Mr.
Thomas Gantt, Mr. Thomas Greenfeild.

Andrew Abington was granted
administration on estate of John Pain
(CV). Security: Capt. Samuell Bourn.
Appraisers: Mr. Francis Collier,
William Haymes.

18 March. Present: Col. Henry Jowles,
Mr. Francis Collier, Mr. James Keech,
Mr. Thomas Gant, Mr. Thomas
Greenfeild.

Thomas Hollyday (also Thomas Holliday)
attorney for William Pagan & Co.
(merchants, London) was granted
administration on estate of William Hunt
(CV), as greatest creditor. Security:
Thomas Gant. Appraisers: David Fall,
Josuah Hall.

Winifred Margrete Brome widow of John
Brome (Calvert Towne, CV) exhibited his
will, made on 5 February 1687. He is
going to ENG.
16:2 Bequests: wife Winifred Margrett Brome
600 a. bought of Nicholas Sporne on
north side of Petuxant River called
"Island Neck", said wife a Negro woman
called Negro Mary bought of John
Willymott, eldest son John Brome 550 a.
called "Flonesby" near Muffett's Island
(if he dies before age 21 or marriage
then to be divided among other
children), daughter Martha Brome 600 a.
called "Hamisted" in freshes of Choptank
(if she dies before age 18 or marriage
then to be divided among other

children), youngest daughter Heneretta
Brome 1000 a. called "Brome's Bloome" in
BA (if she dies before age 18 or
marriage then to be divided among other
children), godson Henry Truman, Jr. mare
on plantation of Edward Hurlock on other
side of Crattle Creek, friends &
neighbors: Henry Truman & wife & son
Henry, Cecill Butler, Henry Fearnly,
George Curwen. Distribution: wife, 3
children.

16:3 Executrix: wife. Witnesses: Cecill
Butler, Henry Trueman, Henry Fernley,
John Ledyatt, Thomas Barnett. Proved on
18 March 1689 by Henry Trueman, Henry
Fernley, John Ledyatt, & Thomas Barnett.
Said Winifred Margrett was granted
administration. Appraisers: MM Francis
Huchinson, Hugh Ellis.

Andrew Abington administrator of John
Pain was granted continuance.

Court Session: Calvert Co. Court at Calvert 1

19 August. Present: Col. Henry Jowles,
Mr. Thomas Greenfeild, Mr. John
Griggs, Mr. Thomas Hollyday, Mr. James
Keech, Mr. Thomas Gant, Mr. William
Parker, Mr. Thomas Parsla.

Exhibited inventory of Mr. John Pain.
Date: 31 January 1689. Appraisers: MM
Francis Collier, William Haimes.
Administrator: Andrew Abington

16:4 List of debts: George Hale, Capt. Burgis
& William Hopkins, Thomas Athow, Mr.
William Britton, Casparus Harman, Mr.
Edmondson, William Blake on Philip Lyne,
Capt. Yeats on John Burringham, John
Burringham, William Humphrys, Philip
Cox,

16:5 George Leifeild, Elias King, William
Settle, Mary Yarsly, John Ledyatt,
Samuel Levett, Mr. John Pain (London),
Samuell Gresly, William Askwith, John
Beenly, Mr. Vanderheyden, Michael
Hiller, Thomas Johnson. Amount:
£140.14.4 & #13951.

Elisabeth Devine executrix of Henry
Devine exhibited his will. Executrix:

wife. Bequests: all to wife, Jeremiah Eldridge. Date: 19 February 1689. Witnesses: Charles Wheeler, Stephen Anshee, Jacob Williams, Elisabeth Onsbee. Proved by Stephen Onsbee, Jacob Williams, Elisabeth Onsbee.

16:6 Said Elisabeth was granted administration. Appraisers: William Head, William Wadsworth. Also exhibited inventory, dated 24 March 1689. Amount: £32.12.0.

Edward Ball was granted administration on estate of Micaell Ball (CV). The wife of said Micaell resigned administration. Securities: MM Thomas Hollyday, David Small.

16:7 Appraisers: James More, Joshua Hall.

Ann Hopewell widow of Hugh Hopewell, Sr. (CV) exhibited his will. Bequests: daughter Mary wife of John Keene, son Hugh, wife Ann land, son Richard, daughter Agnes Negro Peeter (boy), daughter Ann Negro Maria (woman), daughter Susanna Negro Stephen (man). Executrix: wife. Date: 23 May 1687. Witnesses: James Harper, Harry Fitzharbert, Charles Jones. Proved on 20 February 1688 by Harry FitzHarbert.

16:8 Proved on 11 July 1689 by James Harper before Henry Darnall. Said Ann was granted administration. Appraisers: Abraham Roads, William Asquith.

19 August. Present: Col. Henry Jowles, Mr. Thomas Tasker, Mr. Thomas Greenfeild, Mr. Thomas Hollyday, Mr. William Parker, Mr. John Griggs.

John Holdsworth & his wife Isabell executrix of William Martin (Clifts, CV) exhibited his will, made 19 September 1689. Bequests: daughter Elisabeth Martin (under age 16) 100 a. pt. of "Thabush Manning" bought of John Manning if she dies then to next of relatives, said daughter Elisabeth Negro Moll (woman) at age 16, son-in-law Thomas Abbott (under age), son-in-law John Abbott (under age), son-in-law George Abbott (under age), son-in-law William

Abbott (under age), son-in-law Samuell
Abbott. Distribution to: daughter
Elisabeth, wife Isabell. Executrix:
wife.

16:9 Witnesses: Samuell Holdsworth, Ja.
Martin, Thomas How. Proved 21 August
1690 by said Holdsworth & said How.
Said John & Isabell were granted
administration. Appraisers: Thomas How,
William Barton.

16 September. Present: Col. Henry
Jowles, Mr. Thomas Tasker, Mr. Fra.
Collier, Mr. James Keech, Mr. Thomas
Gant, Mr. Francis Hutchins.

Capt. John Bigger attorney for William
Pagan & Co. (merchants, London) was
granted administration on estate of John
Loftis (CV), as greatest creditor. The
widow of said John left, refusing to
administer the estate. Security: Mr.
Hugh Ellis. Appraisers: Mr. Samuell
Goosey, William Williams. Mr. Francis
Hutchins to administer oath.

16:10 George Jones & his wife Johanna relict
of Orlandus Ultrasactinus (CV) was
granted administration on his estate.
Security: Capt. Richard Brightwell.
Appraisers: Samuell Copeland, Henry
Taylor. Mr. Thomas Greenfeild to
administer oath.

Richard Keen was granted administration
on estate of Henry Evens (CV), as
greatest creditor. Appraisers: William
Haymes, John Curry.

16:11 Inventory of John Brome (inn holder,
CV). Appraisers: Francis Hutchins, Hugh
Ellis. Date: 2 September 1690.
16:12 ...
16:13 List of debts: Col. Henry Jowles, Mr.
Henry Parker, Mr. James Cranford, John
Padgett, Seth Biggs, Roger Soreen, John
Biggs, Hugh Jones, Arthur Young, George
Younge, Mr. Francis Collier, William
Martin, Robert Freeland, Sarah Reynolds,
Joseph Strickland, Murphey Ward,
Benjamin Ball, William Gringoe, James
Heath, Francis Hyhum, Mr. John Sallers,

John Reed, George Bussey, Jobe Evans,
Mr. Philip Lynes, Richard Brookes,
Thomas Topping, Jonah Winfeild, Edward
Bankes, Edward Butler, Thomas Crowder,
Joseph Harrison, William Smith, Hugh
Ryley, John Soper, John Veatch, John
Smith at Leonard's Creek, William
Nicholes, Joseph Edlo, William Reed,

16:14 Samuell Preston, George Thompson, Paul
Kisby, Mr. Basill Warren, Owen Sheul,
David Smals, Thomas Hughes, John
Bennett, Nathaniell Vizors, Mr. George
Hawes, Mr. Richard Smith, Jr., Mr.
Bucher, Gilbert Devor, Thomas Sedwicks,
William Creed, Mr. Henry Fernley,
Thomas Ward, John Willimott, John
Powell, John Cowdrey, Maj. Ninion
Beals, Robert Blinkhorne, John Chittam,
Nathaniell Cranford, Francis Freeman,
Capt. Richard Gardiner, Mr. Thomas
Greenfeild, William Harris, Able Imon,
Francis Maulden, William Meceres,
Cornelius Newill, Mr. George Kirker,
Thomas Robison, Robert Reed, William
Shittle, William Turner, Cornelius
Watkinson, William Williams, at Pt.
Patience, Mr. Samuell Tew, Benjamin
Haddock, Richard Jenkins, Ignatius
Craycroft, Edward Isaac, John Burd, Mr.
Thomas Johnson, James Dawsey, Mr.
William Holland, James Mecall, Thomas
Hillary, William Howes, Edward
Armstronge, Mrs. Baker at St. Maries',
Thomas Brigentow, Henry Cox, Mr. Thomas
Constable, John Cave, Edward Daw, Mr.
Henry Dryden, Mr. William Dent, Mr.
Richard Fife, Hugh Stone, William Heard,
David Hellen, Mr. Thomas Holladay, John
Radford, Richard Stallings, Jonathon
King, John Stanley, Joseph Waters, John
White, James Whealer, John Manninge,
Joshua Hollinshead,

16:15 James Empson, Joseph Wilson, Baruch
Williams, Thomas Blanford, Mr. James
Bigger, Mr. Richard Brightwell, Daniell
Armiger, John Brasheir, Jonathon Prater,
Bryant Magdaniell, Henry Devine, William
Collingwood, John Fenwicke, Joseph
Ireland, Richard Keen, William Kempster,
William Moore, Mr. George Plater,
Thomas Tinsly, James Berry, John Browne,
Richard Burke, Ambrose Biggs, Mr. James

Cranford, Dr. Craford, John Cragbourne, Edward Dickinson, Samuell Fowler, Thomas Hardine, Joseph How, John Hedger, William Isenonnger, George Johnson, John Joyce, James Moore, Obadiah Evans, Robert Rouse, John Sanderline, John Scott, Mr. Michaell Tawney, John Hollings, Thomas Pearson, Daniell Sharadine, Robert Anderson, Mr. Edward Batson, William Simons, James Dicke, Mrs. Parker, Capt. Samuell Bourne, Thomas Butterfeild, William Barton, Samuell Copeland, William Meade, Abraham Clarke, Tymothy Gunter, John Godsgrace, Thomas Hinton, Elisha Hall, William Howard, Robert Jervis, John Kent, Peter Lamar, Phillip Lawrence, Mr. Thomas Parslow, Robert Spickernell, Edmond Stow, John Tanman, Mr. William Parker, Mr. Richard Fenwicke, Robert Hobbs, Edward Perdew, William Wood, John Gyatt, Richard Pollard, George Hardesty, Charles Tracy,

16:16 Mr. Robert Carvile, Capt. Timothy Keiser, John Barrett, Thomas Bridges, Capt. Thomas Caggett, Richard Clarke, John Conoway, Nathaniell Dare, Peter Flood, John Ganderell, William Hutchins, Ezekiell Hide, John Nelsone, Thomas Jones, William Needham, Daniel Philipps, Thomas Purnell, Francis Roades, John Skippers, Joseph Wilsone, Richard Shephard, John Lydiatt, Jeremiah Sheirendine, Thomas Smith, Charles Bradley, John Spencer, Jeremiah Johnson, William Haimes, Thomas Biven, David Morgan, Edward Blagbourne, Thomas Clawson, Joshua Welsteede, Mr. George Butler, Mr. John Hance, William Harbott, John Humes, John Sutten, Mr. Andrew Abington, Andrew Brade, John Hollands, William Harris, Mr. George Lingan, Daniell Murrine, William Sturmy, Joseph Woodroffe, Capt. Charles Partis, Edward Harlocke. Amount: £263.3.11 + #93161.

16:17 18 November. Present: Capt. Samuell Bourne, Mr. Thomas Tasker, Mr. Francis Hutchins, Mr. Thomas Greenfeild, Mr. William Baker, Mr. Thomas Gantt.

Inventory of William Martin.
Appraisers: Thomas Howe, William Barton.
Date: 1 October 1690. List of debts:
Mr. John Manninge, Nath. Manning,
Richard Shepherd, Jo. Pardo, Jam.
Craford, Nath. Maning, William
Wilkinson, William Derumple, Mr.
Hollins, Richard Leake, William Barton.
16:18   Amount: £277.17.0 + #24335.

Inventory of John Loftis. Appraisers:
Samuell Goosey, William Williams. Date:
2 October 1690.
16:19   Amount: £14.7.0 + #400.

Inventory of Hugh Hopewell, Sr. (CV).
Appraisers: Abraham Rhodes, William
Asquith.
16:20   Mentions: Negro Stephen (man). Amount:
£142.7.0.
16:21   Date: 12 November 1690.

Inventory of Orlandus Ultrajurtinus.
Appraisers: Samuell Copeland, Henry
Taylor. Date: 14 November 1690 List of
debts: John Davis, Hugh Jones, Joseph
Wilson, Charles Biven, Mr. Thomas
Sprigg, John Kelley, Pearce Nowland,
William Richards, Henry Cranford, John
Tickpenny, Francis Copsen, John Johnson.
Mentions: Capt. Michaell Homes.
Amount: £64.3.6 + #5299.

16:22   Mr. Andrew Abington was granted
administration on estate of Thomas
Broadast (CV). Security: Capt. Samuell
Bourne. Mentions: goods in hands of Mr.
William Nicholes (Clifts, CV).
Appraisers: William Haims, John Curry.
Capt. Samuell Bourne to administer
oath.

Hannah Nevill widow of Cornelius Nevill
(CV) was granted administration on his
estate. Security: Jeremiah Sherindine.
Appraisers: Christopher Banes, Jeremiah
Sherindine.

Thomas Hinton
16:23   was granted administration on estate of
Jeremiah Johnson (CV). Appraisers: John
Bennett, Charles Harrington.

20 January. Present: Col. Henry
Jowles, Mr. Thomas Tasker, Mr. Francis
Hutchins, Mr. Thomas Greenfeild, Mr.
Thomas Holliday, Mr. William Parker,
Capt. Thomas Parslow, Capt. Hen.
Mitchell.

Inventory of Cornelius Nevill.
Appraisers: Christopher Banes, Jeremiah
Sherindine. Date: 24 November 1690.
List of debts: Thomas Sedwick,
16:24 Nath. Cranford, Baruch Williams, Joshua
Cecill, Richard Brasiers, James Cobb,
Col. Jowles. Amount: £17.9.0 + #7558.
Date: 5 February 1690.

Inventory of Jeremiah Johnson.
Appraisers: John Bennett, Charles
Harrington. Date: 17 June 1690. List
of debts: Michaell Yeackly to be paid by
Mr. Richard Johns,
16:25 Robert Stone, Samuell Bagbie. Date: 15
January 1690. Amount: £30.5.8 + #800.

Walter Smith was granted administration
on estate of Lewis Floyde (CV).

17 March. Present: Col. Henry Jowles,
Mr. Thomas Tasker, Mr. Thomas
Greenfeild, Mr. Thomas Gantt, Mr.
James Keetch, Mr. William Parker.

Margarett Russell (now wife of James
Wood) administratrix of John Russell
exhibited accounts. Payments to:
Ernesto Kukabert, John Craycroft, John
Wasker, Capt. Samuell Bourn, William
Johnson, Richard Johns, Michaell Tawney,
Benjamin Ballowing, Joachim Kersteed,
Col. Jowles, Edward Perem paid by
Richard Johns, John Kinsley, William
Cole. Amount of inventory: #7238.
Amount of accounts: #7393. Date: 19
March 1690.

16:26 Ann Simson was granted administration on
estate of her husband (d. October last),
leaving her with 4 small children.
Exhibited was will of Jeremias Simpson
(CV). Date: 29 September 1690.
16:27 Bequests: eldest son Jeremias, 2nd son
John, younger son Thomas. Executrix:

wife. Mentions: Charles Coleman.
Witnesses: William Brooke, John
Skippers, Isaac Baker. Proved on 12
March 1690/1 by Isaac Baker & John
Skippers.

Andrew Abington administrator of John
Payne to exhibit accounts before Capt.
Samuell Bourne & Mr. Thomas Parslow.

Court Session: Calvert Co. Court at Calvert

16:28 5 September. Present: Col. Henry
Jowles, Mr. Thomas Tasker, Mr. Thomas
Greenfeild, Mr. Francis Collier, Mr.
Thomas Holliday, Mr. William Parker,
Capt. Hen. Mitchell, Mr. Thomas Gantt.

Michaell Murreen was granted
administration on estate of Shute Dunn
Veale. Mentions: parents of dec'd,
goods at house of Richard Jenkins.
Appraisers: MM James Keech, Richard
Charlett. Mr. Thomas Gantt to
administer oath.

16:29 17 November. Present: Col. Henry
Jowles, Mr. Thomas Tasker, Mr. Thomas
Greenfeild, Mr. William Parker.

Ann Abington widow of Mr. Andrew
Abington exhibited his will. Bequests:
son John land bought of Richard Keen,
rest of children (under age).
Executrix: wife. Assistants: Capt.
Samuell Bourne, Mr. John Llewellin.
Proved by Capt. Francis Harbin & Mr.
John Edwards on 29 October last before
Thomas Parslow & Henry Hooper. Proved
by George Plater on 19 November 1691
before H. Jowles.

Richard Jenkins exhibited verbal will of
Shute Dunn Veale (alias Mrs. Shute
Dunwell) made on 16 August 1691 at house
of Mr. Richard Jenkins (CV). Bequests:
Mrs. Jenkins & her husband,
16:30 Amey Graves. Mrs. Dunwell died on 23
August. Will proved on 24 September
1691 by Lydia Cobb, Elisabeth Vehatt,
Amey Graves, Robert Gates. Said Robert
Gates deposed. Witnesses: James Clarke,

Lydia Cobb, Elisabeth Vehatt. LoA granted to Michaell Murreen were revoked. Said Jenkins was granted administration.

Marke Smith was granted administration on Richard Weller (CV). Security: William Howes. Appraisers: James Cranford, John Willmott. Thomas Tasker to administer oath.

Thomas Greenfeild was granted administration on estate of Matthew Strickland (CV). Security: Henry Ferneley.

16:31 Mr. Thomas Holliday to administer oath.

19 January. Present: Col. Henry Jowles, Mr. Thomas Tasker, Mr. Thomas Greenfeild, Mr. James Keech.

Michaell Murreen exhibited will of Paul Bertrand (minister, CV). Bequests: wife Mary plantation (Patuxent River, CV) 100 a. called "Coxhay".

16:32 Executrix: wife. Date: 24 March 1686/7. Witnesses: Anthony Underwood, Martha Underwood, John Lowe. [No witnesses found.]

Samuell Holdsworth exhibited will of Richard Ladd (CV). Date: 16 March 1684. Bequests: nephew John Rigdon (under 21, son of sister Ellon) land adjoining James Magrother & bounding "Groom's Lott", wife to be guardian of said John Rigdon, brother John Ladd (Norwich),

16:33 sister Ellon Rigdon 100 a. called "Lad's Desire". Residue: wife including "Groome's Lott", 600 a. then to said nephew then to John Ladd, "Charles' Gift" to Church of ENG to be settled by Richard Smith, Jr. & Thomas Tasker & Michaell Taney & John Hance except for 100 a. sold to William Gumbrell (p). Mentions: nephew Thomas Forman (chirurgeon). Executrix: wife. Witnesses: John Griggs, John Mannyng, William Mitchell, William Harris. Codicil: Overseers: MM Henry Rigdon (brother-in-law), John Hance. Proved on 10 February 1691 by John Griggs before

Henry Mitchell.

16:34   20 January 1691. John Mannyng & William
Harris proved will of Richard Ladd.
Samuell Holdsworth was granted
administration on said estate. Mr.
John Griggs to administer oath.

Edward Daw (son of Nathan Daw & his wife
Mary) was granted administration on both
estates, & exhibited his father's will.
Appraisers: John Hollins, John Jenkis.
Capt. Henry Mitchell to administer
oath. Will of Nathan Daw (Clifts).
Date: 13 May 1688. Executrix: wife
Mary. Bequests: wife Mary,
16:35   son Edward, daughter Mary. Signed:
Nathan Dawe. Witnesses: Samuell
Holdsworth, Jefferey Maneley, William
Wilkinson, Thomas Howes.

John Mannyng exhibited will of James
Cranford (chirurgeon, CV). Executor:
John Mannyng. Date: 26 December 1691.
Witnesses: John Holdsworth, William
Marston, Richard Leake, George Seley.
Proved on 8 January 1691/2 by John
Holdsworth & William Marston before
Henry Jowles & Henry Mitchell. Proved
on 19 January 1691 by Richard Leake.
16:36   Said Mannyng was granted administration.
Appraisers: Thomas Howes, George Seley.
Capt. Henry Mitchell to administer
oath. Provisions given to widow &
orphan, if there is one.

15 March. Present: Mr. Thomas Tasker,
Mr. Francis Hutchins, Mr. James
Keetch, Mr. Thomas Holliday, Capt.
Henry Mitchell.

Ann Gantt widow of Thomas Gantt
exhibited his will. Bequests: wife Ann
plantation,
16:37   eldest son Thomas Gantt (under age 17)
"Marsham's Rest" & "Telerton", daughter
Ann Gant (under age 18) "Bullwick",
daughter Elisabeth Gantt (under age 18)
"Edlowes Choice" on Eastern Shore (DO)
at head of St. John's Creek, son Gantt
Edward. Mentions: John Martin
(overseer). Date: 18 November 1691.

Witnesses: Thomas Brooke, John Smith,
Sam. Peter. Proved by all three on 23
January 1691 before Thomas Tasker &
Thomas Greenfeild. Said executrix was
granted administration.

16:38   Mark Smith administrator of Richard
Weller was granted continuance. Date:
15 March 1691.

John Wilson & his wife Thredwith
executors of James Gardner exhibited
accounts. Appraisers: Thomas Sedgwick,
John Grover. Amount of inventory:
#14372. Payments to: Mr. Taney, Jochem
Kierstead, Richard Cragbourne, William
Smith for child's schooling, Thomas
Cosden. Amount of accounts: #1691.

16:39   Relict of Andrew Abington to exhibit
accounts of John Payne before Capt.
Samuell Bourne & Capt. Thomas Parslow.

John Edwards & his wife Ann executors of
Andrew Abington were granted
administration on his estate.
Appraisers: MM Charles Carroll, Richard
Keen.

Matthew Gautherine & his wife Mary
relict & executrix of William Needham
exhibited his will. Mr. Tasker to prove
said will. Said Mary was granted
administration. Appraisers: William
Turnor, William Howes. Said Tasker to
administer oath.

Richard Brightwell was granted
administration on estate of Edward Banke
(CV). Mr. Thomas Greenfeild to
administer oath.

16:40   Greefe Nugent widow of Henry Nugent was
granted administration on his estate.
Appraisers: John Read, John White. Mr.
James Keech to administer oath.

Exhibited inventory of James Cranford.
Appraisers: Thomas Howes, George Seley.
Date: 27 January 1691.
16:41   Mentions: Mr. Atkey. List of debts:
Nathan Daw, Edward Bedinsher, John

James, Daniell Simons, John Davis,
William Harris, James Holden, William
Migdsley, James Reccinkles, Edward Daw,
Capt. Stevens, George Nokes, John
Holdsworth,

16:42 James Mecall, John Knowell, John White,
Andrew Beard, William Kempster, Thomas
Brigendine, Thomas Spender, Robert Read,
John Hollins, George Seeling, Edward
Cocknell, Andrew StandingStreet, William
Derumple, Thomas Moulden, Thomas
Purnell, Robert Thompson, James
Thompson, Alexander Lewis, Matthew
Curren, John Ball, George Gambrell,
William Browne, Thomas Bull, William
Shittle, Robert Blinkhorne. Amount:
£33.0.0 + #4250.

John Fisher & his wife Elisabeth relict
& executrix of Tobias Miles (p, CV)
exhibited his will.

16:43 Date: 16 August 1691. Bequests: son
John Miles 400 a. called "Miles End",
wife Elisabeth Miles, son Tobias Miles
(under age 18) 100 a. called "Brantry",
daughter Mary Miles (under age 16) 50 a.
part of "Mill Runn", daughter Frances
(under age 16) 50 a. part of "Mill
Runn", daughter Elisabeth Miles (under
age 16) 50 a. of "Mill Runn", son-in-law
Edward Wood. Executrix: wife.
Witnesses: Henry Mitchell,

16:44 Samuell Constable, Francis Maldin,
Richard Kent, Fran. Freeman. Proved on
18 November 1691 by Francis Mauldin &
Capt. Henry Mitchell before Henry
Jowles & William Parker. Proved on 16
March 1691 by Samuell Constable before
Henry Jowles & Thomas Tasker. Said John
& Elisabeth were granted administration.
Appraisers: MM Christopher Banes, Edward
Batson. Capt. Henry Mitchell to
administer oath.

Court Session: Calvert Co. Court at Calvert

21 June. Present: Mr. Thomas Tasker,
Mr. Thomas Greenfeild, Mr. Francis
Hutchins, Capt. Henry Mitchell, Capt.
John Bigger, Mr. Francis Freeman.

Exhibited inventory of Richard Ladd &
Rosamond Holdsworth (late wife of
Samuell Holdsworth). Appraisers: Thomas
Howe, James Duke.
16:45 Date: 25 April 1692.
16:46 ...
16:47 Amount: £451.14.0.

Exhibited inventory of Nathan Daw & Mary
Daw. Appraisers: John Hollins, John
Jenkins. Date: 4 April 1692.
16:48 Amount: £56.4.0.

Inventory of Mathew Strickland.
Administrator: Thomas Greenfeild. List
of debts: Thomas Greenfeild. Amount:
£16.3.11. Appraisers: James Watts,
William Harbert. Date: 17 October 1692.

16:49 Inventory of Richard Weller.
Administrator: Marke Smith. Appraisers:
James Cranford, John Willymott. Date:
20 February 1691. Amount: £8.1.0.

Mathew Gautherine & his wife Mary relict
& executrix of William Needham (CV)
exhibited his will. Bequests: wife
Mary, son James. Date: 26 October 1691.
Witnesses: Mathew Gautherin, James
Needham, John Willymott. Proved by John
Willymott, Mathew Gautherin, & James
Needham (son of dec'd) on 3 March 1692
before Thomas Tasker.
16:50 Inventory of William Needham (p, CV).
Appraisers: William Turnor, William
Howes. Date: 18 June 1692. Amount:
£49.12.0.

16:51-54 <do not exist>

Court Session: 1695

16:55 15 May. [The entry says: Anne Arundel
Co. Court at Ann Arrundell Towne.
However, considering the documents
presented, this must be the Prerogative
Court.] Cleborne Lomax (CH) exhibited:
• will of John Wheeler (CH),
constituting his widow Mary
executrix. She refused
administration.
• will of Humphrey Warren (CH),

constituting his widow Margery & his son Notley Warren executors, proved by 3 witnesses. Said Margery renounced administration. Said Notley was granted administration.

- will of William Smith (CH), constituting his widow Elisabeth executrix, proved by 3 witnesses. Said Elisabeth was granted administration. Also inventory, by appraisers John Godshall & Moses Jones.
- will of Morris Lloyd (CH), constituting Michaell Linge executor, proved by 3 witnesses. Said Linge was granted administration.

16:56 ...

- will of William Burman (CH), constituting his widow & his son Samuell Burman executors, proved by 2 witnesses. Said widow & son were granted administration.
- bond of Robert Laftan son & administrator of Robert Laftan (CH). Securities: Thomas Craxton, John Goversey.
- bond of Henry Gifford administrator of Hugh Gardiner (CH). Security: John Theobalds.
- inventory of John Wright (CH), by appraisers Phil. Hoskins & Thomas Alcock.

Mr. John Thompson (CE) exhibited:
- will of John Adwick (CE), constituting John Hull executor, proved by 3 witnesses. Said Hull refused administration. Gerardus Wessells was granted administration, as greatest creditor. Securities: Edward Skidmore, George Sturton.
- bond of George Sturton son-in-law & administrator of Elinor Neale (CE). Securities: Col. William Pearce, Gerardus Wessells.
- will of John Miller (CE), constituting John Parks, James Course, & Stephen Coleman executors, proved by 3 witnesses. Said Parks & Course refuse administration. Said Stephen Colliman is a Quaker & not

16:57

willing to take oath. John Darke &
his wife Martha relict of said
Miller were granted administration.
Securities: Benjamin Hambline,
Richard Kennard.

- will of Peter Willson (CE), citing
no executor, proved by 2 witnesses.
- additional inventory of Nichollas
Dorrill (CE), by appraisers Ed.
Skidmore & John Atkins.
- inventory of Nicholas Hodson (CE),
by appraisers Ed. Skidmore & George
Sturton.
- inventory of William Burden (CE), by
appraisers Daniell Smith & William
Chamberlin.
- William Walch (CE), by appraisers
Thomas Whitton & William Winfeild.
- accounts of James Willson & his wife
Mary administratrix of William Jones
(CE).

Mr. Samuell Hopkins (SO) exhibited:
- will of Edward Evans (SO),
constituting his widow Mary
executrix, proved by 2 witnesses.
Said Mary died soon thereafter. Mr.
James Round (SO) was granted
administration, as greatest
creditor. Sureties: Robert Johnson,
John Webb. Also inventory, by
appraisers John Franklyn & John
Webb.

Mr. John Rawlings (DO) exhibited:
- bond of Mary Crowe administratrix of
Gournay Crowe (DO). Sureties:
Thomas Clarke, Edward Poole. Also
inventory (unsigned), by appraisers
Obadiah King & Edward Williams.
(Said inventory was returned in
August 1695.)

16:58

- will of Mary Stoaker (DO),
constituting Humphry Hubert &
Charles Powell executors, proved by
2 witnesses before Mr. John
Haselwood.
- bond of Edward Tench administrator
of John Tench (DO). Sureties:
William Willoughby, Edward Williams.

Page 101

Also inventory, by appraisers
Humphry Mould & Morris Mackenny.
- bond of Elisabeth Ford
administratrix of John Ford (DO).
Sureties: Thomas Newton, Edward
Badman. Also inventory, by
appraisers Obadia King & Arthur
Betty.
- bond of Richard Pearce administrator
of John Pearce (DO). Sureties:
Anthony Chilcott, Samuell Brooke.
Also inventory, by appraisers Jo.
Gladstane & William Spencer

Summons were exhibited by:
- Capt. William Holland (high
sheriff, AA).
- Mr. William Parker (high sheriff,
CV).
- Mr. James Smith (high sheriff, TA).
- sheriff (SO).

Andrew Hambleton one of administrators
of James Gill (alias James Gibson, TA)
exhibited accounts.

Hugh Dwyer administrator of Robert Towe
(TA) exhibited accounts. Continuance
was granted.

16:59   Mary Heather (now wife of John Wade)
administratrix of Thomas Gillmun (?)
(DO) exhibited accounts on his estate.
Said Mary administratrix of William
Heather (DO) exhibited accounts on his
estate.

John Nichols administrator of John
Braday (DO) exhibited accounts.

Samuell Johnson administrator of Jane
Wollis (SO) exhibited accounts.

William Jones executor of Cornelius
Johnson (SO) exhibited accounts.

Maj. James Smalwood (CH) administrator
of Robert Thompson (SH) exhibited
accounts. Also exhibited inventory, by
appraisers Samuell Luckes & Cornelius
Maddocks. Continuance was granted.

Court Session: 1695

Capt. John Davis administrator of
Thomas Welsh (TA) exhibited accounts.

Edward Ball (CV) administrator of
Michaell Ball (CV) exhibited inventory,
by appraisers James Moore & Joshua Hall.
Continuance was granted.

Said Edward exhibited that married
Persilla administratrix of William Lyle
& executrix of Henry Dakes. Continuance
was granted.

John Short (CV) administrator of Andrew
Taunhill was granted continuance.

16:60 Benjamin Williams (AA) administrator of
Joseph Williams (BA) exhibited
inventory, by appraisers Leonard Weyman
& John Powell. Continuance was granted.

Faith Gongo executrix of her mother
Faith Gongo (AA) exhibited accounts.

Madam Henrieta Marie Lloyd executrix of
John Loudey (TA) exhibited, by her son,
receipts. Continuance was granted.

Exhibited inventory of John Sunderland
(CV), by appraisers Richard Racke &
William Derumple.

Capt. John King (SO) one of executors
of Nicholas Carpenter (SO) was granted
"quietus est".

David Rogers administrator of John
Burrell (TA) exhibited accounts.

George Burges administrator of William
Walker (AA) exhibited accounts.

Edward Mason & his wife Alice
administratrix of Henry Archer (AA)
exhibited accounts.

Jeremiah Eldridge administrator of Roger
Cooper (CV) exhibited accounts.

Said Eldridge & his wife Elisabeth
executrix of Henry Devins (CV) exhibited
accounts.

16:61 16 May. Philip Clarke procurator for John Mackclester (SO) vs. William Fassitt (SO). Libel was exhibited. Continuance was granted.

17 May. Cornelius Odwyer administrator of Denis Mahony (TA) exhibited that he paid all bills, but cannot exhibit any receipts because his house recently burned. Ruling: dismissal.

18 May. Walter Smith administrator of Henry Taylor (CV) was granted dismissal.

James Stoddart son-in-law of Ann Drifeild administratrix of Thomas Drifeild (AA) exhibited accounts. She is an ancient woman. Continuance was granted.

Thomas Hillary administrator of Baruck Williams (CV) exhibited inventory, by appraisers John Short & Elisha Hall. Continuance was granted.

Hester Baldin administratrix of Nicholas Nicholson (AA) exhibited accounts.

Margarett Newton executrix of Edward Newton (DO) exhibited accounts.

16:62 20 May. Charles Stevens (AA) was granted administration on estate of Michaell Taylor (AA), who died leaving no relations in Province, on behalf of relations in ENG. Sureties: John Rockhould, Peter Bond. Appraisers: John Moriat, Edward Hall.

Elisabeth Lootton widow & executrix of Jacob Lotton (BA) exhibited accounts.

Charles Carroll procurator for Edward Parrish vs. Dr. Wolfran Hunt administrator of Andrew Roberts (AA). Said Hunt exhibited accounts.

Arthur Whitely (DO) exhibited that Charles Wheeler was granted LoA on 1 March 1693 on the estate of William Worgan (DO), unadministered by Dr. John Brookes, in right of their wives Sarah &

Mary only daughters of said Worgan.
Said Charles & Mary have relinquished
administration. Said Whitely was
granted administration. Mr. John
Rawlins to administer oath.

Arthur Whitely vs. Hugh Sherwood (TA)
executor of Judith Brooke relict of Dr.
John Brooke administrator of said
Worgan. Summons for said Sherwood to
render accounts. Complaint exhibited.

Exhibited inventory of Clement Heley
(SM), by appraisers Thomas Clarke &
Thomas Carvile.

16:63   21 May. Col. David Browne (SO)
executor of Archibald Erreskin was
granted continuance.

James Cranford administrator of John
Abington (CV) was granted continuance.

Exhibited will of Robert Dixon (CV),
proved by Nathaniell Dare & John
Wattermore. Executor: Thomas Purnell.

23 May. Edward Boothby (g, BA) was
granted LAC on estate of Arnoldus de la
Grange.

Nicholas Lowe (g, TA) was appointed
Deputy Commissary (TA). Signed: Thomas
Smithson. Mr. Ed. Mann to deliver all
proceedings.

Samuell Hopkins (SO) to continue as
Deputy Commissary (SO). Security: Mr.
William Whittington.

James Cranford (CV) was granted
administration on estate of John
Abington (d. in ENG). Richard Harrison
(CV) & George Lingan (CV) exhibited that
Madam Mariel Parney (London) & Madam
Mariel Abington (London) are
executrices. Said Parney & Abington
have given PoA to said Harrison & said
Lingan. Said Harrison refused to take
oath.

16:64   Said Lingan was granted administration,
unadministered by said Cranford.

Signed: William Turner, Daniell Hully.
LoA to said Cranford are revoked. Will
of John Abington (merchant, London).
Debts to be paid by Mr. Richard
Harrison (MD). Bequests: Dr. Mick
Parney (brother-in-law), sister Mirriell
Parney (wife of said doctor) "The
Living" at Stoake near Bristoll Gloster
in possession of William Worrell, niece
Muriell Parney, niece Mirriell Abington,
Mrs. Alice Nolmes & her sons John &
Charles estate left her by her father in
IRE. Mentions: brother of said Alice.

16:65 Further bequests: John Abington (under
age 21) son of William (dec'd), Mr.
John Pettitt, children (John, Charles,
newborn) of said Alice Nelms land etc.
in MD. Executor: kinsman Mr. John
Abington. Date: 14 January 1692.
Witnesses: Fenton Byund, Hery Damett,
Thomas Freeman.

16:66 [Paragraph in Latin.] PoA before
Jeremiah Jenkins (notary, London) dated
7 December 1694. Madam Mariel Parney
(widow, London) & Madam Mariel Abington
(spinster, London) administratrices of
John Abington (merchant, London) to
Richard Harrison (p, MD) & George Lingan
(p, MD).

16:67 Witnesses: Richard Burke, Henry
Robinson.

16:68 Sir Thomas Lane knight, Lord Mayor of
London affirmed PoA. Signed: (N)
Goodfellow. Date: 11 December 1694.
Affirmed by Jeremiah Jenkins.

16:69 Witnesses: Fran. Harbin, Heneage
Robinson.

24 May. Exhibited will of Mrs. Anne
Chew (AA), proved by 2 witnesses.
Executor refuses administration.

Samuell Browne (BA) executor of Thomas
Thurston (BA) exhibited inventory, by
appraisers George Gunnell & Roger
Mathews. Also exhibited accounts.
Continuance was granted.

16:70 Mr. Henry Wriothesly exhibited LoA to
Mrs. Mary Duvall relict & executrix of
Marren Duvall (AA), granted March last.
Former LoA granted to Mr. John Duvall

by Mr. Henry Bonner revoked.
Securities: Capt. Richard Hill, Samuell
Young.

5 June. Capt. Philip Howard exhibited
oath of Charles Stevens administrator of
Michaell Taylor (AA). Also exhibited
oath of John Marriott & Edward Hall,
appraisers.

17 July. Exhibited inventory of John
Abington (CV), by appraisers William
Turner & Elisha Hall.

24 July. Charles Stevens (AA) exhibited
inventory of Michaell Taylor (AA), by
appraisers John Marriott & Edward Hall.

Mrs. Rachell Procter vs. estate of
Nicholas Moray (AA). Caveat exhibited.

James Harnest vs. estate of Nicholas
Moray (AA). Caveat exhibited.

John Thomas (sheriff, BA) exhibited
summons to George Utie & his wife Mary.

16:71   3 August. Henry Bonner (AA) exhibited:
- bond of Silvester Welch
  administrator of John Welch (AA).
  Securities: Leonard Weyman, Benjamin
  Williams. Also inventory, by
  appraisers Leonard Wayman & Benjamin
  Williams.
- bond of John Gressam administrator
  of Edward Selby (AA).
- bond of Capt. Abraham Wilde
  administrator of Abraham Wilde, Jr.
  (AA). Security: Otho Holland.
- bond of Thomas Tench, Esq.
  administrator of William Harry (AA).
  Security: Benjamin Scrivener.
- bond of Rachell Gray administratrix
  of John Gray (AA). Securities:
  William Browne, Charles Tilby.
- will of John Ray (AA), constituting
  Thomas Hanson executor. Said Hanson
  was granted administration.
- inventory of William Elvidg (AA), by
  appraisers John Gaile & George
  Hollingsworth.
- inventory of Isaack Pettibone (AA),

by appraisers Richard Baily & Edward Chapman.

Charles Carroll procurator for Garrett Murry (CE) & his wife Susanna vs. Edward Jones. Replication of answer.

Exhibited inventory of John Gray (AA), by appraisers Walter Phelps & Robert Hopper.

16:72 6 August. Kenelm Cheseldyn, Esq. exhibited:

- will of William Husculah (SM), constituting Capt. John Dent (SM) executor. Mr. Ralph Foster exhibited oath of Jamina Cabsham (witness) & Walter King (witness). Said Dent was granted administration. Said Foster to administer oath.
- will of William Roswell (SM), constituting his widow Ema executrix. Mr. Samuell Coosey exhibited oath of Anthony Neale (witness), Thomas Torner (witness), William Legg (witness), & William Thomas (witness). Said Ema was granted administration. Said Coosey also exhibited oath of Joshua Guybert & John Dash, appraisers. Said Coosey to administer oath to said Ema. Also exhibited inventory. Said Ema exhibited accounts. Continuance was granted.
- bond of Mary Greengoe relict & administratrix of William Greengoe (SM). Securities: Robert Forguson, William Whirrat. Also exhibited inventory, by appraisers William Whirrett & Robert Fusson [sic].
- bond of William Taylard administrator of James Anderson (SM, died in PA), as greatest creditor. Securities: Robert Mason, John Llewellin.

16:73 ...

- Mr. James Biggers (CV) was granted administration on estate of Thomas Kemp (d. last of April), having no wife or relations. Petition, dated 10 June 1695, sent by Michael

Caterton. Security: Jeremiah
Sheridon. Mr. James Keetch to
administer oath. Continuance was
granted.

- James Nuthorne petition to Francis
Nicholson (Governor). Said Nuthorne
is a poor orphan. His father died
about 10 years ago, leaving him
joint executor with his mother of a
bountiful estate. Soon thereafter,
she married Capt. James Bigger.
Cites "barbarous" usage by said
Bigger. Aunt of said Nuthorne is
only relation. Petition referred to
Commissary General on 11 June 1695.

16:74 ...

Said Bigger appeared & promised to
send the orphans [sic] to school &
to take better care of them.

- Mr. Richard Clouds exhibited
inventory of John Goldsmith (SM), by
appraiser Edward Turner. Mrs.
Judith Clouds is relict.
- inventory of William Mark (CV), by
appraisers Thomas Tucker & William
Morgan. Administrator: John Chittam

Exhibited exceptions to inventory of
Robert Downes (CH). Administrator:
Nicholas Cooper. Administration dbn was
granted to John Morreing father of Mary
Morreing (infant) as next-of-kin to said
Downes. LoA to said Cooper revoked.

John Wheatly executor of Andrew Wheatly
exhibited accounts.

Dorathy Stevens executrix of John
Stevens (DO) exhibited that her husband
made will, constituting her executrix.
Said will was proved before Dr. Jacob
Lookerman. Said Dorathy was dismissed.

16:75 Maj. John Bigger (CV) exhibited:
- will of Francis Higham (CV),
constituting his widow Elisabeth
Higham executrix, proved by 2
witnesses. Said Elisabeth refused
administration.
- will of James Hume (CV),
constituting his widow Sarah Hume
executrix, proved by 3 witnesses.

Said Sarah was granted
administration.
- will of Obadia Evins (CV),
constituting his widow Ann
executrix, proved by 3 witnesses.
Said Ann was granted administration.
- will of Michaell Catterton, Sr.
(CV), constituting his son Marke
Catterton executor, proved by 3
witnesses. Said Marke was granted
administration.
- will of Lawrence Rowland (CV),
specifying no executor, proved by 3
witnesses, bequeathing all to his
widow Grace Rowland.
- will of Thomas Barnard (CV),
constituting his widow Sabina
Barnard & son Luke Bernard
executors, proved by 3 witnesses.
Said Sabina & Luke were granted
administration.
- will of Robert Jarvise (CV),
constituting his widow Dina Jarvise
executrix, proved by 3 witnesses.
Said Dina was granted
administration.

16:76 ...

- bond of Ann Sedgwick administratrix
of Thomas Sedgwick (CV). Security:
Jeremiah Sheriden.
- bond of Henry Trueman administrator
of Henry Pinder (CV).
- will of Ruth Hide (CV), constituting
Isaac Williams executor, proved by 2
witnesses. Said Williams was
granted administration. Security:
Joseph Greare. Also inventory, by
appraisers Thomas Padgett & Joseph
Greare.
- inventory of Benjamin Greare (CV),
by appraisers Thomas Padgett &
Thomas Davis. Administrator: Joseph
Greare.
- inventory of Richard Hill (CV), by
appraisers Richard Brightwell &
Thomas Taney. Administrator: James
Bigger.
- inventory of William Graves (CV), by
appraisers John Morris & Thomas
Davis. Executrix: Elisabeth
(relict).
- inventory of George Carter (CV), by

appraisers Ed. Cowder & Thomas
Coolman. Administratrix: Abigall
wife of Charles Hugh.
- inventory of Thomas Pearson (CV), by
appraisers Jonathon Goozey & Thomas
Lason. Elisabeth Pearson
administratrix exhibited accounts.
- inventory of John Feast (CV), by
appraisers Henry Cox & Thomas
Horner. Elisabeth Feast
administratrix exhibited accounts.

16:77 ...
- inventory of Elisabeth Letchworth
(CV), by appraisers James Bigger &
Jeremiah Sheriden. Thomas Taney
executor exhibited accounts.
- inventory of James Clarke (CV), by
appraisers Thomas Lason & James
Pinher. Thomas Lucas administrator
exhibited accounts.

Maj. John Thompson (CE) exhibited:
- will of John Webster (CE),
constituting Richard Smith executor,
proved by 3 witnesses. Said Smith
was granted administration.
Securities: John Reyley, John
Wridson.
- will of Nicholas Allome (CE),
constituting his widow Anne Allome
executrix, proved by 3 witnesses.
Said Anne was granted
administration. Security: Isaac
Calke.
- bond of Margarett Prior
administratrix of Thomas Prior (CE).
Securities: William Sanders, Thomas
Crestian.
- inventory of John Miller (CE), by
appraisers Richard Kinard & John
James, Jr.
- Diana Jones relict & administratrix
of William Drake (CE) exhibited
accounts.

16:78 Mr. John Rawlings (DO) exhibited:
- bond of Thomas Oliver administrator
of John Stoaker (DO), as greatest
creditor. Sureties: William Mishew,
Dennis Collman. Mary Stoaker relict
died before she could administer the
estate. Also inventory, by

> appraisers Thomas Vickers & David Makall. Also accounts.

- will of Morgan Jones (DO), constituting his widow Jane Jones executrix, proved by Col. Charles Hutchins. Surety: Col. Charles Hutchins. Also inventory, by appraisers Thomas Harpin & Ed. Jones.
- bond of George Barnes administrator of John Barnes (DO). Sureties: Cornelius Johnson, Thomas Harvy. Also inventory, by appraisers John Minifre & John Harman.
- bond of Charles Beadly administrator of Richard Tompson (DO). Sureties: Cornelius Johnson, Thomas Hervy. Also inventory, by John Minifre & Henry Harman.

16:79 Mr. Cleborne Lomax (CH) exhibited:

- will of Ignatius Causin (CH), constituting his widow Jane executrix, proved by 3 witnesses. Said Jane was granted administration. Sureties: Edward Sander, William Forster. Also inventory, by appraisers Marke Lampton & Samuell Luckett.
- bond of Johannah Smithson administratrix of Humphrey Jones (CH). Surety: Thomas Smolt. Also inventory, by appraisers Thomas Smolt & Henry Hawkins.
- bond of William Bishop administrator of John Smith (carpenter, CH). Surety: Richard Harrison.
- inventory of Hugh Gardiner (CH), by appraisers Anthony Neale & Ralph Smith.
- inventory of William Burman (CH), by appraisers William Nicholls & Abel Warkfeild.
- additional inventory of Robert Douglas (CH), by appraisers John Harrison & Walter Story.
- accounts of William Herbert executor of Joseph Cornell (CH).
- accounts of William Herbert executor of John Chirribub. Also inventory, by appraisers Thomas Dixon & John Guyn.

16:80 Mr. Edward Mann (TA) exhibited:
- will of Peter Sides (TA), constituting his widow Alice executrix. She died soon thereafter. John Sides (son & heir) was granted administration. also inventory of estate of both Peter & Alice, by appraisers Jacob Fefe & Thomas Eure.
- will of George Robins (TA), constituting his widow Margarett & his son Thomas Robins executors, proved by 4 witnesses. Said Margarett & Thomas were granted administration. Also inventory, by appraisers Thomas Robins, Sr. & Thomas Smithson.
- will of William Lawrence (TA), constituting his friend Judith Stanley (widow, TA) executrix, proved by 3 witnesses. Said Stanley was granted administration. Also inventory, by appraisers John Cape & Thomas Delahay.
- will of James Sedgwick (TA), constituting his cousin James Murphey & his cousin Mary Wrightson executors. Said Murphey has renounced administration. Said Wrightson was granted administration. Also inventory of said James Sedgweek, by appraisers Lawrence Knowles & Andrew Tonnard.

16:81 ...
- bond of Mr. Nicholas Milburne administrator of Ralph Jackson (TA). Securities: Thomas Delahay, John Ouldham. Also inventory, by appraisers Alexander Willson & Hugh Spedden.
- bond of John Hawkins administrator of Richard & Sarah Collings (TA). Surety: Robert Smith. Also inventory, by appraisers James Smith & William Sparks.
- bond of Robert Grundy administrator of George Hewes (TA). Sureties: John Edmondson, Nicholas Milburne. Also inventory, by appraisers James Bishop & Daniell Morry. Also accounts.
- bond of Peter Watts administrator of

Edward Floyde (TA). Securities:
William Watts, Edward Williams.
Also inventory, by appraisers Thomas
Delahay & William Watts.
- accounts of John Mann administrator
of Thomas Cox (TA).
- accounts of Prudence Bell
administratrix of Joseph Bell (TA).
- accounts of John Needles
administrator of William Rooke (TA).
- accounts of William Carr one of
executors of Joseph Wiggett (TA).
- inventory of Richard Royston (TA),
by appraisers Nicholas Milburne &
Ralph Moone.

16:82 Mr. Samuell Hopkins (SO) exhibited:
- bond of Grizell Latcham executrix of
George Latcham (SO). Surety:
Gabriell Powell. Also inventory, by
appraisers James Round & John Webb.
- bond of Richard Wharton
administrator of Francis Gunbey
(SO). Security: Archibald Holmes.
Also inventory, by appraisers John
Pitts & Archibald Holmes.
- bond of Margery & William Turvile
administrators of William Turvile
(SO). Security: Samuell Hopkins.
Also inventory, by appraisers John
Franklin & John Webb. Also will of
said Turvile, constituting his widow
Margery Turvile & his son William
Turvile executors, proved by 2
witnesses. Said Margery & William
were granted administration.
- bond of Margarett Towers
administratrix of Jonathon Towers
(SO). Surety: Anthony Jones. Also
inventory, by appraisers John
Franklin & John Webb.
- bond of Elisabeth Hamlin daughter &
administratrix of Margrett Hamlin
(widow, SO). Surety: Martin
Kennett. Also inventory, by
appraisers William Tomkins & William
Turvile.

16:83 ...
- accounts of Hannah Clifton
administratrix of Thomas Clifton
(SO).
- accounts of Anne Butcher relict &

administratrix of Robert Butcher
(SO).
- accounts of Elisabeth Kennett relict
& administratrix of William Kennett
(SO).
- accounts of Willmoth Hill
administratrix of Richard Hill (SO).
- accounts of James Dunkin
administrator of William Pattent
(SO).
- additional inventory of Andrew
Whittington (SO), by appraisers
Richard Chambers & William Boseman.

Mr. John Rawlings (DO) exhibited:
- inventory of William Winslow (DO),
by appraisers Andrew Parker & Thomas
Vickars. Mary Winslow
administratrix exhibited accounts.
Quietus est was granted.
- bond of Arthur Whitely administrator
of William Worgan (DO). Securities:
William Trotter, Henry Davis.

Exhibited will of Richard Edlin (SM),
constituting his son Richard & his son
Edward executors, proved by 3 witnesses.
Administration was granted only to said
Richard.

16:84 Mr. Elias King (KE) exhibited:
- will of Samuell Wheeler (KE),
constituting his widow Ruth
executrix, proved by 2 witnesses.
Exhibited was her renunciation, as
she is incapable of managing said
estate. William Bouldin (KE) was
granted administration, as greatest
creditor. Sureties: Michaell
Miller, Mathew Eareskson. Also
inventory, by appraisers Vallentin
Sothern & Henry Carter.
- will of Andrew Toulson (KE),
constituting his widow Sarah Toulson
executrix, proved by 3 witnesses.
Said Sarah was granted
administration on 14 June 1694.
- accounts of Thomas Baxter
administrator of Allexander
Meconikin (KE).
- accounts of Edward Blay (CE) who
married Barbara administratrix of

Court Session: 1695

Josias Lanham (KE).
* accounts of Anna Blay relict of Robert Burman (KE), proved on 1 July 1695.

Exhibited was inventory of Charles Harrington (CV), by appraisers Richard Stallings & Thomas Hinton. Seaborne Tucker & his wife Dorathy administratrix exhibited accounts. Continuance was granted.

16:85 John Willson & his wife Elisabeth administrators of Luke Gregory (AA) exhibited accounts.

Margarett Swift executrix of Michaell Swift (CV) exhibited accounts.

Mathew Gauthering & his wife Mary administrators of William Needham (CV) exhibited accounts.

John Sollers executor of John Shrigley (AA) exhibited additional accounts.

Mr. William Palmer (high sheriff, CV) exhibited summons.

7 August. Benjamin Williams (AA) administrator of Joseph Williams (BA) was granted continuance. Most of the estate is in ENG.

William Clarke executor of Jacob Hollitt (AA) exhibited that said Hollitt was single & bequeathed all to said Clarke. Ruling: dismissed.

Anne Simpson executrix of Jeremiah Simpson (CV) exhibited that the estate was taken away by hardness of time.

Mr. John Stone (high sheriff, CH) exhibited summons.

Capt. William Holland (high sheriff, AA) exhibited summons.

16:86 9 August. John Duvall (AA) son of Marren Duvall (dec'd) was summoned to render accounts.

Court Session: 1695

Col. Henry Ridgley petitioned for
warrants for MM James Sanders & Samuell
Young to appraise estate of Marren
Duvall.

12 August. Mr. Gabriell Parrott (AA)
vs. estate of Thomas Briscoe. Caveat
was exhibited.

William Joseph, Esq. (CV) exhibited that
2 of his servants are lately dec'd:
Oliver Barnwell, William Tent. They
left no relations in the Province.
Administration was granted to said
Joseph.

13 August. Mr. James Smith (high
sheriff, TA) exhibited summons.

Exhibited inventory of George Hardisty
(CV), by appraisers Thomas Hillary &
Jeremiah Eldridg. Cecill Hardisty
relict & administratrix exhibited
accounts.

Exhibited inventory of William Howes
(CV), by appraisers William Whittington
& Nicholas Fountaine. Ursula Howe
relict & administratrix exhibited
accounts.

Thomas Hillary administrator of Baruck
Williams (CV) exhibited accounts.

16:87   Charles Powell for Sarah Pindar
administratrix of John Sutton (DO)
exhibited accounts. Said Sarah
administratrix of Edward Pindar was
granted continuance.

Hugh Ecdleston one of executors of Will.
Hill (DO) exhibited accounts. Petition
for new appraisers to value the
plantation, which is to be sold for the
maintenance of a free school.

John Nicholls executor of John Broaday
(DO) exhibited additional accounts.

Thomas Earle (TA) administrator of
Daniell Bryant (DO) appeared. The
orphans of said dec'd exhibited a

Page 117

petition, dated 23 May 1695, for Mr. Richard Teate to administer said estate. Signed: Mathew Brian, Margarett Brian. LoA to said Earle revoked. Said Teate was granted administration dbn.

16:88 Mr. John Rawlings (DO) to administer oath.

Elisabeth Davis exhibited that John Millar (TA) has falsely obtained LoA on estate of her former husband William Ashely. LoA to said Millar revoked. Said Davis was granted administration dbn. Mr. Nicholas Lowe (TA) to administer oath.

Philip Clarke attorney for John Duvall (AA) administrator of his father Marren Duvall exhibited accounts. Mr. Robert Carvile is attorney for Col. Henry Ridgley (plaintiff). Maj. John Hammond & Capt. Richard Snowden to examine.

John Turner administrator of Thomas Cornwell (CV) was granted continuance.

John Scott was granted continuance to examine accounts of John Holsworth. Summons to: John Maning, John Mackdowell, John Holland.

Exhibited inventory of richard Land (CH), by appraisers Ralph Smith & William Harbert

16:89 14 August. Penolope Land administratrix of Richard Land (CH) exhibited accounts.

Mr. Henage Robinson (merchant, CV) exhibited inventory of Thom. Herman, by appraisers John Whittington & James Smoth.

Edward Daw executor of Nathan Daw (CV) exhibited accounts.

Thomas Tench, Esq. administrator of Col. Lionell Copley petitioned for court date.

Ed. Parrish vs. Dr. Wolfran Hunt. Said Hunt to be kept in custody.

Ralph & John Dawson (TA) vs. Ralph
Fishborne. Plaintiffs exhibited that
said Fishborne has refused to give
satisfaction. Said Fishborne found in
contempt. Said Fishborne appeared.
Sheriff (AA) to keep him in custody.

16:90 Dr. Jacob Lookerman administrator of
Henry Raddon (DO) exhibited inventory,
by appraisers John Kirke & Roger
Woolford. Also exhibited accounts.

Maj. John Bigger administrator of John
Loftis (CV) exhibited accounts.

Edward Swan who married Mary relict &
executrix of Francis Buxton (CV)
exhibited accounts. Also exhibited
inventory, by appraisers George Young &
Hezkiah Hussee.

Robert Sumnar who married Margarett
relict & administratrix of John
Sunderland (CV) exhibited accounts.

John Fisher who married Elisabeth
executrix of Tobias Miles (CV) exhibited
accounts.

15 August. Mr. James Cranford
administrator of John Abington exhibited
accounts. Mr. George Lingan & Richard
Harris to examine said accounts. Mr.
Robert Carvile for Mr. George Lingan
exhibited libel.

16:91 Nuteley Warren one of executors of Col.
Humphrey Warren (CH) exhibited
inventory, by appraisers John Courts,
Jr. & John Wilder. Mrs. Margery Warren
relict petitioned that her 1/3rds are
being detained by him. Mr. William
Dent for said Margery & Capt. John Bain
for said Notley to make division.

John Short administrator of Andrew
Tanehill (CV) exhibited inventory, by
appraisers George Lingan & David Small.
Continuance was granted.

Exhibited was inventory of Hugh
Hopewell, Jr. (CV), by appraisers Mr.

John Griggs & John Wiseman. Elisabeth relict was granted continuance.

16 August. Daniell Ingerson who married Seth relict & administratrix of Henry Pratt (TA) exhibited inventory, by appraisers Thomas Youell & Isaack Winchester. Also exhibited accounts.

Christopher Williamson (SM) was granted administration on estate of Nathaniell Button (SM), as greatest creditor. Appraisers: Giles Willson, Henry Norris. Mr. Samuell Cooksey to administer oath.

16:92　Maj. Sewall (CV) exhibited bill per George Plater, Esq. administrator of Robert Doyne (CH): Robert Doyne (g, CH) is indebted to Madam Jane Calvert (widow, London). Date: 25 (N) 1688.

Edward Ball administrator of Michaell Ball (CV) exhibited accounts. Quietus est was granted.

John Elsey was authorized to examine effects of Mr. Thomas Briscoe (CV, dec'd) at the house of Mr. Thomas Witchall & to create an inventory. Date: 16 August 1695 at Annapolis.

17 August. Edward Walwin (CE) who married Susanna executrix of Philip Davis (KE) exhibited accounts. Continuance was granted.

William Harris (CE) exhibited will of Thomas Parker (KE), constituting him executor. Witnesses are not here. Mr. Edward Sweatnam to prove said will. Said Harris was granted administration. Appraisers: John Carville, Charles Hinson. Said Sweatnam to administer oath.

16:93　Humphry Tilton (g, CE) to examine accounts of Anne James administratrix of Richard Whitton (CE), now wife of Mr. John James.

Mr. William Dent one of executors of John Lambert (CH) was granted continuance.

Mr. Edward Mann (TA) exhibited that the following administrations need to be completed:

- Mr. Robert Smith executor of Mr. Male.
- Mr. Robert Smith administrator of Michaell Hackett.
- Mr. Milborn administrator of Alderman Medkuff.
- Mary Royston widow & administratrix of Richard Royston.
- William Watts administrator of Capt. William Bexbye.
- William Watts administrator of William Bird (Old ENG).
- Mr. William Alden administrator of (N) Ey.
- Elisabeth Seatam widow & administratrix of John Stannard.
- Mr. John Salter administrator of Thomas Hutchins.
- Mr. William Coursey administrator of (N) Atcchesson.
- Mr. Andrew Kinimon executor of John Kinimon.
- Robert Betts administrator of William Cass.
- Mr. William Hemslye administrator of John Rice.

Said Mann to complete said administrations. Date: 20 August 1695.

Maj. Cornelius Comigges administrator of William Lathrop (KE) was granted continuance.

Mr. Richard Boulton (CH) was appointed Deputy Commissary. Signed: Mr. William Dent.

16:94 19 August. Exhibited inventory of Robert Loften (CH), by appraisers Thomas Craxon, Sr. & John Gourley.

Mr. Gouldesborough attorney for Alexander Forbes (merchant, TA) vs. Mr. Carroll attorney for William Taylard (g, SM). Said Forbes is administrator of James Anderson (died in TA), granted by Mr. Nicholas Lowe (TA), as greatest creditor. Said Taylard was granted administration on the same estate. Mr. Robert Carvile for said Taylard requested that said Forbes file his libel. Said libel exhibited. Said Anderson had neither wife nor kindred in this Province.

16:95 Ruling: administration to said Taylard revoked. Said Forbes is greatest creditor.

Hugh Montgomery (CV) administrator of George Parker was cited with attachment of contempt.

Nicholas Evans (SO) vs. Edward Day (p, SO) who married Jane executrix of Thomas Walker. Said Day summoned to answer libel.

Mr. John Elsey (CV) exhibited that, as commanded, he went to the house of Mr. Thomas Witchell. But 3 weeks ago, Mr. Briscoe took the keys to the widow Bourne. Date: 18 August 1695.

Michaell Miller administrator of James Boulay (KE) was granted continuance.

16:96 <does not exist>

16:97 20 August. Mr. Richard Marsham (CV) administrator of James Minney exhibited that both appraisers died before an appraisal was made. New appraisers: John Snuggs, John Forrest. Mr. Thomas Greenfeild to administer oath.

Richard Keene vs. Mr. Robert Carvile procurator for Joseph Edloe (CV) executor of Edward Mollins. Demurrer to libel exhibited.

Richard Purnall for Daniell Richardson vs. Silvester Welch administrator of John Welch (AA). Inventory examined & no objections proved.

Joseph Willson who married Anne relict & executrix of Richard Smith (CV) exhibited inventory, by appraisers Ralph Smith & Thomas Taylor. Also exhibited

Court Session: 1695

accounts.

Thomas Hussey (CH) executor of William
Langworth (SM) exhibited accounts.

Thomas Whichaley & his wife Elisabeth
administratrix of Edward Ford (CH)
exhibited accounts.

16:98   Mr. Samuell Watkins administrator of
William Johnson exhibited that he had
not been sworn as administrator. Mr.
John Edmondson (TA) was restored as
administrator, as formerly granted to
Thomas Donnelan. Appraisers: Daniell
Walker, Robert Gofe. Mr. Nicholas Lowe
to administer oath.

Clement Seales (TA) was summoned to
prove his bill paid by James Bishop
executor of Thomas Browne. Said Bishop
was granted continuance.

21 August. John Hall & his wife Martha
executrix of George Gouldsmith (BA)
exhibited accounts.

Mr. Edward Boothby to examine accounts
of William Osborne & his wife Mary
executrix of John Walston (BA).

Samuell Watkins administrator of Thomas
Broadus (CV) exhibited inventory, by
appraisers William Turner & John
Ledyatt. Also exhibited accounts.

Exhibited inventory of Peter Lemare
(CV), by appraisers John Gillum & John
Price. Col. Jowles for widow Francis
Lemare exhibited accounts. Said
accounts were returned as they were
unsigned.

16:99   Rachell Procter (AA) widow of Robert
Procter was granted administration on
his estate. Sureties: Richard Beard,
Thomas Richardson. Appraisers: Andrew
Norwood, Samuell Howard. Mr. John
Dorsey to administer oath.

Mr. Gabriell Parrott (AA) was granted
administration on estate of Thomas

Briscoe (CV), as greatest creditor.
Sureties: George Burges, Thomas
Blackwell.

Dr. John Harrison (CH) administrator of
Alexander Fulerton (CH) exhibited
inventory, by appraisers Anthony Neale &
Randolph Brandt. Also exhibited
accounts.

23 August. Mr. Robert Carvile
procurator for Mr. George Lingan vs.
Charles Carroll procurator for James
Cranford. Answer exhibited. Response
to answer exhibited.

Robert Carvile procurator for Philip Cox
(CV) vs. Thomas Courtney. Response to
insufficient answer.

26 August. MM Richard Harrison (CH) &
William Stone (CH) to examine estate of
John Ward (dec'd), per agreement between
Milsted & Sergent.

16:100   George Plater & Philip Clarke attorneys
for King & creditors of Gov. Lionell
Copley vs. Thomas Tench, Esq. one of
administrators of said Copley.
Continuance was granted.

Alice Watkins administratrix of William
Barnett (CV) exhibited accounts.

Robert Smith, Esq. (TA) administrator of
Humphrey Devonport exhibited additional
accounts. Former accounts passed by
former judge.

Margery Gardiner relict & executrix of
Richard Gardiner (SM) exhibited
accounts.

Exhibited inventory of Alexander Currey
(SM), by appraisers Anthony Seemes &
Gilbert Cropper.

Robert Grundy one of executors of Edward
Pollard (TA) exhibited accounts.

Garrett Murrey vs. Robert
Gouldesborough procurator for Edward

Court Session: 1695

Jones (CE). Rejoinder to replication.

16:101   Robert Carvile procurator for George
Lingan (CV) administrator of Andrew
Abington (merchant, London) vs. Charles
Carroll procurator for James Cranford.
Said Abington died in June 1694 in
London, with a will constituting his
kinsman Mr. John Abington executor, who
renounced administration. The
Metropolitan of ENG granted
administration to Mrs. Maryell Perry
(sister) & Maryell Abington (niece).
Said Perry & Abington gave PoA to
Richard Harrison & George Lingan. Said
Harrison refused to take oath.
16:102-103 ...
16:104   Mentions: said Harrison is greatest
creditor by marriage of his wife & on
her account is debtor to the estate.
Ruling: plaintiff.
16:105   Said Cranford exhibited caveat to the
estate & exhibited accounts. Payments
to: David Small, Thomas Hedge, James
Cranford. Amount: £170.15.4¼. On 9
September 1695, said Cranford entered
appeal.

16:106   4 September. Dr. Mordica Moore for
self & other creditors of George Parker
(CV) vs. Hugh Montgomery & wife
executrix of said Parker. Attachment
granted.

11 September. Henry Bonner (AA) was
granted administration on estate of
Nicholas Morrey (AA). Sureties: John
Tunner, Robert Hopper.

17 September. Charles Carroll
procurator for John Scott (CV) vs. John
Holsworth administrator of (N) Martin.
Exceptions to accounts exhibited.

20 August. James Bigger (CV) was
granted administration on estate of John
Houseing, as greatest creditor. Mr.
John Bigger to administer oath.

2 October. William Parker (sheriff, CV)
exhibited attachment against Hugh
Montgomery & his wife.

Mrs. Mary Eagle administratrix of Jacob Orick was granted continuance.

Mr. Edward Swetnam exhibited will of Thomas Parker (KE), proved by 5 witnesses. Also exhibited oath of Mr. William Harris & Elisabeth Parker executors. Also oath of Thomas Joce & Thomas Pyner, appraisers.

16:107 3 October. Thomas Hopkins, Jr. administrator of Jacob Abraham was granted continuance.

Said Thomas Hopkins, Jr. for his father Thomas Hopkins administrator of Clement Hopkins was granted continuance.

Anthony Smith (AA) who married Diana executrix of Thomas Knigton (AA) exhibited inventory, by appraisers William Holland & Robert Orme.

Dr. Mordecai Moore vs. Hugh Montgomery & his wife administratrix of George Parker. Caveat exhibited. Said Montgomery was granted continuance.

John Cross administrator of Robert Owens (AA) exhibited accounts.

Benjamin Williams (AA) administrator of Joseph Williams (BA) exhibited additional inventory.

Mr. Elias King (KE) exhibited:
- will of William Deane (KE), constituting his widow Sarah Deane executrix, proved by 3 witnesses. Said Sarah was granted administration. Also inventory, by appraisers Richard Louder & William Edwin.
- bond of Ann Davies relict & administratrix of John Davies (KE). Surety: Edward James. Also inventory, by appraisers Math. Eareckson & Ed. James.

16:108 4 October. John Dawson (TA) exhibited inventory of Bryan Omaley, by appraisers James Benson & Daniell Sherwood.

Court Session: 1695

Michaell Catterton (CV) was granted administration on estate of his brother Marke Catterton, as next of kin. Appraisers: John Godsgrace, Gabriell Burnham. Mr. William Barton to administer oath.

Exhibited inventory of Michaell Catterton (CV), by appraisers Hugh Ellis & Ed. Wenman. Also exhibited itemization of estate of Marke Catterton, by Hugh Ellis & James Catterton, made 20 September last.

Maj. James Smallwood (CH) administrator of Robert Thompson (CH) exhibited additional accounts.

Mr. John Wattson (SM) who married relict of Thomas Spinke (SM) administrator of Jane Paine (SM) exhibited accounts of said Jane Payne.

Samuell Warner who married Sarah relict of Francis Dorrington (CV) exhibited accounts.

Mary Wolsted administratrix of Joshua Wolsted (CV) exhibited accounts.

Exhibited inventory of Lawrence Rouland (CV), by appraisers John Chittam & Alexander Beall.

16:109 Mrs. Jane Truman (CV) widow of Henry Truman was granted administration on his estate. Mr. John Bigger to administer oath.

Charles Powell attorney for Mrs. Sarah Pindar widow & administratrix of Edward Pindar exhibited accounts.

Mr. John Thompson (CE) exhibited:
- inventory of John Webster (CE), by appraisers Philip Holleadger & William Sanders.
- inventory of Nicholas Allum (CE), by appraisers William Pearce & Henry Rigg.
- inventory of Thomas Pryer (CE), by appraisers Thomas Christian &

Page 127

William Sander.
• additional inventory of William
Drake (CE), by appraisers John
Waggott & Mathias Hendrickson.

5 October. Mr. Richard Marsham (CV)
administrator of James Miney (CV)
exhibited inventory, by appraisers John
Snugg & John Forrest. Also exhibited
accounts.

Said Marsham who married relict of Henry
Brent (CV) exhibited list of debts.

Mr. Richard Keene was appointed Deputy
Commissary (CV).

16:110   7 October. Robert Carvile procurator
for Mr. Henry Lowe (CV) vs. Col. Henry
Darnall. Libel exhibited.

John Moreing (CH) vs. Nicholas Cooper
administrator of Robert Downes (CH).
Said Cooper summoned to show cause why
administration should not be revoked.

Mathias Vanderheyden (CE) exhibited will
of his daughter-in-law Rebecca Ward, who
bequeathed all to her brother & sisters
(under age): Henry Ward, Jane
Vanderheyden, Ariana Frances
Vanderheyden, Augustina Vanderheyden.
Said will was proved by 4 witnesses.
Said Mathias was granted administration
on her estate, for said minors.
Sureties: Col. Casparus Herman, Ed.
Jones.

Robert Carville procurator for Nicholas
Evans & his wife Susanna daughter of
Thomas Walker (SO, dec'd) vs. Edward
Day & his wife Jane relict & executrix
of said Walker. Libel exhibited.

William Jones (CV) who married Mary
relict of William Hichock (CV) exhibited
accounts.

8 October. Mr. Henry Lowe vs. Charles
Carroll procurator for Col. Henry
Darnall. Defendant was granted
continuance.

Thomas Whitton (CE) vs. John James & his wife Ann administratrix of Richard Whitton. Said James summoned to render accounts.

16:111 Charles Carroll for John Scott vs. Robert Carvill for John Holsworth. Said Holsworth exhibited accounts on estates of (N) Abbott & (N) Martin.
- Col. Henry Mitchell deposed that he received from John Holsworth on account of bill of William Martin.
- William Barton & Thomas How deposed that they appraised the estate of (N) Martin.
- John Scott petitioned that Jacob Accuot (?) (a servant) was not appraised.
- John Mackdowell deposed that he received from (N) Martin in his lifetime & from John Holsworth the remainder of his wife's legacy.
- Mr. Maning & Mr. Freeman, 2 neighbors, are to value the rent of the land. Mentions: 5 children (2 of which are already paid).
- John Holsworth exhibited additional accounts of William Martyn.

9 October. James Crowley (TA) & his wife Jane relict of Benjamin Pride (TA) exhibited accounts.

Dr. Mordica Moore administrator of William Elvidge (AA) exhibited accounts.

Exhibited inventory of Thomas Ploumer (AA), by appraisers William Goodman & Mark Richardson.

16:112 Maj. dead Ridgely Henry (AA) who married Mary relict & executrix of Marren Duvall (AA) exhibited inventory, by appraisers MM James Sanders & Samuell Young. Also exhibited an additional inventory. Also exhibited commission to Maj. John Hammond & Capt. Richard Snowden, with accounts adjusted between John Duvall (former administrator) & said Ridgely (now administrator).

Mr. Samuell Hopkins (SO) exhibited:
- will of Ellenor Cane (SO), constituting her son Lazarus Maddox executor, proved by 2 witnesses. Said Maddox was granted administration. Also exhibited discharge by Blandina Bosman for her legacy.
- accounts of Robert Cattlin administrator of Dennis Miller.
- accounts of Jane Sewell executrix of Thomas Sewell.
- accounts of Mariane Smith administratrix of James Smith.
- accounts of Martha Poole (alias Martha Makey) administratrix of John Makey.
- accounts of Elisabeth Linch administratrix of Henry Linch.

11 October. Walter Lane executor of Josias Seward (SO) exhibited accounts.

Robert Grundy (TA) one of executors of Edward Pollard (TA) exhibited additional accounts.

16:113 Garrett Murrey (CE) vs. Edward Jones (CE). Accounts examined.

14 October. Elisabeth Peacocke executrix of Richard Freeman (CV) exhibited accounts.

Alexander Forbes administrator of James Anderson vs. William Taylard. Libel exhibited.

Exhibited inventory of James Graves (CV), by appraisers Thomas Wells & Em. Stowe.

Mr. Nicholas Milburne (TA) administrator of Ralph Jackson (TA) exhibited accounts.

15 October. Mrs. Marjery Warren relict of Col. Humphrey Warren (CH) petitioned that she be allowed her goods. Ruling: granted.

At request of Mr. Michaell Turbott
(TA), Ignatius Craycroft for himself &
his wife Sophia released any claims to
Elisabeth Coursey relict &
administratrix of Henry & Sophia Bedell
(AA). Witnesses: R. Gouldesborough,
Cha. Ridgely, Micha. Turbott.

16:114 Mr. Alexander Forbes (merchant, TA)
administrator of James Anderson
(merchant) petitioned for Robert
Gouldesborough to examine witnesses.
Mentions: libel against William Taylard,
Mr. John Watson (g, SM), Mr. Samuell
Hopkins (g, SO), Mr. William Dent (g,
CH), Mr. John Pollard (g, DO), Mr.
William Harris (g, CE).

Alexander Forbes vs. Mr. William
Taylard (g, SM). Answer exhibited.

James Bishop executor of Thomas Browne
(TA) was granted continuance.

16:115 17 October. Exhibited inventory of
Joseph & Elisabeth Fry (CV), by
appraisers Ignatius Craycroft & Thomas
Lauson.

19 October. Mr. Philip Clark (SM) &
his wife Hannah administratrix of George
Meekall (SM) petitioned that his
accounts be perfected.

Michaell Miller (KE) administrator of
James Boulay exhibited accounts.
Continuance was granted.

Exhibited additional inventory & list of
debts of Col. Nehemiah Blackiston (SM).

22 October. James Macklester (SO) vs.
William Fassit (SO). Said Fassit
summoned to answer libel.

Col. David Browne administrator of
Archibald Erreskin (SO) exhibited
accounts.

Mr. Robert Gouldesborough (g) was
appointed Deputy Commissary (TA).

Henry Reed who married relict of John Smock (SO) exhibited accounts.

16:116 2 November. Exhibited inventory of Philip Wiott (TA), by appraisers Daniell Walker & William Gary.

12 November. Franc. Collier (CV) who married Sarah relict of John Evans (CV) exhibited inventory, by appraisers Richard Hen & John Reade.

16 December. Mr. Edward Mann (TA) exhibited:
- will of Capt. William Bexley (TA), constituting his widow Margarett executrix. Also exhibited bond of Peter Watts administrator. Securities: Peter Wats, Thomas Earle. Also exhibited inventory, by appraisers Thomas Robins, Sr. & James Saywell.
- bond of Elisabeth Seaton administratrix of Joseph Seaton (TA). Sureties: Joseph Bird, William Johnson. Also exhibited inventory, by appraisers Isaac Seserson & John Stonnard.
- bond of Robert Bets administrator of William Cross (TA). Securities: William Hartford, John King. Also inventory, by appraisers Isaac Winchester & William Clayton.
- bond of William Coursey administrator of Luke Atchison (TA). Surety: John Hawkins. Also inventory, by appraisers Edward Purie & William Hemsley.

16:117 16 November. Mr. Nicholas Lowe (TA) exhibited:
- will of Henry Woolchurch (TA), constituting James Ridley & his 2 daughters Rebecca Anderson & Mary Barker executors, proved by 3 witnesses. Said Ridley, Anderson, and Barker were granted administration. Also exhibited inventory, by appraisers Samuell Abbot & John Swallow. Accounts were exhibited by John Barker & his wife Mary one of the executors.

- inventory of John Kinimont (TA), by appraisers Daniell Walker & Alexander Ray.
- bond of Alexander Forbes administrator of James Anderson. Securities: Nicholas Milburne, William Scott.

Mary Crouch (AA) with her grandfather Morris Baker exhibited will of William Sutton (AA), constituting her executrix, proved by 2 witnesses: John Gill, Philip Jones. Said Crouch was granted administration. Appraisers: John Rockhold, Richard Sorrill. Mr. John Worthington to administer oath.

16:118 18 November. William Clarke (AA) was granted administration on estate of John Crowley (AA), who died leaving 3 young children & no relations. Sureties: Thomas Dawson, Alexander Garner. Appraisers: Francis Made, William Pennington.

21 November. John Batie (AA) who married Sarah relict & executrix of Roger Bishop (AA) exhibited his will. Seth Biggs (AA) to prove said will. Appraisers: Nicholas Terrett, David Small. Said Biggs to administer oath.

27 November. Richard Chishire (AA) was granted administration on estate of his overseer Charles Roberts, as principle creditor. Sureties: Mordica Price, Richard Goodt. Appraisers: said Price, said Goodt.

28 November. Capt. John Dorsey vs. estate of Robert Maine (AA). Caveat exhibited. Said Dorsey is principle creditor.

16:119 14 January. Mary Mading (CV) widow of Dennis Mading was granted administration on his estate. Thomas Greenfeild (g) to administer oath. "She is a poor widow."

Michaell Catterton (CV) eldest son of Michaell Catterton petitioned for LoA on his father's estate. Also said Michaell

(son) petitioned for LoA on estate of
his brother Marke Catterton.

15 January. Gabriell Parrott (AA) vs.
John Elsey administrator of Thomas
Briscoe (CV). Said Elsey summoned to
render accounts.

Dr. Mordica Moore (AA) exhibited will
of John Suallwell (CH), constituting him
executor. Said Moore was granted
administration. Surety: Richard Jones.
Capt. John Addison to prove said will.

17 January. John Worthington exhibited
oath of John Rockhold & Richard Sorrill,
appraisers of William Sutton.

16:120 Mr. Edward Boothby (BA) exhibited:
- bond of Mary Utye widow &
  administratrix of George Utye (BA).
- will of John Durham (BA),
  constituting his son John Durham
  executor, proved by 4 witnesses.
  Said John (son) was granted
  administration. Also inventory, by
  appraisers James Maxwell & Moses
  Groome.
- will of Robert Gates (BA),
  bequeathing to Thomas Liton, proved
  by 2 witnesses. Said Liton, as
  chief legatee, was granted
  administration. Also inventory, by
  appraisers Moses Groome & John
  Webster.
- bond of Jonas Bowin administrator of
  James Robeson (BA). Sureties: John
  Thomas, Richard Samson. Also
  exhibited will, constituting said
  Bowin supervisor. Said Bowin was
  granted administration. Also
  inventory, by appraisers Rowland
  Thornbery & Robert Willmott.
- Martha Lovell relict of John Lovell
  (BA) was granted administration on
  his estate. Also inventory, by
  appraisers John Rouse & Nicholas
  FitzSimons.
16:121 ...
- will of John Hill (BA), constituting
  his son William Hill executor,
  proved by 2 witnesses. Said William

was granted administration. Also
inventory, by appraisers Richard
Adams & Michaell Judd.
- will of Benjamin Bennett (BA),
  proved by 2 witnesses.
- will of Robert Jones (BA), proved.
- will of Joseph Simmons (BA), proved.
- additional inventory of John Harding
  (BA), by appraisers William
  Wilkinson & John Hayes.

16:122 Mr. Samuell Hopkins (SO) exhibited:
- will of John Tarr (SO), constituting
  his widow Elisabeth executrix,
  proved by 3 witnesses. Said
  Elisabeth was granted
  administration. Sureties: John
  Sanders, Samuell Hopkins. Also
  inventory, by appraisers Walter Read
  & John Pope.
- will of William Onorton (SO),
  constituting his son John Onorton
  executor, proved by 3 witnesses.
  Said John was granted
  administration. Surety: Robert
  Tyre. Also inventory, by appraisers
  John Powell & James Walke.
- will of Charles Hall (SO),
  constituting his widow Alice
  executrix, proved by 3 witnesses.
  Said Alice was granted
  administration. Sureties: George
  Lane, Mary Fountaine. Also
  inventory, by appraisers Stephen
  Horsey & Michaell Gray.

John Rockhold (AA) vs. estate of John
Lary (AA). Caveat exhibited. Said
Rockhold is greatest creditor.

16:123 21 January. Kenelm Cheseldyn, Esq.
exhibited:
- will of Thomas Salmon (SM),
  constituting his friends William
  Shirtly & Michaell Realy executors,
  proved by 3 witnesses. Said Shirtly
  & Realy were granted administration.
  Also inventory, by appraisers
  William Husband & Charles Daft.
- will of Henry Spinke (SM),
  constituting his sons Henry &
  William Spinke executors, proved by

4 witnesses, including Mr. William
Husband. Said Henry (son) & William
were granted administration. Also
inventory, by appraisers William
Sheirtliffe & Thomas Dant.

- verbal will of John Little (SM),
  bequeathing land to his son John
  Little & residue to his wife Mary
  Little, proved by 2 witnesses. Said
  John (son) & Mary were granted
  administration.
- inventory of John Lidyatt (CV), by
  appraisers William Haimes & Mathew
  Lewis.
- list of debts of estate of William
  Roswell (SM), by Emma Roswell.
- additional inventory of Lionell
  Copley (late Governor), by
  appraisers John Lowe & Ed. Heliard.

16:124 ...

- will of Elisabeth Young (SM),
  constituting William Boarman, Jr.
  (SM) executor. Said Boarman was
  granted administration. Appraisers:
  Benjamin Hall, John Higdon. Capt.
  John Beane to administer oath.

24 January. Exhibited inventory of
Robert Procter (AA), by appraisers
Samuell Howard & Orlanda Greenslade.

27 January. Michaell Catterton (CV) was
granted administration d.b.n. on estate
of his father Michaell Catterton (CV),
unadministered by Marke Catterton (CV).
Thomas Greenfeild (g) to administer
oath. Also said Michaell (son) was
granted administration on estate of his
brother Marke Catterton.

6 February. Capt. John Dorsey (AA) was
granted administration on estate of
Robert Maine (AA), as principle
creditor. Surety: Thomas Blackwell.
Appraisers: Cornelius Howard, Joseph
Howard. Maj. John Howard to administer
oath.

16:125 [from f. 88.] 13 August 1695. Mr.
Robert Carvile procurator for Col.
Henry Ridgley & his wife Mary executrix
of Marren Duvall vs. Philip Clarke

procurator for John Duvall. Said Duvall exhibited accounts on estate of his father said Marren. Maj. John Hamond & Capt. Richard Snowden to examine said accounts.

16:126 Maj. John Hamond & Capt. Richard Snowden (alias Richard Snowden, Sr.) exhibited their report, dated 29 August 1695. Accounts: mentions: Negro Doctor, William Roper, Henry Bonner, Robert Snoden, Sr., Solomon Stinson, Elisabeth Duvall, 4 children.

16:127 Also exhibited inventory. Mentions: Robert Procter,

16:128 Negro Toney (man) sold to Richard Snoden, Negro Sampson (boy) sold to L. Wayman, Negro Jacob (boy) sold to James Lewis, William Cotter.

16:129 Received from: Hugh Abrahams, Robert Goldsborough, Leon. Wayman, Robert Gott, John Nicholson, John Larkins. Amount of accounts: £171.12.10 + #7477.

10 February. John Thomas for Sarah Norris (BA) widow of Edward Norris (BA) was granted administration on his estate. Mr. George Ashman to administer oath.

14 February. Elisabeth Hawkins, wife of Joseph Hawkins, relict & administratrix of Christopher Rolls (AA) exhibited accounts. Distribution: residue to orphans.

18 February. Alice Gott (AA) widow of Robert Gott exhibited his will, constituting her executrix, proved by 3 witnesses: James Ford, Elisabeth Ford, John Hopkins. Said Alice was granted administration. Appraisers: James Ford, John Watters.

24 February. Exhibited inventory of Robert Maine (AA), by appraisers Cornelius Howard & Jos. Howard.

16:130 26 February. Jane Highland (CE) widow of John Highland was granted administration on his estate. Sureties: John Cross, Nicholas Sporne.

Court Session: 1695

Thomas Whitton (CE) vs. John James &
his wife Ann relict & administratrix of
Richard Whitton. Attachment to said
James for not having rendered accounts.

Benjamin Williams administrator of
Joseph Williams was granted continuance.

27 January. Exhibited will of Maj.
John Cambell (SM), constituting his
widow Katherine Cambell & his eldest son
Thomas executors, proved by 3 witnesses.
Said Katherine renounced administration.
Said Thomas was granted administration.
Sureties: James Greenwell, John
Woodward. Appraisers: MM Robert Mason,
William Husband.

Exhibited inventory of Nathaniell Buton
(SM), by appraisers Giles Willson &
Henry Hony.

Exhibited inventory of John Little (SM),
by appraisers William Watts & Peter
Watts.

16:131 Mr. William Dent attorney for Dr.
Mordica Moore (AA) vs. Mr. Hugh
Montgomery administrator of George
Parker. Caveat exhibited, against the
passing of the accounts.

Mr. William Parker (high sheriff, CV)
exhibited summons & brought into court
Mr. James Bigger, who was ordered to
remain in custody.

Col. John Bigger vs. James Bigger.
Said John is security on estate of Mr.
James Nutwell & his brother James
married the widow. The children are
coming of age. Summons to said James to
render accounts.

Richard Watkins (CV) who married Ann
relict & administratrix of William Obery
(CV) exhibited inventory, by appraisers
James Drinkwatter & William Barham.
Also exhibited accounts.

28 February. Exhibited inventory of
Henry Truman (CV), by appraisers John

Hance & Henry Ferneley.

Orphans of Mordica Hunton vs. Hugh
Ellis (CV). Said Ellis appeared.
Ruling: dismissed. Said Ellis exhibited
that the estate of (N) Cosden & (N)
Hunton are intermingled. Continuance
was granted.

16:132 Mr. James Bigger (CV) exhibited
inventory of John Howson (CV), by
appraisers Thomas Lawson & William
Madding.

Said Bigger also exhibited inventory of
Thomas Kemp (CV), by appraisers Thomas
Taney & Jeremiah Shaderin.

Richard Bennett, Esq. for his mother
Madam Henrieta Marye Lloyd (TA)
petitioned that Col. George Robotham
administer oath to her for additional
account on her husband's estate.

Richard Bennett, Esq. (Wye River)
exhibited that Metropolitan of ENG
granted Elisabeth Howell relict of John
Howell (mariner, Stockton on Tease,
Durham, ENG) administration on his
estate. Said Elisabeth gave PoA to said
Bennett. Said Bennett was granted
administration on said estate. Signed:
John Edmondson, John Emerson. Text of
PoA.
16:133 Date: 19 October 1695. Witnesses:
Thomas Sutton, William Broad. Said PoA
proved before James Murphey (g, TA) &
Thomas Smithson (g, TA) on 31 January
1695. [Paragraph in Latin.]

16:134 Robert Gouldsborough (TA) exhibited:
- George Ellett executor of John
Ellett (TA) was granted
administration on his estate. Also
exhibited will, proved by 4
witnesses.
- Elisabeth & Thomas Coursey 2 of
executors of Col. Henry Coursey
(TA) were granted administration on
his estate. Also exhibited will,
proved by 3 witnesses.
- Isaack Winchester executor of his

father Isaac Winchester (TA) was granted administration on his estate. Also exhibited will, proved by 3 witnesses.

- Thomas Roe & William Jump executors of James Silvester (TA) were granted administration on his estate. Also exhibited will, proved by 3 witnesses. Also inventory, by appraisers William Purnell & Sam. Crayker. Also accounts.
- bond of John Davis & his wife Elisabeth administrators of William Ashley (TA). Sureties: Richard White, Henry Woollman. Also inventory, by appraisers Thomas Clements & William Carr.
- Ann Watkins relict of Peter Watkins (TA) was granted administration on his estate. Also inventory, by appraisers William Coursey & John Sergeant.
- Thomas Clements was granted administration on estate of William Inchbud (TA).
- Mary Mountichew relict of William Mountichew (TA) was granted administration on his estate.

16:135 ...

- John Sargeant was granted administration on estate of John Gibson (TA). Also inventory, by appraisers Jacob Seth & Robert Robinson.
- John Glovar was granted administration on estate of Henry Boston (TA). Also inventory, by appraisers John Swallow & William Gwin.

Mr. Richard Boughton (CH) exhibited:
- verbal will of Abraham Sapcoate, proved by 2 witnesses. Morris Fitzgerrell was granted administration. Also inventory, by appraisers James Kirke & (N).
- bond of May Mire widow & administratrix of Christopher Mires. Security: William Dent.
- Mr. Richard Harrison was granted administration on estate of Richard Carver. Also inventory, by

appraisers John Dearman & Robert Lee.
- inventory of John Smith, by appraisers Francis Harrison, John Brooke, & Thomas Wharton.
- inventory of Morice Lloyd, by appraisers John Godshall & Moses Joanes.
- accounts of William Dent & Thomas Mitchell executors of John Lambeth. Continuance was granted.

16:136 Mr. Samuell Hopkins (SO) exhibited:
- will of Frances Gunby [!], constituting Richard Wharton executor, proved by 2 witnesses. Said Wharton was granted administration. Also accounts.
- bond of John Cornish administrator of Henry Dingley. Security: William Fassitt. Also inventory, by appraisers Peter Dent & Edmund Howard.
- will of Alexander Thomas, constituting Mr. John Huett executor, proved by 3 witnesses. Said Huett was granted administration. Sureties: Robert Colier, Thomas Holbrooke. Also inventory, by appraisers James Wetherle & John Bud.

Mr. John Rawlings (DO) exhibited:
- will of John Ross (DO), which did not cite an executor, proved by 3 witnesses. Mabeth Ross relict was granted administration. Also inventory, by appraisers Thomas Allmen & David Macall. Also accounts.
- will of Henry Aldred, constituting his widow Mary Aldridg executrix, proved by 1 witness. Said Mary was granted administration.
- bond of Thomas Earle (TA) administrator of Elenor Corkeron. Securities: Elisabeth Mackey, Edmond. Branock.

16:137 ...
- bond of Mary Aldredge administratrix of Henry Aldredge (DO). Securities: Anthony Thompson, Thomas Newton.

Page 141

Also inventory, by appraisers Arthur Whiteley & William Mishew.
- bond of Elisabeth David administratrix of Jeremiah David. Securities: William Mishew, Richard Owen. Also inventory of said Jeremiah Davis, by appraisers Benjamin Hunt & John Kirke.
- accounts of Hann Prichett administratrix of William Prichett (DO).
- accounts of Mary Crow administratrix of Gourney Crow.
- accounts of Elisabeth Ford administratrix of John Foord.
- accounts of Grace Clyford administratrix of William Norcomb.
- accounts of James Foxon administrator of Simeon Hubbart.
- accounts of Edward Tench administrator of John Tench.
- Jane Jones administratrix of Morgan Jones.
- accounts of Richard Pearce administrator of John Pearce.
- inventory of George Hooper (DO), by appraisers Timothy Nemare & Samuell Mileton. will, constituting his son William Hooper executor, proved by 3 witnesses. Said William was granted administration. Securities: John Meridith, Richard Parson.
- inventory of Thomas Cooke (DO).

16:138 29 February. Mr. Richard Keene (CV) exhibited:
- bond of Elisabeth Morris administratrix of John Morris (CV). Securities: Joseph Greare, Richard Wollis.
- bond of Thomas Taney administrator of Thomas Earle (CV). Securities: John Elsey, Clarke Skinner.
- bond of Mathew Gardiner administrator of James Gardiner (CV). Securities: Charles Stinnett, John Barker. Also inventory, by appraisers James Cob & Nicholas Willson.
- bond of Jane Trueman administratrix of Henry Trueman (CV). Securities: William Joseph, Michaell Taney.

- inventory of John Pecocke (CV), by appraisers John Leach & John Davis. Administratrix: Elisabeth Pecocke.
- inventory of Thomas Sedgwick, by appraisers Michaell Taney & Ignatius Sawell.

Exhibited inventory of Thomas Cooke (DO), by appraisers Hugh Eccleston & Andrew Parker. Also exhibited accounts.

John Edmondson (TA) administrator of William Johnson exhibited that he finds nothing to appraise, except stock & the plantation in the hands of Joseph Rogers for 7 years. Said Rogers refuses to give accounting. Attachment issued to said Rogers. Summons to Philip Lynes & John Atkey to testify concerning said estate.

16:139   At request of John Edmondson (TA), Mr. Nicholas Milburne testified to tobacco shipped on ship John Anderson of New Castle. Said Edmondson petitioned for allowance from estate of Ralph Moore.

2 March. Henry Reed who married Parthenia relict & executrix of John Smocke (SO) petitioned that since he obtained quietus est, he has been sued numerous times for debts to said estate. In each case, the ruling was: no action. Said Reed was granted to exhibited additional inventory & additional accounts.

Capt. John Davis administrator of Philip Wyott (TA) exhibited accounts.

Dr. Mordicay Moore (AA) administrator of John Suallwell exhibited inventory, by appraisers Daniell Elliett & Hugh Hamilton. John Addison, Esq. exhibited will of said John Swallwell, proved by 2 witnesses.

16:140   Edward Jones (CE) who married Mary relict & administratrix of William Brokas (CE) exhibited accounts of payments to Garrett Murrey & his wife Susanna only daughter & heiress to dec'd.

Charles Carroll procurator for Garrett
Murrey vs. Mr. Robert Gouldesborough
procurator for Ed. Jones. Ruling:
plaintiff.

Ralph Moone (TA) administrator of his
father Ralph Moone exhibited accounts.

James Bigger (CV) administrator of
Richard Hill (CV) exhibited accounts.

3 March. Mr. John Hawkins (TA)
administrator of Richard & Sarah
Collings (TA) exhibited accounts.

Maj. Nicholas Sewall, Esq. (CV) was
granted LAC on estate of Col. Edward
Pye (CH).

William Sparks (TA) administrator of
Nicholas Hudson (CE) exhibited accounts.

John Dorsey administrator of Robert
Maine (AA) exhibited additional
inventory & accounts.

16:141   Mr. Richard Johns for Madam Bourne (CV)
vs. Michaell Millar administrator of
James Boulay. Exceptions to accounts
exhibited. Continuance was granted.

Richard Galloway (AA) who married
Elisabeth relict & executrix of Benjamin
Lawrence exhibited accounts.

Archibald Edmondson (CV) son of Robert
Edmondson was granted administration on
his estate. Securities: Otho Holland,
John Meritton. Appraisers: David Small,
Joshua Hall. Mr. Thomas Greenfeild to
administer oath.

John Stuard who married Mary relict &
executrix of Robert Winsmore (DO)
exhibited accounts.

John Holsworth (CV) administrator of (N)
Abbott & administrator of (N) Martyn
exhibited accounts. Mentions:
exceptions by John Scott.

16:142 <u>4 March</u>. James Carvile (high sheriff, CV) exhibited summons to Edward Blay & his wife Ann relict of Robert Burman to answer Samuell Manthrop.

Said Carvile exhibited summons to John James & his wife Ann to render accounts on estate of Richard Whitton.

Edward Blay (CE) administrator of (N) Whitton was granted continuance, due to hardness of winter & sickness of his wife.

John Underwood (BA) who married relict of Henry Wollin (BA) was granted administration on his estate. Mr. George Ashman to administer oath.

Capt. John Beane administrator of William Longe (SM) vs. Mr. Philip Clarke procurator for George Short. Regarding: administration of said estate. Ruling: if said Short pays said Beanes, then LoA will be granted.

William Harris one of executors of Thomas Parker (CE) petitioned for appraisers.

<u>6 March</u>. John Macklester vs. Charles Carroll procurator for William Fassett. Capt. William Whittington (high sheriff, SO) exhibited summons of attachment to William Fassett. Libel exhibited. Attachment renewed.

16:143 <u>7 March</u>. Francis Collier (CV) who married Sarah relict & executrix of John Evans (CV) exhibited accounts. Continuance was granted.

Mr. Humphrey Chilton (CE) exhibited accounts of Anne James wife of John James on estate of Richard Whitton (CE).

Samuell Browne executor of Col. Thomas Thurston (BA) exhibited additional accounts.

Exhibited inventory of Bazill Warren (CV), by appraisers Mr. Thomas

Court Session: 1695

Greenfeild & Thomas Garrett.

Joseph Edloe executor of Ed. Meillings
vs. Mr. Philip Clarke procurator for
Richard Keene. Answer exhibited.

James Bigger (CV) exhibited that LoA
were granted to him & Mr. Thomas
Greenfeild on estate of Richard Charlett
(CV) as attorneys for Mr. Richard Kings
(merchant, London) executor of said
Charlett. Said Greenfeild refused to be
concerned with the estate. Said Bigger
was granted sole administration. Mr.
Richard Keene to administer oath.

16:144 10 March. Mrs. Mary Eagle wife of
Robert Eagle (away in ENG) exhibited
accounts on estate of her 2 former
husbands: James Orrocke & Jacob Preene.
Mentions: 3 orphans (under full age)
desire security for their estate.
Continuance was granted.

11 March. Mr. Edward Boothby (BA) to
examine accounts of Mary Freesland,
Martha Hall, Mary Utie, James Philips, &
Elisabeth Gibson of their
administrations.

18 March. Dr. Mordicay Moore vs.
Rachell Gray administratrix of John
Gray. Caveat exhibited.

Exhibited inventory of Robert Gott (AA),
by appraisers James Ford & John Watters.

19 March. Samuell Watkins (CV) vs.
estate of James Harper (AA). Caveat
exhibited.

Court Session: 1696

4 April. Seth Biggs (g, AA) exhibited
will of Roger Bishop (AA), proved by 2
witnesses. Also bond of John Batie who
married Sarah executrix. Securities:
Nicholas Terrett, David Small.

9 April. Mr. George Lingan (CV)
administrator of John Abington exhibited
list of debts.

16:145 Mr. Elias King (KE) exhibited:
- will of John Biddle (KE), constituting Simon Wilmer executor, proved by 2 witnesses. Said Wilmer was granted administration.
- William Frisby & Michaell Miller were granted administration on estate of Lawrence Vanderbush (KE). Appraisers: Richard Lowder, Robert Peack.
- Mary Rouse widow of John Rouse (KE) was granted administration on his estate. Appraisers: Edward James, Mathew Earekson.
- John Oliver was granted administration on estate of John Row (KE).

13 April. Mr. George Asman (g, BA) exhibited:
- bond of Sarah Norris administratrix of Edward Norris (BA). Securities: Jonas Bowen, John Thomas. Also inventory, by appraisers John Mounfeild & Jonas Bowen.
- bond of John Underwood who married relict & administratrix of Henry Wellden (BA). Securities: Isaack Jackson, Joseph Toullson. Also inventory, by appraisers James Jackson & William Sladen.

21 April. Katherine Carrington (BA) widow of John Carrington (BA) exhibited his will. Mr. George to Ashman prove said will. Said Katherine was granted administration. Appraisers: John Willman, John Broad. Said Ashman to administer oath.

16:146 23 April. Mr. Robert Gouldesborough (TA) exhibited:
- will of Warner Sudall, constituting his friend John Emerson executor, proved by 3 witnesses. Said Emerson was granted administration.
- will of William Simson (TA), constituting his landlord George Hadaway executor, proved by 3 witnesses. Said Hadaway was granted administration.
- bond of Nicholas Millburn

administrator of Richard Metcalf (TA). Securities: Robert Ungle, Thomas Bennett.

- bond of Katherine Finey administratrix of William Finey (TA). Securities: David Blaney, William Clayton.
- bond of Isaac Winchester administrator of Isaac Winchester (TA). Securities: Robert Smith, John Hawkins.
- bond of Ann Watkins administratrix of Peter Watkins. Securities: Robert Broadaway, John Worley.
- bond of John Sergeant administrator of John Gibson. Securities: William Clayton, Moses Harris.
- bond of John Glovar administrator of Henry Boston. Security: Stephen Dardeen.

24 April. Exhibited inventory of Roger Bishop (AA), by appraisers Nicholas Terrett & David Small.

16:147 30 April. Mr. Richard Keene exhibited regarding the estate of (N) Charlett:
- Mr. James Bigger has proposed Mr. Richard Clouds (CH) & Mr. Serjant (CH) as securities. The Commissary General is not convinced of their solvency. Date: 23 March 1695.
- Bigger responded that Keene says there is hardly any man in the county worth so much. Mr. Keene lives a great way from me, over the river; my brother lives nearby. Date: 27 March 1696.

16:148 ...
- Letter from Keene. Date: 6 April 1696.
- Letter from Keene, citing that he has granted LoA to Mr. Thomas Greenfeild on estate of Richard Charlett. Securities: William Barton, Thomas Taney. [Amount: £2500.0.0 sterling.] Date: 14 April 1696.
- bond of Thomas Greenfeild, William Barton, Thomas Taney. Witnesses: John Wight, Josh. Cecell, Henry Croft.

16:149 ...

- bond of James Bigger administrator of John Honsong (CV). Security: Robert Curron.
- bond of James Catterton (CV) administrator of Michaell Catterton (CV). Securities: Mathew Burnham, John Hedger.
- bond of James Catterton (CV) administrator of Marke Catterton (CV). Securities: Mathew Burnham, John Hedger.
- administration formerly granted to Michaell Catterton & returned for want of good security.
- Mary Samwes administratrix of Jonathon Samwes (CV). Securities: Paul Rawlens, Hugh Williams.
- will of Francis Billingsley (CV), constituting his widow Sarah Billingsley & only daughter Rebeckah Birkhead executrices, proved by 2 witnesses. Said executrices are Quakers; no LoA were granted. Also inventory, by appraisers James Height & John Leach.
- inventory of John Morris (CV), by appraisers Isaack Williams & William Willson. Elisabeth administratrix exhibited accounts. Estate is overpaid.

30 April. Exhibited inventory of Maj. John Cambell (SM), by appraisers Robert Mason & William Husband.

Exhibited additional inventory of William Hill (DO), by appraisers Mr. Thomas Ennalls & Thomas Hicks. A tract of land is appraised at £45.0.0, to be used for maintenance of a free school. Mr. Hugh Eccleston is one of executors.

16:150 Mr. Robert Mason (g, SM) & Mr. Philip Clarke (g, SM) were granted administration on estate of Capt. Thomas Meech. Securities: Michaell Browne, James Bland. Mr. Henry Denton (clerk of Council) exhibited books of accounts of said Thomas Meetch. Appraisers: Col. David Browne, George Layfeild, Esq., Maj. Robert King.

Cornelius Danman who married Jane relict
& administratrix of John Bould (CH)
exhibited accounts.

George Layfeild, Esq. vs. Mr. Thomas
Jones & Mr. King administrators of
Stephen Luffe (SO). Caveat exhibited.
Continuance was granted.

2 May. Christopher Thompson & his wife
Grace executors of Laurence Rouland (CV)
exhibited accounts. Quietus est was
granted.

16:151   Maj. James Smallwood (CH) administrator
of Robert Thompson (CH) exhibited
additional accounts. Estate is
overpaid. Quietus est was granted.

Sarah Teal (BA) administratrix of Edward
Teal exhibited accounts. She is a poor
widow.

Mr. John Gresham vs. Mr. Gabriell
Parrott administrator of Thomas Briscoe.
Caveat exhibited.

Said Gresham administrator of Edward
Selby exhibited that no effects could be
found. Continuance was granted.

Mr. Thomas Hamon & his wife Rebecka
executrix of Thomas Lytfoote (BA)
exhibited inventory, by appraisers John
Thomas & Christopher Gift. Also
accounts. Estate is overpaid.

James Harper (Annapolis, AA) died
intestate. Samuell Watkins (CV) in
right of his wife Anne executrix of
Andrew Abington petitioned for
administration, as greatest creditor.
Said Anne & said James were copartners
in keeping an ordinary in CV.
16:152   Mr. Charles Carroll, Mr. Robert
Carvile, William Joseph, Esq., & Mr.
John Lewellin were authorized to take
accounting of said estate. Mr. Charles
Carroll was excused, with Mr. James
Browne put in his place. Said Joseph,
Llewellin, and Browne returned:
16:153   Said Harper was indebted to said Samuell

Watkins.
16:154 Date: 20 May 1696. Signed: William
Joseph, John Llewellin, Ja. Browne.
16:155 Also exhibited inventory. Mr. Samuell
Watkin was granted administration, as
greatest creditor. Securities: William
Joseph, Esq., George Plater, Esq.

Darby Henley (CV) exhibited inventory of
Obidath Evans (CV), by appraisers James
Dicke & Joseph Dawking.

Capt. Richard Brightwell executor of
Robert Kent (CV) exhibited inventory, by
appraisers John Blandid & George Nelor.
16:156 ...

16:156 4 May. Penelope Land (CH) widow of
Richard Land exhibited additional
accounts. Mentions: bill due Jonas
Kingsbury. Estate is overpaid.
Discharge was granted.

Silvester Welch administrator of John
Welch (AA) exhibited additional
inventory, by appraisers Leonard Wayman
& Benjamin Williams.

Mr. George Ashman (g, BA) exhibited
will of John Carrington (BA),
constituting his widow Katherine
Carrington executrix, proved by 3
witnesses. Said Katherine was granted
administration. Also exhibited
inventory, by appraisers John Wilmot &
John Broad.

Henry Lowe & his wife Susanna vs.
Charles Carroll procurator for Col.
Henry Darnall. Answer exhibited.

Maj. Thomas Ennalls (DO) administrator
of Edward Conner exhibited accounts.

Col. David Browne (SO) executor of
Archibald Erreskin was granted "quietus
est".

16:157 7 May. Mr. Thomas Greenfeild returned
LoA for Michaell Catterton on estate of
his father Michaell Catterton & LoA on
estate of his brother Marke Catterton.

Said Michaell was not able to produce security.

Col. George Robotham exhibited his examination of accounts of Madam Henrietta Lloyd (TA) on estate of her husband Col. Philemon Lloyd.

11 May. John Robinson (CV) who married Frances relict & executrix of James Graves (CV) exhibited accounts.

12 May. Nathaniell Wickham (CV) who married Sabena relict & executrix of Thomas Barnard (CV) exhibited inventory, by appraisers Samuell Magruder & Simon Nickholls. Also accounts.

The following exhibited summons:
- William Holland (sheriff, AA).
- John Thomas (sheriff, BA).
- William Parker (sheriff, CV).
- John Coode (sheriff, SM).
- William Whittington (sheriff, SO).
- John Cambell (DO).
- James Smith (sheriff, TA).
- John Carvile (sheriff, CE).
- John Stone (sheriff, CH).

16:158 13 May. Mr. Thomas Nicholls (merchant, Clifts, CV) exhibited will of Joseph Fary (merchant, London), constituting his mother Mary Fary executrix. Said Mary was granted administration by Metropolitan of London, & she executed a PoA to said Nicholls. Said Nicholls was granted administration on said estate, on behalf of said Mary. Securities: William Nicholls,, John Dorman. Appraisers: MM Thomas Blake, William Nicholls. Capt. Thomas Tasker to administer oath. PoA of Mrs. Mary Fary to said Nicholls, before Nicholas Hayward (notary). Date: 13 November 1695.

16:159 Mentions: plantation of said Joseph at Clifts, adjoining William Nicholls. Witnesses: Nath. Dare, Nathaniell Palmer, Richard Clarke.

16:160 Will of Joseph Fary. Date: 2 February 1692. Bound for VA on ship Ruth. Bequests: brother Francis Fary & brother

Robert Fary, mother Mary Fary (widow, London). Mentions: sister Mary Wagstaff wife of James Wagstaff, brother Charles Fary. Executrix: mother.

16:161 Attested by: William Broxton, Benjamin Edmonds his servant, John Marriott. Date: 7 November 1695.

John Macklester vs. Charles Carroll procurator for William Fassett (SO). Answer exhibited.

Elenor Howard (AA) exhibited will of her husband John Howard, constituting her executrix, proved by 3 witnesses: Henry Wriothesly, Edward Rumney, James Leyler. Said Elenor was granted administration. Maj. John Hamon to administer oath.

John Ford (CV) who married Diana relict & executrix of Robert Jarvise (CV) exhibited accounts.

Darby Henly (CV) who married Ann relict & executrix of Obadia Evins (CV) exhibited accounts.

Capt. Richard Brightwell executor of Robert Keemp (CV) exhibited accounts.

Benjamin Ball (CV) who married Martha relict & executrix of Robert Freeland (CV) exhibited accounts.

Exhibited inventory of Robert Jarvise (CV), by appraisers William Meads & Abraham Clark.

16:162 14 May. John Mackdowell who married Mary relict & administratrix of John White (CV) exhibited inventory, by appraisers Evan Rice & Edward Dickson. Also exhibited accounts.

15 May. Jane Raullings (AA) widow of Richard Raullings exhibited his will, which cited no executor, proved by 2 witnesses. Said Jane was granted administration. Securities: Daniell Edge, Richard Everard. Capt. John Dorsey to administer oath.

Court Session: 1696

16 May. Col. John Thomas on behalf of
Robuck Lynch (BA) was granted
administration on estate of Samuel
Greenwood (BA), for the use of the
orphans. Capt. John Ferry to
administer oath.

John Stevens & his wife Ann executrix of
Thomas Cooke (DO) exhibited additional
inventory & additional accounts.
Continuance was granted.

Henry Gifford administrator of Hugh
Gardiner (CH) exhibited accounts.

Nehemiah Covington executor of John
Covington (SO) exhibited accounts.

Jesse Houlton administrator of Cornelius
& Mary Mulraign (TA) exhibited accounts.

16:163   Anthony Smith (AA) who married Diana
relict & executrix of Thomas Knighton
(AA) exhibited accounts.

John Sides (TA) administrator of his
father Peter Sides exhibited accounts.
Discharge was granted.

Madam Elisabeth Blackiston (SM)
administratrix of Col. Nehemiah
Blackiston exhibited additional
inventory, by appraiser Capt. Thomas
Attoway. Also exhibited accounts.

William Dare (CE) was granted
administration on estate of Thomas
Killger. Securities: William Mansfeild,
Thomas Whitton. Appraisers: Garrett
Murrey, Thomas Whitton.

Richard Wade one of administrators of
John Wright (CH) exhibited accounts.
Continuance was granted.

Alice Bridges (alias Ellis Bridges, TA)
widow of Thomas Bridges (who died March
last) exhibited his will, constituting
Mr. John Hawkins executor. Said
Hawkins has seized all. Sheriff (KE) to
summon said Hawkins, to show cause why
he detains the widow's 1/3rd & to

exhibited inventory.

16:164 Evan Rice vs. Nathaniell Dare (CV).
Mentions: Mich. Yokley, Samuell Groome,
wife of said Rice. Said Rice is due
1/4th of estate of (N).

John Macklester vs. William Fassitt
(SO) administrator of Andrew Whittington
(SO). Said Fassitt to exhibited
accounts & distribute 1/3rd to said
Macklester & his wife.

Exhibited inventory of Isaac Winchester
(TA), by appraisers MM Robert Smith &
John Hawkins. Amount: £553.7.7.

Exhibited inventory of William Simson
(TA), by appraisers Thomas Evans & Peter
Hadaway.

16:165 Mr. Robert Gouldesborough (TA)
exhibited will of Thomas Bridges (TA),
constituting Mr. John Hawkins executor,
proved by 3 witnesses. Said Hawkins was
granted administration.

Mr. Samuell Hopkins (SO) exhibited:
* bond of Francis Jenkins
  administrator of William Coleburne.
  Security: Samuell Hopkins. Also
  inventory of said William Colburne,
  by appraisers Richard Tull & Peter
  Lowder.
* will of Samuell Long, constituting
  his son John Long executor, proved
  by 3 witnesses. Said John was
  granted administration. Securities:
  Richard Tull, John More. Also
  inventory, by appraisers Jeffris
  Mitchell & John Heath.
* bond of Thomas Addams administrator
  of Philip Addams. Securities:
  Rouland Bevins, John Tayler. Also
  inventory of said Phillips Addams,
  by appraisers Thomas Dixon & John
  Tayler.
* bond of William Fassett
  administrator of Samuell Tomlin
  Security: William Boseman. Also
  inventory, by appraisers William
  Boseman & John Polk.

Mr. Elias King (KE) exhibited:
- bond of William Frisby & Michaell Miller administrators of Lawrence Vanderbuss.
- bond of Mary Rouss administratrix of John Rouss. Securities: William Elliott, Edward Rallinges. Also inventory of said John Rouse, by appraisers Matthew Erreckson & Edward James.

16:166 ...
- will of John Trew (KE), constituting his only brother William Trew executor, proved by 3 witnesses. Said William is Quaker. Said William was granted administration.
- bond of Peter Allabie administrator of William Webb (KE). Securities: John Heathcot, Abraham Ambross, Jr.
- bond of Simon Willmer administrator of Lambert Willmer (KE). Security: Charles Tilden.

Morris Slany who married Elisabeth relict & administratrix of Morriss Wollohand (KE) exhibited accounts.

Mr. John Thompson (CE) exhibited:
- bond of Alexander Simms administrator of Samuell Underhay (CE). Surety: Mr. William Harris.
- bond of Mr. John Carvile administrator of John Cuffe (free Negro, CE, died by drowning), as greatest creditor. Surety: Robert Drury.
- bond of Abraham Redgrave who married Margaret relict & administratrix of John Morris. Sureties: John Carvile, Charles Bass.
- bond of John Sequence administrator of John Bevell, Sureties: Ralph Rutter, Peter Clauson.
- additional accounts of Diana Jones relict & administratrix of William Drake (CE).
- accounts of Christopher Mounts administrator of Nicholas Dorrill.
- accounts of Thomas Browning & his wife Anne relict of Darby Nolan (CE).

16:167 Mr. Richard Boughton (CH) exhibited:
- bond of Richard Harrison administrator of Richard Carver. Security: Henry Wharton.
- bond of William Hall administrator of Thomas Taft. Sureties: Ralph Shaw, George Godfrey.
- accounts of Francis Bullery & his wife Ellenor relict & administratrix of Edward Frawner (CH).

18 May. Robert Grundy who married Debora relict & executrix of Thomas Impey (TA) exhibited accounts.

Ralph Moone (TA) administrator of his father Ralph Moone exhibited additional accounts.

John Edmondson vs. Samuell Watkins procurator for John Rogers (TA). Petition for said Edmondson to file libel.

19 May. Exhibited inventory of Richard Edlen (SM), by appraisers William Boarman, Jr. & Anthony Sims.

20 May. Mrs. Judith Stanley executrix of Maj. John Stanley (TA) exhibited accounts.

Quietus est was granted to:
- Mr. John James administrator of Richard Whitton (CE).
- Michaell Courtois (SM) administrator of Capt. Justinian Gerrard.
- Thomas Roe & William Jump executors of James Silvester (TA).

Philip Clark procurator for ;Mr. John Edmondson vs. John Rogers. Libel exhibited.

16:168 Mr. Thomas Brooke, Esq. exhibited:
- bond of Richard Southerne & Richard Brightwell administrators of Mary Trueman (widow, CV), dated 28 July 1686. Securities: Ninian Beall, John Buras.
- will of Arthur Storer (CV), dated 25 November 1686. Ann Skinner & Martha

Greenfeild were granted administration.

- bond of Ann Skinner administratrix of Robert Skinner (CV), dated 14 February 1686. Securities: Thomas Greenfeild, Richard Brightwell.
- will of William Truman (CV), dated 18 March 1684/5, constituting his cousin Thomas Greenfeild executor, proved by 3 witnesses.
- will of Jonathon Pearce (CV), dated 17 April 1685, proved by 2 witnesses. Bequests: all to friend James Moore.
- will of Basill Waring (CV), dated 8 December 1688, proved by 3 witnesses. Sarah Waring executrix & his father Richard Marsham executor for his 2 sons Marsham Waring & Basill Waring, & his father John Hance executor for his son Samson Waring were granted administration.
- bond of Thomas Braine administrator of Arthur Ludford (CV), dated 11 September 1686. Securities: Richard Clarke, Joseph Fry.
- bond of Hugh Stone administrator of Robert Treuant (CV), dated 15 December 1687. Securities: Philip Laurence, Mathew Scrukin.
- bond of Rebecca Finch administratrix of Guy Finch (CV), dated 7 January 1688. Securities: James Moore, Jos. Hall.

16:169 ...

- bond of Col. Henry Darnall administrator of Madam Mary Darnall (CV), dated 24 May 1694. Security: Thomas Brooke.

Thomas Tench, Esq. administrator of Lyonell Copley exhibited accounts. Mentions: debts due: the King, Mr. Robert Mason, husband (dec'd) of Mrs. Blackistone.

22 May. Mr. Thomas Coursey (TA) & Madam Elisabeth Coursey executors of Col. Henry Coursey petitioned for appraisers: Col. John Hinson, Maj. Thomas Smithson, Mr. William Coursey. Mr. Robert Gouldesborough to administer

oath.

23 May. Samuell Weathers (KE) was
granted administration on estate of
Charles Feris (TA), as greatest
creditor. Securities: John Edmondson,
John Whrightson.

16:170   Mr. William Cooper (g, PG) to prove
will of Thomas Lewis (PG) & to
administer oath to Katherine relict &
executrix.

Mr. Edward Boothby (BA) exhibited:
* accounts of Elisabeth Boyce
administratrix of Cornelius Boyce.
* accounts of Moses Edwards
administrator of Robert Skinner
(BA).
* accounts of Joseph Perrigoy on
behalf of Ann Mumfort administratrix
of Edward Mumfort.
* accounts of William Farfar
administrator of Lewis Barton (BA).
* accounts of Michaell Gormack & his
wife Judith administratrix of Andrew
Peterson.
* accounts of Francis Smith & his wife
Elisabeth administratrix of Daniell
Laurence (BA).
* accounts of John Endsor
administrator of John Maynard (BA).
* accounts of Thomas Stone & his wife
Mary executrix of William Gayne
(BA).
* accounts of John Lockett
administrator of Richard Gwins (BA).
* accounts of Christopher Shaw
administrator of John Ashes (BA).
* accounts of Richard Thompson
administrator of Richard Rutter
(BA).
* accounts of David Thurston & his
wife Martha administratrix of Robert
Cage administrator of Mark Childs
(BA).
* accounts of John Devegha who married
relict & administratrix of William
Deyson (BA).
* accounts of Robert Olees & his wife
Margarett administratrix of William
Westburges (BA).

16:171 ...

- accounts of John Love executor of Robert Love (BA).
- accounts of John Love executor of his father Robert Love administrator of Elisabeth Hempstead (BA).
- accounts of William Yorke administrator of John Woods (BA).
- accounts of John Keemble administrator of Robert Keemble (BA).
- accounts of William Yorke & his wife Elisabeth executrix of Jacob Lotton.
- accounts of James Frizle & his wife Mary executrix of William Yorke (BA). will of William Yorke (BA), dated 23 November 1690, constituting his widow Mary executrix. Also inventory, by appraisers Richard Adams & Thomas Reston. Also additional inventory.
- bond of William Yorke administrator of John Wood (BA), dated 15 April 1693. Securities: Robert Owlas, Will. Leanox.
- will of Elisabeth Hempstead (BA), constituting her friends Mr. Thomas Staley & Robert Love executors, dated 9 December 1690. Said Love was granted administration. Securities: Samuell Sickmore, John Fuller. Also inventory, by appraisers Moses Growin & Samuell Sikmore.

16:172 ...

- bond of Christopher Shaw administrator of John Ashes (BA). Date: 20 October 1692. Securities: Rouland Thornbury, Edmond Baxter. Also inventory, by appraisers Luke Raven & William Fairfar.
- bond of John Ensor administrator of John Maynard. Date: 1 August 1691. Securities: Hugh Jones, William Game. Also inventory, by appraisers said Jones & said Game.
- bond of Margarett Westberry administratrix of William Westberry. Date: 3 March 1690/1. Securities: Robert Olas, Thomas Staley, Mich. Judd. Robert Olas married said Margarett. Also inventory, by

appraisers John Hall & James Maxwell.

- bond of Richard Thompson administrator of Richard Rutter (BA). Date: 1 August 1691. Securities: John Ferrey, John Arden. Also inventory, by appraisers John Arden & Richard Samson.
- will of Robert Love (BA), constituting his son John executor, proved by 3 witnesses on 7 June 1692. Also inventory, by appraisers John Fuller & Moses Groome.
- bond of Francis Smith & his wife Elisabeth relict of Daniell Laurence (BA). Date: 8 December 1690. Also inventory, by appraisers Robert Draysdaill & Richard Perkins.

16:173 ...

- inventory of Jacob Lotton (BA), by appraisers George Oldfeild & Francis Smith.
- inventory of John Wood, by appraisers Thomas Jones & (N).
- inventory of John Hathway, by appraisers William Osborn & George Gunnell.
- bond of Judith Dorman administratrix of Andrew Peterson. Date: 7 May 1692. Securities: John Hayes, Sellah Dorman. Also inventory, by appraisers Edmond Baxter & John Harden.
- bond of John Kemble administrator of Robert Kemble. Date: 6 July 1691. Securities: August Herman, Richard Askew.
- bond of William Fairfar & his wife Judith relict of lewis Barton (BA). Date: 4 March 1692/3. Securities: John Hayes, Richard Gardiner.

John Edmondson vs. Samuell Watkins (g) administrator of William Johnson (mariner). Per Mr. John Edmondson, Mr. Philip Lynes was summoned to give testimony. Date: 25 May 1696.

16:174 Christian Godard (DO) exhibited that her father Elias Godard is dec'd & that she had proved his will. But her grandfather Thomas Skillington came to

her father's plantation & locked it up.
Petition for estate to be returned.
Date: 11 May 1696. Said Thomas
Skillington petitioned that he is
willing to permit the appraisement
providing notice be taken of estate of
Salomon West (dec'd) which is
intermingled. And if Mathias Alford
should marry said Christian (under age),
then said Alford is to give security.
Notice to such given to Deputy
Commissary.

26 May. Capt. George Brent (g, VA) on
behalf of Francis Hamersley
administrator of Nathan Barton (CH)
exhibited additional accounts, allowed
by Justices of Stafford Co. (VA).

29 May. Exhibited inventory of Mrs.
Ann Chew (AA), by appraisers Richard
Johns & Neh. Birchead.

9 June. Mr. Gabriell Parrott (AA) vs.
estate of John Powell (AA). Caveat
exhibited.

30 June. Exhibited inventory of Joseph
Fary, by appraisers Thomas Blake &
William Nicholls.

16:175   1 July. Elisabeth Higham (CV) executrix
of Francis Higham (CV) was granted
administration on his estate. Said
Elisabeth widow of Christopher Bains was
also granted administration on his
estate. Appraisers: Thomas Howe, James
Martyn. Mr. Francis Freeman to
administer oath.

2 July. Mr. Samuell Hopkins (SO)
exhibited:
- will of Gilbert Taylor (SO), proved
  by 3 witnesses. Judith Taylor
  relict & administratrix was granted
  administration. Securities: Walter
  Taylor, Thomas Quillam. Also
  inventory, by appraisers Peter
  Lowder & Rowland Beavins.
- will of Christopher Reynolds, proved
  by 3 witnesses. Elisabeth Reynolds
  executrix was granted

administration. Securities: William
Bowin, Samuell Hopkins. Also
inventory, by appraisers Thomas
Morris & John Law.

- will of David Richardson (SO),
constituting his son William
Richardson executor, proved by 3
witnesses. Said William was granted
administration. Securities: Mathew
Scarbrough, Samuell Hopkins. Also
inventory, by appraisers Robert
Johnson & Samuell Hopkins, Jr.
- accounts of John & Thomas Purnell
executors of Thomas Purnell.

16:176 ...

- will of William Tomkins (SO),
constituting Elisabeth Wale, Jr.
daughter of Edward & Elisabeth Wale
executrix, proved by 2 witnesses.
Said Elisabeth Wale, Jr. was granted
administration. Securities: Edward
Wale, Charles Wale. Also inventory
of said William Thomkins, by
appraisers John Franklyn & Edward
Green.
- will of Walter Powell, constituting
William Powell, John Powell, & Henry
Scholdfield executors, proved by 3
witnesses. Said John, William, &
Henry Scholfield were granted
administration. Securities: Robert
Peell, Francis Thorowgood. Also
inventory, by appraisers Peter Dent
& Alexander Maddox. Also additional
inventory, by appraisers John
Cornish & Peter Dent.
- will of Richard Holland,
constituting his widow Frances
Holland & his eldest son Nehemiah
Holland executors, proved by 2
witnesses. Said Frances & Nehemiah
were granted administration.
Security: Samuell Hopkins, Sr. Also
inventory, by appraisers Walter
Scarbrough & William Cord.
- bond of Cornelius Innes
administrator of William Innes.
Security: Aaron Bishopp. Also
inventory, by appraisers Edward
Green & Thomas Morris.

16:177 ...

- accounts of Mr. James Round

administrator of Edward Evins.
- accounts of Grizell Latcham administratrix of George Latcham.
- accounts of Margery & William Turvile executors of William Turvile (SO).
- accounts of Margaret Towers administratrix of Jonathon Towers.
- accounts of Elisabeth Hamelin administratrix of Margarett Hamelin.

Mr. John Rawlings (DO) exhibited:
- bond of Mary Sealous administratrix of Stephen Sealous (DO). Security: James Foxon. Also inventory, by appraisers Richard Meekins & William Shenton.
- accounts of Jane Bosewell administratrix of Robert Boswell (DO).
- accounts of William Hooper administrator of George Hooper.
- accounts of Charles Bradly (DO) administrator of Richard Thompson (DO).

Mr. Elias King (KE) exhibited:
- will of William Hodges (KE), constituting John Hurt & Richard Mason trustees, proved by 3 witnesses. Said Hurt & Mason were granted administration.
- inventory of Mr. Laurence Vanderbush (minister, KE), by appraisers Richard Lowder & Robert Peck.
- inventory of William Webb (KE), by appraisers John Heathcot & William Smith.

16:178 Mr. Richard Boughton (CH) exhibited:
- bond of Barbare Gourley administratrix of John Gourley (CH). Securities: John Wood, Evan Jones. Also inventory, by appraisers said Wood & said Jones.
- accounts of Dorathy Graves relict & administratrix of Joshua Graves.
- inventory of Christopher Myers, by appraisers John Barker & John Booker.

Court Session: 1696

Mr. William Cooper (PG) exhibited:
- will of Thomas Lewis (PG), proved by 2 witnesses. Katherine Lewis relict & executrix was granted administration.
- inventory of Robert Edmondson, by appraisers David Small & Jo. Hall. Also accounts of Archibald Edmondson administrator of his father said Robert, proved before MM Ro. Bradly & David Small.

Maj. William Whittington exhibited a list of fees.

Mr. Edward Boothby (BA) exhibited a list of fees.

Mr. Walter Campbell (high sheriff, DO) exhibited a list of fees.

Exhibited inventory of William Sutton, by appraisers John Rockhould & Richard Sorrell.

16:179 3 July. Mr. John Thompson (CE) exhibited:
- bond of William Jones administrator of Francis Bellowes (CE). Security: Richard Kinnard.
- accounts of Anne Allum relict & executrix of Nicholas Allum (CE).
- accounts of John Daring & his wife Martha relict & administratrix of John Miller (CE).
- inventory of John Morris (CE), by appraisers Mathias Mathiason & Thomas Kelton. Administrators: Abraham Redgrave & his wife Mary.
- inventory of John Beavell (CE), by appraisers William Currer & Humphrey Kitly.
- accounts of Thomas Windall & his wife Anne relict & executrix of Henry Higgs (CE).

Mr. Robert Gouldesborough (TA) exhibited:
- will of Zerobabell Wells (TA), constituting his friends MM John Cheirs & John Hamer executors, proved by 3 witnesses. They both

Page 165

renounce administration. Catherine
Wells widow was granted
administration. Securities: John
Hamer, Ambrose Kinimont.
- will of Edmond Fish (TA),
  constituting his widow Joane Fish
  executrix, proved by 2 witnesses.
  Said Joane was granted
  administration.
- will of Thomas Yovell (TA),
  constituting Sarah Yovell & Thomas
  Yovell executors, proved by 3
  witnesses. Said Sarah & Thomas were
  granted administration.

16:180 ...
- will of Michaell Turbott (TA),
  constituting his widow Sarah Turbott
  executrix, proved by 3 witnesses.
  Said Sarah was granted
  administration.
- bond of Mr. Edward Mann
  administrator of William Bird (TA).
  Securities: Nicholas Milburn, John
  Tiley.
- bond of Mary Baggs administratrix of
  Thomas Baggs (TA). Securities:
  Edward Mann, William Catrop.
- inventory of Warner Sudall (TA), by
  appraisers John Salter & Christopher
  Higgs.
- inventory of William Mountichew
  (TA), by appraisers John Davis &
  William Jones.
- inventory of Richard Metcalfe, by
  appraisers Ra. Moone & Edward Scott.

Commissary General exhibited:
- accounts of Richard Clouds & his
  wife Judith relict & executrix of
  John Goldsmith (SM).
- additional inventory & accounts of
  Thomas Ross & his wife Jane
  executrix of Emanuell Pitcher (SM).
- accounts of Charles Daft & his wife
  Anne administratrix of William
  Medley (SM).
- accounts of Katherine Cambell
  executrix of William Bevins (SM).
- additional inventory of Maj. John
  Cambell (SM), by appraisers Mr.
  Robert Mason & William Husband.
- bond of Elisabeth Morgaine

administratrix of Robert Large (SM). Securities: John Symons, William Garratt.
- accounts of Mr. Clement Hill & Luke Gardiner executors of Richard Gardiner (SM).

16:181 Alice Egion (AA) widow was granted administration on estate of Benjamin Gargill (AA), as greatest creditor. Surety: Edward Sanders. Appraisers: Hugh Merickan, Jonathon Neale. Mr. Henry Constable to administer oath. Also inventory, exhibited on 13 July. Also accounts. Discharge was granted.

Andrew Kinimont (TA) was granted administration on estate of his brother John Kinimont. Securities: Ambros Kinnimont, Alexander Raye.

Charles Carroll procurator for Col. Henry Darnall vs. Henry Lowe & his wife Susanna Maria. Libel exhibited.

Mr. Samuell Watkins (now of SM) administrator of James Harper vs. William Morrison (TA). Libel exhibited.

4 July. Exhibited inventory of John Hayland (CE), by appraisers Edward Jones & William Dare.

Thomas Hanson (AA) executor of John Ray (AA) exhibited inventory, by appraisers William Pennington & Richard Bayly. Also accounts.

16:182 Capt. John Beane exhibited will of Elisabeth Young (SM), proved by 2 witnesses.

Stephen Willson & his wife Mary petitioned that Lt. Col. Finney (TA) died leaving 2 children: a son, & Mary (petitioner). Petition for Katherine Finney relict & executrix to show why the petitioner should not have her share. Sheriff (TA) to summon said Katherine to render accounts.

Thomas Greenfeild administrator of
Richard Charlet (CV) petitioned that he
can not inventory said estate without
the books, etc., kept by Capt. James
Bigger. Sheriff (CH) to summon said
Bigger to show cause why he detains the
papers.

6 July. Gabriell Parrott administrator
of Thomas Briscoe vs. John Elsey. Said
Elsey cited to render accounts of said
estate in his hands. Sheriff (CV) to
render an attachment.

16:183   Gilbert Clarke petitioned that Mr.
Clarke & Mr. Carvile on behalf of Capt.
Pheppard have notice regarding accounts
of (N) Plater, Esq. Also to summon
William Neagle & his wife Mary
administrators of Henry Payne to render
accounts, as said Gilbert is greatest
creditor. Date: 27 June 1696 at Charles
Town. Also petition that Mr. Carroll &
Your Honor finish the award between Mr.
Smith & myself.

Joseph Pettibone (AA) administrator of
his brother Isaacke Pettibone exhibited
accounts.

7 July. Philip Body (CV) who married
Sarah relict & administratrix of Thomas
Robinson (CV) exhibited accounts.

Samuell Watkins administrator of James
Harper. vs. Robert Goldesborough
procurator for William Morrison (TA).
Answer exhibited.

11 July. Exhibited will of Madam Jane
Long (BA), constituting her daughter
Jane Peck overseer for benefit of son
(under age 19) of said Long, proved by 3
witnesses.

14 July. Exhibited inventory of John
Howell (TA), by appraisers James Scott &
William Scott.

16:184   11 August. Mr. Samuell Hopkins (SO)
exhibited:
• will of Charles Rackliffe (SO),

constituting his widow Elisabeth &
son Rackliffe Charles executors,
proved by 3 witnesses. Said
Elisabeth and Charles were granted
administration. Securities: Edward
Wale, Samuell Hopkins. Also,
inventory by appraisers John
Franklin & Edward Greene.

- will of William Porter (SO),
constituting his widow Elisabeth
Porter executrix, proved by 2
witnesses. Said Elisabeth was
granted administration. Securities:
George Bonto, John Turpin. Also
inventory, by appraisers Richard
Chambers & Ephraim Willson.

Exhibited inventory of Charles Roberts
(AA), by appraisers Mordica Price &
Richard Gott.

Mr. Robert Carvile procurator for
Edward Wood & his wife Sarah one of
daughters of Mordica Hunton (CV) vs.
Hugh Ellis (CV). Libel exhibited.

29 August. William Mote (AA) who
married Susanna relict of John Smart
(AA) was granted administration on his
estate. Securities: Richard Baily,
Jonathon Neale. Appraisers: said Baily,
said Neale.

16:185 5 September. Mr. Edward Boothby (BA)
exhibited:
- will of Col. George Wells (BA),
constituting his son Benjamin Wells
executor, proved by 2 witnesses.
Said Benjamin was granted
administration. Also inventory, by
appraisers James Phillips & Dan.
Palmer.
- will of Rowland Thornburgh (BA),
constituting his widow Ann
Thornburgh executrix. Said Ann was
granted administration. Also
inventory, by James Strawbridge &
William Wilkison.
- will of Nathaniell Henchman (BA),
constituting his friend Jonas Bowen
overseer for Benjamin (under age 18,
son of said Jonas), proved by 2

witnesses. Also inventory, by John
Thomas & Charles Meriman.
- will of Robert Wilmott (BA),
constituting his widow Joane
Willmott executrix, proved by 3
witnesses. Said Joane was granted
administration. Also inventory, by
appraisers Jonas Boyan & John
Mounfeild.
- accounts of George Gunnell
administrator of Edward Gunnell.

16:186 ...
- will of Thomas Morris (BA),
constituting his widow Anne Morris
executrix, proved by 2 witnesses.
Said Anne was granted
administration. Also inventory, by
appraisers Jonas Bowen & John
Enswer.
- verbal will of Francis Watkins (BA),
proved by 4 witnesses before Mr.
John Ferry. Mary Watkins relict &
William Barker were granted
administration. Securities: John
Hayes, Nicholas FitzSymons. Also
inventory, by appraisers said Hayes
& said FitzSymons.
- bond of Robuck Lynch administrator
of Samuell Greenwood (BA).
Securities: Nicholas FitzSymons,
William Terfer. Also inventory, by
appraisers Luke Raven & William
Tarfer.
- inventory of George Utie (BA), by
appraisers Lodwick Martin & Daniell
Palmer.
- inventory of Madam Jane Long (BA),
by appraisers William Wilkinson &
William Farfare.
- inventory of Simeon Jackson (BA), by
appraisers Lodwick Martin & Daniell
Palmer.

16:187 Mr. James Phillips (BA) executor of his
father James Phillips (BA) exhibited
accounts, proved before Mr. Edward
Boothby.

7 September. Mr. Richard Keene (CV)
exhibited:
- will of Christopher Banes (CV),
constituting his son Christopher

Banes executor, proved by 3
witnesses. Said son was granted
administration.
* bond of Ann Johnson administratrix
  of George Johnson (CV). Securities:
  Thomas Tucker, William Herbert.
  Also inventory, by appraisers
  William Feild & William Morgan.
* bond of John Jenkins administrator
  of Henry Thomas (CV). Securities:
  Richard Kent, James Beauchamp.
* bond of Ann Cosden administratrix of
  Alphonso Cosden (CV). Securities:
  Christopher Banes, Robert Brooke.
* inventory of Richard Bowen (CV), by
  appraisers Jeremiah Eldridge & Darby
  Sulivan.

9 September. Jeremiah Sheridan for Ann
Sedgwick administratrix of Thomas
Sedgwick (CV) exhibited accounts.

Charles Harrison who married Johanna
relict & administratrix of Anthony
Arnoll (AA) exhibited accounts. [See
will & inventory in book of Mr. Henry
Bonner (AA).]

16:188 Mr. Elias King (KE) exhibited:
* will of John True (KE), constituting
  his brother William True executor.
  Said William is a Quaker. Upon
  further consideration, he complied &
  was granted administration.
* bond of John Hurt & Richard Mason
  administrators of William Hedges
  (KE). Security: Morgan Jones. Also
  inventory, by appraisers Charles
  Hynson & William Glanrell.
* bond of Elisabeth Powell
  administrator of Cornelius Powell
  (KE). Security: Michaell Millar.
  Also inventory, by appraisers
  Benjamin Ricaud & Thomas Ricaud.

16 September. The Commissary General
exhibited from SM:
* will of John Heard (SM),
  constituting his widow Susanna
  executrix, proved by 4 witnesses.
  Said Susanna was granted
  administration. Securities: Henry

Court Session: 1696

Spink, William Spink.
- bond of Payne Turberfeild & his wife Ann relict, administrators of Robert Taylor. Securities: Gilbert Turbervile, John Cooper. Also inventory, by appraisers Gilbert Turbervile & Barnabe Anctell.
- accounts of Maj. Sewall administrator of Col. Edward Pye (CH).
- inventory of Robert Large (SM), by appraisers Henry Smith & Richard Atwood.

16:189 ...
- additional accounts of Emma Roswell executrix of William Roswell (SM).
- accounts of Robert Thomas & his wife Mary executrix of John Little (SM).
- accounts of John Newman & his wife Rebecka executrix of John Barcraft (SM).
- inventory & accounts of estate of Alexander Currey (SM), per his father Hubbart.
- additional accounts of Tomasine Damer administratrix of Thomas Dammer (SM).
- accounts of Jane Skipper administratrix of James Skipper.
- accounts of Charles Daft administrator of William Medley (SM).
- accounts of William Shirtley & Michaell Reyly executors of Thomas Sallman (SM).
- accounts of Henry Spinke executor of his father Henry Spinke (SM).
- accounts of Elisabeth Warren administratrix of William Warren (SM).

MM Robert Mason & Philip Clarke exhibited inventory of Capt. Thomas Meech, by appraisers MM Thomas Beale & Richard Benton.

Letter from S. Hopkins to Commissary General. Mentions: Col. Browne on 28 July last, Maj. Whittington, (N) Stockdale who married Jane Sewall.

Court Session: 1696

16:190 Ann Smith widow of James Smith (AA)
exhibited his will, constituting her
executrix, proved by 2 witnesses. Said
Ann was granted administration.
Appraisers: Richard Bayly, Jonathon
Neale.

17 September. Mr. John Rawlings (DO)
exhibited:
- will of Elias Godward (DO),
  constituting his daughter Christian
  executrix, proved by 3 witnesses.
  Said Christian was granted
  administration. Securities: John
  Allford, Jr., Mathias Alford. Also
  inventory, by appraisers Richard
  Sowter & John Nicholls.
- bond of Richard Teate administrator
  of Daniell Bryan. Securities:
  Richard Adams, Edward Poole. Also
  inventory, by appraisers Obadiah
  King & Edward Williams.
- will of John Mackeel (DO),
  constituting his 2 sons William &
  Thomas Mackeell executors, proved by
  1 witness. Said William & Thomas
  were granted administration. Also
  bond ob William Mackeell & Thomas
  Mackell administrators of John
  Mackeell. Securities: Jacob
  Lookerman, Edmond Branock. Also
  inventory, by appraisers John Kirk &
  Benjamin Hunt.
- accounts of Elisabeth Davis
  administratrix of Jeremiah Davis
  (DO).
- accounts of Mary Selous
  administratrix of Stephen Sealous.
- additional inventory of George
  Hooper.

16:191 18 September. Mr. Robert
Gouldesborough (TA) exhibited:
- bond of Mary Vickars administratrix
  of Franc. Vickars (TA). Securities:
  Jeremiah Hooke, Roger Hooke.
- bond of Joshua Atkins administrator
  of Maurice Neal. Security: Clement
  Sayle.
- bond of William Alderne
  administrator of James Eley.
  Securities: Thomas Bennett, Ralph

Moone.
- bond of Joan Fish executrix of Ed. Fish (TA). Securities: Christopher Spry, Will. Bush.
- inventory of William Finney, by appraisers William Tench & John Salter.
- inventory of Thomas Baggs, by appraisers William Catrop & C. Delahay.
- inventory of Michaell Turbott, by appraisers Will. Lowrey & Nich. Hemsly.
- inventory of Thomas Yeovell, by appraisers David Blaney & William Clayton.

21 September. Mr. Scarborough for his daughter Hanna Maynard was granted continuance on estate of her husband.

22 September. Andrew Kininmont administrator of his brother John Kininmont (TA) exhibited accounts.

Exhibited inventory of Francis Higham (CV), by appraisers Thomas Howe & Ja. Martin.

Mr. Robert Mason (high sheriff, SM) exhibited summons.

16:192 Elisabeth Brace widow of John Brace (CE) was granted administration on his estate. Securities: Robert Hews, Thomas Lindsey.

Elisabeth White executrix of Edward White (DO) petitioned for Mr. John Rawlings to examine her accounts.

23 September. Richard Harrison (g, CH) & William Stone (g, CH) exhibited depositions regarding estate of (N). Ward.

Exhibited inventory of Jonathon Samway (CH), by appraisers George Naylor & Thomas Lawson.

25 September. Nathan Vitch (CV) administrator of John Vitch exhibited

accounts.

26 September. David Small (PG) was granted administration on estate of William Cooper (PG), as greatest creditor. Mr. Thomas Greenfeild to administer oath.

Exhibited inventory of Garratt Killger (CE), by appraisers Garrett Morrey & Thomas Whitton.

Elizabeth Smith executrix of William Smith (CH) petitioned for Mr. Cleborne Lomax to examine accounts.

Richard Cheshire & his wife Mary executrix of Samuell Ramiger (AA) exhibited accounts.

Said Cheshire administrator of Charles Roberts was granted continuance.

16:193 **30 September.** Richard Edlen executor of his father Richard Edlen exhibited accounts.

Ubgatt Reeves who married Jane relict & executrix of Ignatius Causin (CH) exhibited accounts.

Isaack Williams (PG) executor of Ruth Hide (PG) exhibited accounts.

Joseph Greares administrator of Benjamin Greares (PG) exhibited accounts.

John Forrist administrator of Philip Larrance (PG) exhibited accounts. Continuance was granted.

Maj. Henry Ridgley who married Mary relict & executrix of Marren Duvall (AA) exhibited accounts. Continuance was granted.

John Newman & his wife Rebecka executrix of John Bercraft (SM) exhibited accounts.

William Dent for Ann Wheilden widow of Isaack Wheilden (PA) exhibited that Mr.

Edward Green (SO) is indebted to said estate. Said Ann is very poor. Said Ann was granted administration. Securities: Joseph Wheilden (her son), Garret Morrey.

16:194 Mary Bagg administratrix of Thomas Bagg (TA) petitioned for Mr. Gouldesborough to examine accounts.

Robert Summar who married Margarett relict of John Sunderland (CV) exhibited accounts.

Capt. John Dent executor of William Husculah exhibited accounts. There is no inventory; the dec'd left nothing but land.

1 October. Christopher Beanes who was summoned to render accounts on estate of Francis Higham exhibited that as his father's executor, he will exhibit what he can.

Exhibited inventory of John Duncan (PG), by appraisers John Snuggs & John Rawlings. Administrator: William Barne.

Philip Willis executor of Joseph & Elisabeth Fry (PG) exhibited accounts.

Mr. Thomas Greenfeild (PG) exhibited will of Capt. William Penn (mariner), constituting his widow Elisabeth executrix. She is in ENG. Said Greenfeild was granted administration, for said Elisabeth.

2 October. Exhibited inventory of Thomas Parker (KE), by appraisers John Ward & Thomas Pinner.

Samuell Manthrop vs. Edward Blay & his wife Ann. Said Blay appeared & division was ordered by the Judge.

16:195 Mr. Samuell Hopkins (SO) exhibited:
• will of Hope Taylor (SO), constituting Donnock Dennis, Sr. executor. Said Dennis was granted administration. Security: Hugh

Porter. Also inventory, by
appraisers John Taylor & Donnack
Dennis, Jr.
• will of John Ruske (SO),
constituting his widow Ann Ruske
executrix. Said Ann renounced
administration. Mr. John Purnell
was granted administration, as
greatest creditor. Security:
Samuell Hopkins. Also inventory, by
appraisers William Cord & Parker
Selby.
• bond of Mary Jones administratrix of
Mathew Jones (SO). Security:
Anthony Jones. Also inventory, by
appraisers Thomas Morris & John
Gray.

Hugh Ellis executor of Mordica Hunton
(CV) exhibited accounts.

Elisabeth Powell widow of John Powell
(AA) was granted administration on his
estate. Securities: John Green, John
Edwards. Appraisers: John Solman, G.
Weston.

3 October. Walter Emerton administrator
of William White (AA) exhibited
accounts.

16:196 Samuell Holsworth who married Elenor
relict & executrix of Thomas Parslow
(CV) exhibited accounts.

John Edmondson (TA) exhibited that
Thomas Donnelan was granted
administration on estate of William
Johnson for said Edmondson. Said
Donnelan refuses to continue. Said
Edmondson was granted administration.
Security: Philip Lynes. Renewed: 29
December 1697.

6 October. Edward Ball (CV) who married
Persilla relict & administratrix of
William Lyle exhibited accounts.
Distribution: 4 shares. Also exhibited
accounts on estate of Henry Dakes.

Notley Rozier (g, CH) was granted
administration on estate of Col. Edward

Pye (CH), as next of kin. Securities: Maj. Nicholas Sewall, Mr. Cecill Butler. Appraisers: Maj. James Smallwood, Mr. Thomas Hussey. Maj. Nicholas Sewall & William Joseph, Esq. to make accounting of bills, books, etc.

Madam Henrieta Maria Lloyd executrix of John Louden (TA) petitioned for Mr. Gouldesborough to examine accounts.

16:197 Notley Warren (CH) executor of his father Humphrey Warren exhibited accounts.

Charles Stevens (AA) administrator of Michael Taylor (AA) exhibited accounts.

Mrs. Katherine Montgomery (alias Katherine Parker) administratrix of George Parker exhibited additional inventory. Her present husband is absent.

Capt. John Bayne vs. George Short. Re: estate of William Longe. Capt. John Bayne exhibited depositions of Richard Dudson & John Wilder, dated 7 July last. Ruling: said Bayne was granted administration.

Capt. John Beane (CH) who married Ann relict & executrix of Thomas Gerrard exhibited accounts.

Ralph Moone (TA) administrator of his father Ralph Moone was granted "quietus est". Estate is overpaid.

7 October. Exhibited inventory of John Trew (KE), by appraisers Charles Tilden & Thomas Piner.

John Stevens who married Ann relict & executrix of Thomas Cooke exhibited additional accounts. Estate is overpaid.

16:198 Capt. James Bigger (CH) exhibited:
- accounts of John Howsin.
- accounts of Richard Hill.
- accounts of Thomas Keemp.

- accounts of James Nutwell.

9 October. Capt. John Hawkins (KE) administrator of Thomas Bridges exhibited inventory, by appraisers Robert Smith & Richard Jones Also exhibited accounts. Mentions: widow Alice Bridges is allowed her 1/3rds, including land.

Maj. Robert King & Mr. John West executors of Capt. John King (SO) were granted continuance.

John Emerson (TA) executor of Warner Sudall (TA) exhibited accounts.

Sarah Humes executrix of James Humes (CV) exhibited inventory, by appraisers John Hunt & Marke Clare. Also exhibited accounts.

16:199 **10 October.** John Edmondson vs. Joseph Rogers. Continuance was granted.

William Hemsley (g, TA) was granted administration on estate of Francis Armstrong, as greatest creditor. Securities: Michaell Earle, Moses Harris.

Alexander Gardiner (AA) was granted administration on estate of Thomas Pennington (AA), as greatest creditor. Securities: John Hurst, William Clarke. Appraisers: Joshua Merriken, Robert Handcock.

Katherine Constable widow of Henry Constable exhibited his will, constituting her executrix, proved by 3 witnesses. Said Katherine was granted administration. Appraisers: Mr. John Worthington, Humphrey Boone.

George Layfeild, Esq. (SO) was granted administration dbn on estate of Col. William Steevens (SO), unadministered by his widow Elisabeth (now dec'd). Also exhibited accounts.

George Lingan (CV) administrator of John
Abington exhibited accounts.

John Willson & his wife Elisabeth
executrix of Luke Gregory (AA) exhibited
additional accounts.

16:200   13 October.   Mr.   Edward Boothby (BA)
exhibited:
- accounts of Joseph Strawbridge & his
  wife Sarah executrix of John Arden
  (BA).
- accounts of William Hill executor of
  John Hill (BA).
- accounts of Thomas Litton executor
  of Robert Gates (BA).
- accounts of Thomas Bowen
  administrator of Nathaniell Henchman
  (BA).
- accounts of said Jonas Bowen
  administrator of James Robertson
  (BA).
- will of John Nicholls (BA),
  constituting his widow Mary Nicholls
  executrix.   Said Mary was granted
  administration in 1691.   Also
  inventory, by appraisers Edward
  Hansley & Thomas Heath.
- accounts of Thomas Staley & Robert
  Olesse administrators of Mary
  Warforte late Mary Nichollson
  executrix of above John Nichollson.

Henry Bonner administrator of Nicholas
Morrey (AA) was granted continuance.

Robert Smith, Esq. (TA) was granted
administration on estate of Morris Neale
(TA), as greatest creditor.   Security:
John Edmondson.

James Bishop (TA) executor of Thomas
Browne exhibited accounts.

George Burges (AA) administrator of
William Walker exhibited accounts.
Estate is overpaid.   "Quietus est" was
granted.

16:201   Elisabeth White executrix of Ed. White
(DO) petitioned for Mr.   John Rawlings
to examine accounts.

Court Session: 1696

Elisabeth Smith executrix of William
Smith (CH) petitioned for Mr. Cleborne
Lomax to examine accounts.

14 October. (N) Milstead vs. Mr.
Charles Carroll procurator for William
Sergeant & his wife Damarias. Re:
estate of (N) Ward. Continuance was
granted.

15 October. Mr. Philip Clarke
procurator for Thomas Warren vs. Notley
Warren (CH). Libel exhibited.

Said Clarke exhibited inventory of Capt.
Thomas Meech, by appraisers Thomas Beal
& Richard Benton

George Plater, Esq. who married Ann
relict & administratrix of Robert Doyne
(CH) exhibited accounts. Continuance
was granted.

Madam Elisabeth Blackiston
administratrix of Col. Nehemiah
Blackiston exhibited additional
accounts.

Thomas Tench, Esq. administrator of Col.
Lyonell Copley exhibited accounts. Some
are challenged.

Maurice Baker for Mary Crouch executrix
of William Sutton (AA) exhibited
accounts.

16:202 30 October. Richard Boughton (CH)
exhibited:
• bond of Joseph Willson administrator
  of James Turner (CH). Security:
  Henry Hawkins.
• bond of Elisabeth Ogden
  administratrix of Andrew Ogden (CH).
  Securities: Thomas Lawson, John
  Stope.
• inventory of abovesaid James Turner,
  by appraisers Ralph Smith & Walter
  Story.
• inventory of Thomas Tafft, by
  appraisers George Godfrey & Ralph
  Shaw.
• accounts of William Bishop

Page 181

administrator of John Smith.

16:203 10 November. Jane Terrett (AA) widow of
Nicholas Terrett exhibited his will,
constituting her executrix. The
witnesses are far removed; Mr. Seth
Biggs to prove said will. [Said will
proved by 2 witnesses.] Said Jane was
granted administration. Said Biggs to
administer oath.

2 December. Mr. Richard Boughton (CH)
exhibited:
* accounts of Richard Harrison
  administrator of Richard Carver.
* accounts of Michaell Linge executor
  of Morris Lloyd (CH).
* accounts of Morrice Fitzgerrald
  executor of Abraham Sapcoate (CH).

Mr. Thomas Greenfeild (PG) exhibited
inventory of Richard Charlett, by
appraisers George Naylor & Joshua
Cecill.

Exhibited inventory of Thomas Briscoe,
by appraisers Clementius Davis & John
Powell & approved by Robert Hopper &
Christopher Waters.

4 December. Thomas Brooke, Esq. & Col.
Ninian Bell are to administer oath to
Madam Darnall to the answer exhibited by
Col. Darnall to libel of Mr. Henry
Lowe.

Edward Swan (CV) & his wife Mary relict
& executrix of Francis Buxton exhibited
additional accounts.

16:insert Exhibited appeal by (N) Lingan. Date:
9 October 1695.

16:204 Commissary General exhibited:
* will of John Brassier (CV),
  constituting his widow Anna
  executrix, proved by 3 witnesses.
  Said Anna was granted
  administration. Appraisers: John
  Scott, William Derumple.
* bond of Amy Read administratrix of
  John Read (SM). Securities: Philip

Clarke, John Lowe.
- inventory of Elisabeth Young (SM), by appraisers Benjamin Hall & John Higton.
- will of John Marke (CV), proved by 2 witnesses before Mr. Tobias Norton on 10 March 1676. Executor: Richard Charletton.

Mr. Robert Gouldesborough (TA) exhibited:
- bond of John Pitt administrator of Thomas Cooke (TA). Security: John Edmondson.
- bond of William Hemsley administrator of Arthur Pursinah (chirurgeon). Security: John Salter.
- bond of John Latte administrator of William Jones (TA). Security: Nic. Lowe. Thomas Nicholson (p, KE in PA) renounced administration. Date: 19 November 1696.
- accounts of Madam Henrieta Lloyd administratrix of John Loudey, exhibited on 3 October last.

16:205 Mr. Luke Gardiner (SM) exhibited accounts of 1/5th part of his father's estate, put in the hands of Mr. Richard Gardiner for use of his brother Thomas Gardiner.

Gabriell Parrott administrator of Thomas Briscoe vs. John Elzey (g, CV). Attachment for said John Elsey to render accounts of effects he has of said Briscoe.

Hugh Ellis (coroner, CV) to administer attachment of contempt to James Cranford to answer regarding estate of (N) Abington.

Sheriff (KE) to administer attachment of contempt to John Jordain & his wife administrators of Richard Tydins for the answer.

Sheriff (SM) to administer attachment of contempt to Mr. Henry Lowe for no answer to libel of Col. Darnall.

Court Session: 1696

William Colvert (mariner, London) exhibited will of William Robinson (chirurgeon), constituting him executor, proved by 3 witnesses. Said Colvert was granted administration. Appraisers: Dr. Robert Jones, Charles Kibburne. Mr. James Cullins to administer oath.

7 December. Sheriff (TA) to administer attachment of contempt to Joseph Rogers to answer libel of John Edmondson.

16:206 Exhibited inventory of John Howard (AA), by appraisers John Rockhold & Thomas Blackwell.

Exhibited inventory of John Smart (AA), by appraisers Jonathon Neale & Richard Bayly.

Exhibited inventory of Samuell Osborne (KE), by appraisers Mathew Erreckson & Francis Stevens.

Mr. John Rawlings (DO) exhibited:
• bond of Elisabeth Troughton administratrix of Roger Troughton (DO). Securities: Arthur Whiteley, David Mackall. Also inventory, by appraisers John Draper & William Mishew.
• accounts of William Lawyer & his wife Grace administratrix of John Barnes (DO).

Administration of Maj. Nicholas Sewall & William Joseph, Esq. administrators of Col. Edward Pye was renewed.

Mr. James Wroth (CE) was granted administration on estate of William Nowell (CE), who died leaving no relation in the Province, as greatest creditor. Appraisers: Syrack Whitworth, Richard Peacock. Mr. Edward Blay to administer oath.

16:207 9 December. John Bartlett (TA) son of Sarah Bartlett was granted administration on her estate. Securities: Nicholas Milburne, William Aldern. Appraisers: John Pope, Nicholas

Milburne.

John Edmondson for self & Maj. Thomas
Raynolds, Thomas Higgs, & William Sharp
securities for Sarah Pindar
administratrix of Edward Pindar
petitioned that the said Sarah be
summoned to give new security.

Capt. James Bigger exhibited the
petition of John Muth dated 1 December
1696. Mr. Richard Charlett (dec'd) was
executor of will of John Murke, father
of petitioner, & Mr. Thomas Greenfeild
administrator of said Charlott to pay
said orphan (now of age).

10 December. Notley Roziers (g, CH)
exhibited that as administrator of Col.
Pye, he finds said estate intermingled
with that of his father Benjamin Rozier,
since his mother married said Pye. Said
Notley was granted administration dbn on
estate of said Benjamin, unadministered
by Ann Rozier (alias Ann Pye).
Appraisers: Maj. James Smalwood, Mr.
Thomas Husey. Mr. John Stone (g, CH)
to take security. Mr. Philip Hoskins
to administer oath.

16:208 Mr. James Cranford administrator of
John Abington appeared. Mr. George
Lingan refused to pay said Cranford to
be paid to Richard Harrison as a just
debt. [See f. 105.] Ruling: defendant.
Signed: John Freeman.

16:209 Madam Henrietta Marya Lloyd vs. estate
of Mr. Edward Lloyd (London). Caveat
exhibited.

11 December. Mr. George Lingan (CV)
administrator of John Abington exhibited
additional accounts.

12 December. Timothy Lane who married
Margarett relict & executrix of Capt.
Henry Alexander (TA) exhibited accounts.

14 December. Mr. John Thompson (CE)
exhibited:
• will of Ezekill Jackson (CE),

constituting Sarah Jackson
executrix, proved by 3 witnesses.
Said Sarah renounced administration.
William Elmes (CE) was granted
administration, as greatest
creditor. Security: Edward Beck.
• renunciation of Mary Dermont relict
of Abraham Hollins (CE). Date: 2
December 1696. Witnesses: John
Thompson, Mary Atkinson.
• inventory of Elinor Neale (CE), by
appraisers Gerardus Wessells &
Thomas Powell. Administrator:
George Sturton.

16:210 15 December. Court at SMC on 15 August
1696. Robert Carvile procurator for
Philip Cox (p, CV) & his wife Sarah
relict & administratrix of John Johnson
(SM) for self & Sarah daughter of said
Johnson by said Sarah vs. Capt. Samuell
Watkins procurator for Thomas Courtney
(SM) & his wife Elinor. Mentions: Fobbe
Roberts (SM) 20 years ago went to
Holland. Said Roberts made will
bequeathing to nephew John Johnson &
niece Elinor Courtney. Said Courtney
detains the estate.
16:211 Mentions: Edward Ward, Mr. Robert
Ridgely.
16:212 Ruling: plaintiff.

Mr. Joshua Cecill was appointed Deputy
Commissary (PG).

16 December. Thomas Kinniston (PG) was
granted administration on estate of
Richard Bayly, as greatest creditor.
Appraisers: Robert Orm, John Smith. Mr.
William Barton to administer oath.

MM William Dent & Robert Carvile
procurators for (N) Milstead vs. Mr.
Charles Carroll procurator for (N)
Sergeant. Continuance was granted.

16:213 Mr. Richard Bennett (TA) administrator
of John Howell petitioned for Mr.
Robert Gouldesborough to examine
accounts.

Court Session: 1696

Mr. Robert Goldesborough (as King's Councell) vs. Mr. Thomas Tench administrator of Lyonell Copley, Esq. Caveat exhibited.

31 December. Thomas Freeburne (AA) & Richard Kilburne (AA) executors of Elisabeth Barnett (AA) exhibited accounts.

12 January. Exhibited inventory of Thomas Pennington (AA), by appraisers Joshua Meriken & Robert Handcocke.

Exhibited inventory of William Bird (TA), by appraisers Thomas Robins & Thomas Clemens.

22 January. Exhibited inventory of Thomas Lewis (PG), by appraisers Mr. William Hatton & William Hutchison.

3 February. Mr. Roger Newman (merchant, AA) was granted administration on estate of Thomas Darbin, as greatest creditor. Securities: John Kemble, James Read.

11 February. Mary Welsh (AA) widow of Richard Welsh was granted administration on his estate. Securities: William Jefferys, Richard Garrett. Appraisers: Jacob Harnest, Laurence Drappier. Capt. Richard Hill to administer oath.

16:214 17 February. Alice Austin (AA) widow of Samuell Austin was granted administration on his estate. Securities: William Jeffris, John Fairebrother. Appraisers: John Fairebrother, Robert Ward.

18 February. John Scutt who married Katherine relict of Stephen Hart (BA) was granted administration on his estate. Appraisers: James Jackson, Christopher Coxe. Mr. George Ashman (g, BA) to administer oath.

20 February. Patience Collins (AA) widow of Josias Collins was granted administration on his estate.

Securities: Richard Killburne, William Freeman.

Richard Beard (sheriff, AA) exhibited summons.

Mr. Nicholas Lowe (high sheriff, TA) exhibited summons.

23 February. Mr. Benjamin Hall (CH) who married Mary relict & executrix of James Bouling (SM) exhibited accounts. Discharge was granted.

16:215 Mr. Robert Gouldesborough (TA) exhibited:
- will of James Coursey, constituting his mother Elisabeth Coursey & his brother Thomas Coursey executors.
- will of John Boone (TA), constituting his widow Jane executrix. Said Jane was granted administration. Securities: Nicholas Banks, John Edmondson.
- will of Thomas Ree (TA), constituting his friends Andrew Price & William Scoott executors, proved by 3 witnesses. Said Price & Scoott were granted administration.
- will of Thomas Thompson (TA), constituting William Jackson executor, proved by 3 witnesses. Said Jackson was granted administration.
- will of John Swaine (TA), constituting his widow & Richard Tilghman executors. Said Swaine & Tilghman were granted administration.
- will of Thomas Booker (TA), constituting his widow, son Thomas, & son John executors, proved by 3 witnesses. Said Thomas & John were granted administration. Security: Joseph Rogers.
- inventory of Zerobabell Wells, by appraisers William Coursey, & Mich. Earle.

16:216 ...
- will of John Boram (TA), constituting his friend William Sharp executor, proved by 3

witnesses. Said Sharp was granted administration.
- bond of Hannah Batson administratrix of Christopher Batson (TA). Securities: John Cape, William Anderson.
- bond of John Edmondson administrator of Samuell Millson (TA). Security: William Aldern.
- bond of Thomas Robins, Sr. administrator of John Robins (TA). Security: Thomas Robins, Jr.
- inventory of William Jones (TA), by appraisers John Pemberton & Moses Harris.
- inventory of Edmond Fish (TA), by appraisers Christopher Spire & Philemon. Joane Fish executrix exhibited accounts.

Mr. Hennage Robinson (merchant, PG) administrator of Thomas Harman exhibited accounts.

Exhibited inventory of James Smith (AA), by appraisers Richard Bayly & Jonathon Neall.

24 February. Silvester Welsh administrator of John Welsh (AA) exhibited accounts.

16:217 Mr. George Lingan (CV) administrator of John Abington exhibited additional accounts. Mentions: John Elley.

Mr. John Elsey (CV) exhibited list of items in his hands regarding: estate of Thomas Briscoe. Administrator: Gabriell Parrott. Given to: William Parker (sheriff, CV).

Mr. Richard Boughton (CH) exhibited:
- bond of Sarah Cooksey widow & administratrix of Philip Cooksey (CH). Securities: William Smith, Thomas Price.
- bond of Joane Regon widow & administratrix of James Regon (CH). Securities: Patrick Anderson, Evan Jones.
- inventory of Andrew Ogdon, by

appraisers John & Thomas Losson.
- accounts of Robert Loften
  administrator of Robert Loften (CH).

16:218 Mr. Samuell Hopkins (SO) exhibited:
- will of Edward Prise (SO),
  constituting his widow Jane Price
  executrix, proved by 4 witnesses.
  Also bond of Jane Prise
  administratrix. Securities:
  Benjamin Sumers, Cornel. Ward. Also
  inventory, by appraisers William
  Coulbourne & Benjamin Sumers.
- will of James Dunkan (SO), proved by
  3 witnesses. Elisabeth Dunkan widow
  was granted administration.
  Securities: Samuell Hopkins, William
  Shankland. Also inventory, by
  appraisers Edward Greene & Adam
  Spence.
- will of Daniell Selby (SO),
  constituting his widow Mary Selby &
  son Parker & son Thomas executors,
  proved by 3 witnesses. Said Mary,
  Parker, & Thomas were granted
  administration.
- accounts of Grace Scholfeild
  executrix of Robert Houston (SO).

Mr. John Thompson (CE) exhibited:
- bond of Edward Johnson administrator
  of Abraham Hollens. Said Johnson is
  greatest creditor. Mary widow
  renounced administration. Sureties:
  William Chamberlin, John Bovington.
- bond of Rosemond Steevens
  administratrix of George Steevens
  (CE). Securities: Henry Rigg,
  Guisbert Cocke.
- accounts of Daniell Macklen & his
  wife Margaret executrix of William
  Burden (CE).

16:219 Exhibited inventory of Ezekill Jackson
(CE), by appraisers John Carvile & John
Ellis

John Edmondson vs. Robert
Gouldesborough procurator for Joseph
Rogers (TA). Answer exhibited.

Court Session: 1696

Commissary General exhibited:
- list of Maj. Nicholas Sewall &
  William Joseph, Esq. regarding
  estate of Col. Pye.
- inventory of John Read (SM), by
  appraisers John Nutthall & Robert
  Clarke.
- additional accounts of Walter Lane
  (SO) administrator of Josias
  Seaward.
- accounts of Penellope Waters
  executrix of John Waters.

6 March. Joshua Meriken (AA) exhibited
will of Richard Bayly (AA), constituting
him executor, proved by 2 witnesses.
Said Meriken was granted administration.
Appraisers: Capt. Humphry Boone, Edward
Gibbs.

8 March. Exhibited inventory of Edmond
Stow (CV), by appraisers James Berry &
John Willymott.

9 March. Exhibited inventory of John
Powell (AA), by appraisers John Sellman
& George Westall.

16:220 Mr. John Rawlings (DO) exhibited:
- bond of Edward Taylor, Jr.
  administrator of Mordant Thacker
  (DO). Security: Henry Davis. Also
  inventory, by appraisers Peter
  Williams & David Makall.
- accounts of Elisabeth White
  executrix of Edward White.
- accounts of Richard Teate
  administrator of Daniell Bryant.
- accounts of James Petterkin executor
  of John Salsbury.

15 March. Exhibited inventory of
Richard Welch (AA), by appraisers
Laurence Draper & Jacob Harnis, sworn by
Capt. Richard Hill.

Edward Hall (AA) vs. estate of Henry
Ballard. Said Ballard died at said
Hall's house. Caveat exhibited. On 17
March, George Brufs (AA) was granted
administration on said estate, as
greatest creditor. Said Ballard had

been a lodger at said Brufs' house for
several years. Said Ballard has no
relations in the Province, but a wife &
children in ENG. On 27 March, bond was
exhibited. Securities: Robert Hopper,
Richard Killburne. Appraisers: Leonard
Wayman, Robert Hopper.

16:221 17 March. Dr. Louis de Rochebrune (KI,
TA) was granted administration on estate
of Maurice Hooper (cooper, KI), who died
having no relations in this country.
Security: William Rabetts. Mr. John
Coppedge to administer oath.

23 March. Mr. George Ashman (BA)
exhibited oath of John Scutt & his wife
Katherine administrators of Stephen Hart
(BA). Securities: Thomas Hooker, Robert
Parker. Also inventory, by appraisers
James Jackson & Christopher Cox.

Court Session: 1697

30 March. Nicholas Greenbury for Hanah
widow of Nicholas Lambe (AA) exhibited
his will, constituting said Hannah Lambe
widow executrix. Mr. John Worthington
to prove said will. Said Hannah was
granted administration. Appraisers:
Thomas Beson, Sr., William Clarke. Said
Worthington to administer oath. Note:
she is a poor widow.

2 April. William Liddell (AA) who
married Jane relict & executrix of
Nicholas Terrett (AA) petitioned for
renewal of warrants for appraisers. Mr.
Seth Biggs to administer oath.

12 April. Mr. John Thompson (CE)
exhibited accounts of Margarett Pryor
administratrix of Thomas Pryor.

16:222 22 April. Mr. Richard Keene (CV)
exhibited:
- will of Henry Orton (CV),
  constituting his friends Richard
  Johns, William Mears, Daniell
  Rawlings, & Athur Young executors,
  proved by 2 witnesses. Said Johns,
  Mears, & Rawlings renounce

administration. Said Young was
granted administration. Also
inventory, by appraisers Robert Day
& Robert Shepard.
- will of Walter Gillett (CV),
constituting his friend Peter Sawell
executor, proved by 3 witnesses.
Said Sawell was granted
administration. Also inventory, by
appraisers Robert Skinner & John
Grover.
- bond of James Heigh administrator of
Peter Goodard (CV). Security:
William Derumple. Also inventory of
said Peter Godard, by appraisers
John Leach, Jr. & Benjamin Ball.
- bond of Jane Stow administratrix of
Edward Stow (CV). Security: John
Taman.
- bond of Col. John Bigger
administrator of Robert Curry (CV).
Security: Robert Skinner.
- inventory of Christopher Beans (CV),
by appraisers James Duke & John
Turner.
- inventory of Alphonso Cosden (CV),
by appraisers James Duke & John
Turner.

His Lordship vs. estate of Col.
Casparus Augustin Herman. Caveat
exhibited, for finishing work on
Statehouse by Henry Denton. Date: 26
April 1697.

16:223 29 April. Exhibited additional
inventory of James Turner (CH), by
appraisers Ralph Smith & Walter Story.
Joseph Willson administrator exhibited
accounts. Continuance was granted.

John Sumerland (AA) was granted
administration on estate of Thomas Wood,
as greatest creditor. Securities:
Richard Horne, Stephen Handcock.
Appraisers: said Horne, said Handcock.

4 May. Exhibited will of David Steward
(AA), constituting his widow Margarett
Steward executrix. Capt. Nicholas
Gasway to prove said will. Appraisers:
Stephen Warman, Thomas Carter. Said

Court Session: 1697

Gasway to administer oath.

George Brufs administrator of Henry
Ballard (BA) exhibited inventory, by
appraisers Robert Hopper & Leonard
Wayman. Continuance was granted.

5 May. Ann Austin administratrix of
Samuell Austin (AA) exhibited inventory,
by appraisers John Fairebrother & Robert
Ward.

16:224   8 May. Exhibited inventory of Thomas
Wood (AA), by appraisers Frances Mead &
John Hurst.

13 May. Mr. Richard Boughton (CH)
exhibited:
- will of Thomas Mudd (CH),
  constituting his widow Ann Mudd &
  son Thomas Mudd executors, proved by
  3 witnesses. Said Ann & Thomas were
  granted administration. Securities:
  William Boarman, Sr., William
  Boarman, Jr.
- bond of Magdlen Tailler
  administratrix of William Tailler
  (CH). Securities: Mathew Sanders,
  John Willkinson. Also inventory of
  said William Tailer, by appraisers
  said Sanders & said Willkinson.
- bond of Grace Collier administratrix
  of Giles Collier (CH). Securities:
  Mathew Sanders, John Parker. Also
  inventory, by appraisers said
  Sanders & said Parker.
- will of Dr. William Hall (CH),
  constituting his widow executrix,
  proved by 2 witnesses. Mary Hall
  executrix was granted
  administration. Sureties: Ralph
  Shaw, John Godshall.
- inventory of James Regon (CH), by
  appraisers Patrick Anderson & Evan
  Jones.

16:225   Mr. Samuell Hopkins (SO) exhibited:
- will of Stephen Costin (SO), proved
  by 4 witnesses. Comfort Costin
  relict was granted administration.
  Securities: William Warwicke,
  William Smillin. Also inventory, by

appraisers Miles Gray & Richard Chambers.

- will of John Bishop (SO), constituting his widow Mary executrix, proved by 3 witnesses. Said Mary was granted administration. Securities: Charles Williams, Sall. Hopkins. Also inventory, by appraisers Mathew Scarbrough & Thomas Selby.
- bond of Elisabeth Robins administratrix of William Robinson (SO). Securities: James Hardy, Henry Freces. Also inventory, by appraisers Thomas Winder & Benjamin Cottman.
- bond of Mary Swaine administratrix of John Swaine (SO). Security: John Webb. Also inventory, by appraisers John Webb & John Hendry. Also accounts.
- accounts of John Long executor of Samuell Long.
- accounts of Thomas Adams administrator of Philip Adams.
- accounts of Judith Taylor executrix of Gilbert Taylor.
- accounts of Elisabeth Reynolls executrix of Christopher Reynolls.

16:226 ...

- additional inventory of Henry Lynch (SO), by appraisers Peter Dent & George Lean.

Mr. John Rawlings (DO) exhibited:

- will of George Prouse (DO), constituting his widow Mary Prouse executrix, proved by 3 witnesses. Also bond of said Mary Prous administratrix of said George Prous. Securities: John Allford, Mathias Allford. Also inventory, by appraisers John Nicholls & John Wade.
- bond of Alice Kennerly administratrix of William Kennerly (DO). Securities: Henry Beckwith, Thomas Hicks. Also inventory, by appraisers Thomas Vickers & William Dossey.

Mr. John Thompson (CE) exhibited:
- Benoni Clarke (CE) who married Mary daughter of Jacob Young was granted administration on his estate. Said Clarke was granted LoA in PA. Securities: John Sequence, Thomas Whitton.
- inventory of George Steevens (CE), by appraisers Edward Laddemore & Christopher Mounts.

16:227 Mr. Robert Gouldesborough (TA) exhibited:
- will of William Anderson (TA), which cited no executor. Sarah Anderson relict was granted administration.
- will of Edward Mann (TA), in the form of a letter to Edward Pollard. There are no witnesses. Lucy Mann was granted administration on his estate. Securities: Robert Smith, Esq., Nicho. Milburne.
- bond of Christopher Santee administrator of John Quan (TA). Security: Richard Hazledine.
- bond of Elisabeth Coursey administratrix of Thomas Blackader (TA). Security: John Lillingston.
- bond of John Pitt administrator of JOhn Estell (TA). Security: William Dixon.
- will of Elisabeth Dixon (TA), constituting her husband William Dixon executor, proved by 3 witnesses. Said William was granted administration.
- will of William Parratt (TA), constituting his friend John Pemberton & his son John Parratt executors, proved by 4 witnesses. Said Pemberton renounced administration. Said John Parratt was granted administration.
- inventory of Christopher Betson (TA), by appraisers John Cape & William Anderson.
- inventory of John Boon (TA), by appraisers Nicholas Banks & Robert Bryan.
- inventory of Thomas Roe (TA), by appraisers John Browne & William Jackson.

- inventory of Thomas Thompson, by appraisers Andrew Price & William Scoot.

16:228 ...

- inventory of James Eley (TA), by appraisers Thomas Bennett & Ralph Moone.
- accounts of Mr. Richard Bennett administrator of John Howell.
- accounts of Ann Watkins administratrix of Peter Watkins (TA).

Mr. Elias King (KE) exhibited:
- will of John Power (KE), constituting his widow Bridgett Power executrix, proved by 3 witnesses. She has since married Jacob Taylor (KE). Said Jacob & Bridgett were granted administration.
- will of Richard Lowder (KE), constituting his widow Susanna Lowder executrix, proved by 2 witnesses. Said Susanna was granted administration.
- will of John Tillotson (KE), which cited no executor. The widow has since married John Hughson. Both were granted administration.
- bond of Amoss Chadburn administrator of William Jones (KE). Security: Mr. Edward Wallwin.
- accounts of John Hurt & Richard Mason administrators of William Hodges (KE).
- accounts of Peter Allabee administrator of William Webb (KE).

Exhibited will of John Chew (BA), constituting his brother Samuell Chew executor, proved by 2 witnesses. Said Samuell is gone to ENG.

16:229 14 May. Mr. Richard Keene (CV) exhibited nuncupative will of William Moss, attested by 2 oaths, bequeathing to Michaell Taney. Also exhibited petition of Mr. Ellis for LoA, as having a greater right. Date: 11 May 1697.

Hugh Ellis vs. estate of William Moss.
Caveat exhibited. Date: 10 May 1697.
* John Stephens, age 24, deposed that
on 1 May instant, he heard William
Moss give all to Michaell Taney.
* John Stephens, age 18, deposed that
in April he heard William Moss give
all to Michaell Taney.
Mr. Michaell Taney was granted
administration on said estate. Col.
John Bigger to administer oath.

Mr. George Lingan vs. Richard Harrison
& his wife Elisabeth. Mr. George
Lingan administrator of John Abington
exhibited the award made by MM Richard
Johns (CV) & Samuell Chew (AA)
concerning the protested bills by Mr.
Richard Harrison.
16:230 Ruling:
* Richard Harrison to give said Lingan
bills of exchange.
* Said Harrison to pay charges.
* Said Harrison to give receipt &
discharge.
* said Lingan to deliver to said
Harrison his wife's protested bills.
Date: 20 May 1696. Mentions: Elisabeth
Hall now wife of Richard Harrison,
Benjamin Hall, John Hyde per John Smith,
James Cranford.

16:231 Mr. Henry Lowe (SM) exhibited:
* will of John Currey (SM),
constituting his friends Mr. Edward
Cole & James French executors,
proved by 2 witnesses. Said Cole &
French were granted administration.
Also inventory, by appraisers John
Fenwicke & Thomas Dillon.
* bond of Rose Mooney administratrix
of Thomas Mooney (SM). Security:
Thomas Dillon. Also inventory, by
appraisers John Godard & Timothy
Mahony.
* bond of Susannah Andrews relict of
Anthony Andrews (SM). Securities:
Thomas Rose, Charles Smith.
* additional accounts of Henry Lowe,
Esq. administrator of John Darnall.

Mr. William Husband exhibited bond of Frances Vanroswicke administrator of John Vanroswicke (SM). Securities: John Tant, Charles Daft. Also exhibited oath of appraisers: Stephen Gough, Thomas Kirtly.

MM Clement Hill & Luke Gardiner executors of Richard Gardiner exhibited additional accounts.

Samuell Lee & his wife Susanna administratrix of Edward Baxter (SM) exhibited accounts.

16:232 Mr. Richard Clouds exhibited:
- will of Thomas Turner (SM), constituting his widow Elisabeth executrix, proved by 3 witnesses. Said Elisabeth was granted administration. Security: Joshua Guybert. Also exhibited oath of appraisers: Joshua Guybert, Luke Gardiner.
- bond of Joshua Guybert administrator of Thomas Turpyn (SM). Security: Henry Poulter. Also inventory, by appraisers Henry Poulter & Edward Feild.
- bond of Roderick Lloyd administrator of Owen Newton (SM). Securities: Notley Maddox, John Ocaine.

Joshua Cecill (PG) exhibited:
- bond of Mary Floyd administratrix of David Floyd (PG). Securities: John Fowler, John Miller.
- inventory of William Cooper (clerk, PG), by appraisers John Cussons & Benjamin Berry.

Mr. Cleborne Lomax exhibited accounts of Elisabeth Smith executrix of William Smith (CH).

George Plater, Esq. who married Ann relict & executrix of Robert Doyne exhibited additional accounts.

16:233 Exhibited inventory of Francis Vickars (TA), by appraisers Thomas Delahay & Bryan Scuty.

Court Session: 1697

John Dobs who married Mary relict &
administratrix of John Meconikin (KE)
exhibited accounts.

Col John Bigger administrator of Robert
Currey (CV) exhibited inventory, by
appraisers William Head & Robert
Skinner. Also exhibited accounts.

Michaell Higgins administrator of John
Guyatt (CV) was granted continuance.

John Jordain (KE) who married Charity
daughter & executrix of Richard Tydins
(AA) exhibited accounts. Continuance
was granted.

Sarah Yovell & Thomas Yovell executors
of Thomas Yovell (TA) exhibited
accounts.

William Trew executor of John Trew (KE)
exhibited accounts.

Richard Edlen executor of his father
Richard Edlen exhibited additional
accounts.

Capt. Richard Brightwell executor of
Robert Keemp (CV) exhibited accounts.

Samuell Watkins procurator for Gabriell
Parrott (AA) administrator of Thomas
Briscoe vs. John Elsey (CV). Libel
exhibited.

16:234 15 May. Sarah Cockey (AA) widow of
William Cockey was granted
administration on his estate.
Securities: George Eager, Joshua
Merickin. Appraisers: Edward Fowler,
William Penington.

John Elsey petitioned for continuance to
answer Gabriell Parrott on estate of
Thomas Briscoe.

Mathias Vanderheyden (CE) who married
Anna Margeritta relict & administratrix
of Henry Ward exhibited additional
accounts.

Exhibited inventory of Thomas Darbin
(BA), by appraisers William Willkinson &
Stephen Johnson.

Exhibited inventory of John Brassur
(CV), by appraisers John Scott & William
Derumple.

John Downes (KE) administrator of Paul
Winbrough exhibited accounts, proved
before Robert Smith, Esq.

Jane Hyland widow & administratrix of
John Hyland (CE) was granted
continuance.

17 May. John Swinstire (AA) & his wife
the relict of Richard Deavor were both
granted administration on his estate.
Appraisers: Daniell Browne, Robert Wood.
Capt. William Holland to administer
oath.

16:235   Mary Rouse administratrix of John Rouse
(TA) exhibited accounts.

Edmond Goodman (TA) who married Sarah
relict & executrix of Andrew Toulson
exhibited accounts.

Mr. John Turner (CV) administrator of
Thomas Cornwell exhibited the receipt of
Col. Anthony Cornwell (merchant,
London). Signed: Thomas Blake.

Elenor Howard (AA) executrix of John
Howard exhibited accounts.

Thomas Brooke, Esq. exhibited oath of
Madam Darnall to the answer of the libel
of Mr. Henry Lowe.

George Hadaway (TA) executor of William
Simson exhibited accounts.

Samuell Browne (BA) executor of Thomas
Thurston exhibited additional accounts.

Katherine Carrington executrix of John
Carrington (BA) exhibited accounts.
Mentions: 8 children. Also inventory,
by appraisers John Gaither & Amos

Peirpoint.

Elisabeth Hyam (alias Elisabeth Banes)
executrix of Francis Higham was granted
continuance.

16:236 Gerrardus Wessell (CE) administrator of
John Adwick exhibited accounts. Also
inventory, by appraisers Robert Gibson &
Ezakell Jackson.

18 May. Phillip Griffin (AA) who
married Jane relict & executrix of
Richard Rawlings exhibited inventory, by
appraisers John Gaither & Amos
Peirpoint. Also exhibited accounts.
Mentions: 5 children.

John Short (CV) who married Ann relict &
administratrix of Andrew Tanehill
exhibited accounts. Continuance was
granted.

Jane Kendle relict of John Quatermus
(DO) exhibited inventory, by appraisers
Timothy Nemara & John Merideth.

John Scott for Mary Hickman (widow, CV)
exhibited will of William Hickman. Said
John was granted administration, for
said Mary. Appraisers: John Scott,
James Heath. Mr. William Nicholes to
administer oath.

Mr. John Wright (PG) who married Ann
relict & executrix of Thomas Gant
exhibited inventory, by appraisers
Robert Marsham & Thomas Brooke. Also
exhibited accounts. Continuance was
granted, as there are effects in ENG.

16:237 19 May. Thomas Taney (CH) who married
Jane Trueman relict & administratrix of
Henry Trueman (CV) exhibited additional
inventory, by appraisers John Hume &
Henry Ferneley.

Said Taney executor of Thomas Earle
exhibited inventory, by appraisers
William Smith & Thomas Price. Also
exhibited accounts.

said Taney also exhibited inventory of Henry Pinder, by appraisers Ignatius Craycroft & Hugh Ellis. Also exhibited accounts.

Said Taney administrator of his father Michaell Taney was granted continuance.

Said Taney administrator of Henry Trueman was granted continuance.

James Cullens one of executors of Marke Cordea exhibited accounts.

Richard Teate (DO) administrator of Daniell Bryant exhibited accounts.

Edward Turner vs. Joseph Willson administrator of James Turner (CH). Said Edward is a brother of the whole blood; wife of said Willson is a sister of the half-blood. Said Willson summoned.

16:238   Thomas & Abraham Warren vs. Notley Warren (CH). Continuance was granted.

John Worthington (g, AA) exhibited will of Nicholas Lamb, proved.

Mary Wells (AA) widow of Richard Wells was granted administration on his estate. Appraisers: Morgan Jones, Edward Masson. Capt. William Holland to administer oath.

20 May. Hugh Sherwood executor of Judith Brooke was granted continuance.

21 May. Charles Carroll procurator for Col. Darnall vs. Robert Carvile procurator for Henry Lowe, Esq. (SM) & his wife Susanna Maria. Answer exhibited.

MM Richard Keene & Henry Fernley for said Henry Lowe, Esq. vs said Col. Darnall. Replication exhibited.

Said Henry Lowe administrator of John Darnall exhibited additional accounts.

George Plater, Esq. administrator of Robert Doyne (CH) exhibited additional accounts.

William Jones (CV) who married Mary relict of William Hitchcock exhibited additional accounts.

16:239 Elisabeth Peacocke (CV) administratrix of John Peacocke exhibited accounts.

Jane Stowe (CV) administratrix of Edmond Stowe exhibited accounts.

William Boarman (CH) executor of Elisabeth Young exhibited accounts.

<u>22 May</u>. Samuell Wethers (TA) was appointed Deputy Commissary (TA). Securities: John Edmondson, William Sharp.

Mary Baggs administratrix of Thomas Baggs (TA) petitioned for Mr. Samuell Wethers to examine accounts, since she is incapacitated to come over the Bay.

John Edmondson (TA) administrator of William Johnson exhibited accounts.

Sarah Turbott (TA) executrix of Michaell Turbott exhibited accounts.

Robert Grundy (TA) who married Deborah relict & executrix of Thomas Impey exhibited additional accounts.

Robert Grundy who married Judith relict & executrix of Maj. John Stanley exhibited additional accounts.

Richard Wells, age 48, deposed on 7 December 1695 that "Kingsale" 300 a. on Patuxon River was given to John Hume & his heirs by Jeremiah Sulivant. The deponent is the writer of the will, though not so expressed in said will. Before: Thomas Brooke, Thomas Greenfeild.

16:240 Capt. Nicholas Gassaway (g, AA) exhibited will of David Steward (AA),

proved by 2 witnessed. Also inventory,
by appraisers Stephen Warman & Ed.
Carter.

24 May. Capt. George Brent (VA) who
married Mary relict & executrix of Col.
William Chandler (CH) petitioned to
exhibit inventory & accounts on said
estate. On 7 June, Mr. Charles Carroll
& said Brent exhibited inventory, by
appraisers John Wheeler & William
Barton. Date: 9 June 1685.

25 May. William Sharp (TA) exhibited
will of William Dorrington (DO),
constituting his son William Dorrington
(under age) & daughter Ann Dorrington
(under age) executors. Said Sharp was
granted administration, on behalf of the
children.

16:241   Capt. Richard Hill (AA) exhibited that
Patience Collings relict of Josias
Collings (AA) had LoA, but no
administration was done on the estate.
Said Patience is runaway. Said Hill was
granted administration, as principle
creditor. Securities: James Baker,
Thomas Reynolds. Appraisers: MM Richard
Killburne, Thomas Blackwell. Inventory
was exhibited on 21 June.

William Clarke (p, AA) administrator of
John Cooley (AA) exhibited inventory, by
appraisers William Penington & Francis
Moyd. Also exhibited accounts.

John Chittam (CV) administrator of
William Marks (CV) exhibited accounts.

26 May. Mr. Anthony Neale (CH) one of
& surviving executor of Joseph Piles
(SM) exhibited additional accounts.

Amey Roswell (SM) executrix of William
Roswell (SM) exhibited additional
accounts.

Susanna Andrews (SM) was granted
administration on estate of Anthony
Andrews (SM). Securities: Thomas Ross,
Charles Smith.

16:242 Mr. Baker Brooke (SM) administrator of Garrett Comberford was granted continuance. Estate consists only of goods in the hands of Capt. Kersey in ENG. Date: 12 May 1697.

27 May. Exhibited inventory of Sarah Bartlett (TA), by appraisers Nicholas Milburne & William Aldern.

Exhibited inventory of William Harry (AA), by appraisers Edward Masson & Thomas Hugh.

Mr. Thomas Coursey (TA) administrator of his father was re-summoned.

Bridgett Moore (CE) widow of Thomas More exhibited that his will is in the hands of Henry Anderson (Farly Creek, CE). Mentions: 2 children. Appraisers: Dr. Sydrock Whitworth, Stephen Wix. Said Anderson summoned.

16:243 MM Alexander Forbes & William Taylard administrators of James Anderson were granted continuance.

29 May. Mr. William Coursey (TA) administrator of Luke Atchison exhibited accounts.

Mr. Scarborough for Hannah Maynard executrix of James Maynard (SO) was granted continuance.

Mr. Elias King (KE) to examine accounts of Col. John Hinson administrator of Joseph Wicks.

Mr. Thomas Smithson (TA) to examine accounts of Katherine Finey administratrix of William Finey.

Dr. Wolfran Hunt (AA) exhibited a discharge from Edward Parrish on estate of Andrew Roberts. Date: 27 May 1697. Witness: Charles Carroll. Before: Mr. Richard Beard.

GENERAL INDEX

(no surname)
　Benjamin 20
　John 190
　Philemon 189
　Richard 64
　William 31

Abbington
　John 77
Abbot
　Samuell 36, 132
Abbott
　(N) 129, 144
　George 33, 34, 54,
　　80, 88
　Isabella 33
　John 88
　Samuell 30, 36, 89
　Thomas 88
　William 89
Abeston
　William 77
Abington
　(N) 183
　Adrew 65
　Andrew 17, 86, 87,
　　91, 92, 94, 97,
　　125, 150
　Ann 94
　John 75, 76, 94,
　　105, 106, 107,
　　119, 125, 146,
　　180, 185, 189,
　　198
　Mariel 105, 106
　Maryell 125
　Mirriell 106
　William 106
Abraham
　Jacob 126
Abrahams
　Hugh 137
　Jacob 30
Abrams
　John 8
Accuot
　Jacob 129
Acton
　John 4, 12

Adams
　David 5, 13
　Philip 195
　Richard 34, 65,
　　135, 160, 173
　Thomas 195
Addams
　Philip 155
　Phillips 155
　Thomas 155
Addison
　Alexander 10
　Ann 6, 10
　John 41, 72, 134,
　　143
Aderson
　William 43
Adison
　Alexander 6
Adwick
　John 100, 202
Agambra
　Domindigo 3
Aisbrooke
　James 38
Alcock
　Thomas 100
Alden
　William 121
Aldern
　William 184, 189,
　　206
Alderne
　William 173
Aldred
　Henry 141
Aldredge
　Henry 141
　Mary 141
Aldridg
　Mary 141
Alexander
　Henry 70, 185
　Margarett 70
Alford
　Mathias 162, 173
Allabee
　Peter 197
Allabie
　Peter 156

Allein
  Zachary 63
Allford
  John 173, 195
  Mathias 195
Allmen
  Thomas 141
Allome
  Anne 111
  Nicholas 111
Allum
  Anne 165
  Nicholas 127, 165
Ambross
  Abraham 156
Anctell
  Barnabe 172
Anderson
  Henry 206
  James 108, 121,
    130, 131, 133,
    206
  Patrick 189, 194
  Rebecca 132
  Robert 91
  Sarah 196
  William 36, 43, 44,
    64, 189, 196
Andrews
  Anthony 198, 205
  Susanna 205
  Susannah 198
Anshee
  Stephen 88
Arbuckle
  Robert 8, 25
Archer
  Allix 22
  Henry 22, 103
  Jacob 78
  Mary 78
Arden
  John 64, 161, 180
  Sarah 64
Armiger
  Daniell 90
Armstrong
  Francis 179
Armstronge
  Edward 90
Arnold
  Benjamin 19
Arnoll
  Anthony 171

Ashcom
  Charles 29
Ashely
  William 118
Ashes
  John 159, 160
Ashhurst
  William 83
Ashley
  William 140
Ashlye
  William 36
Ashman
  George 40, 66, 137,
    145, 151, 187,
    192
  George to 147
Asiter
  Anne 58
Askew
  Richard 161
Askue
  Richard 5, 13, 14
Askwith
  William 87
Asman
  George 147
Asquith
  William 46, 58, 59,
    61, 62, 88, 92
Assiter
  Anne 26
Ataway
  Thomas 48
Atcchesson
  (N) 121
Atchison
  Luke 132, 206
Athow
  Thomas 87
Atkey
  John 143
  Mr. 97
Atkins
  John 23, 77, 78,
    101
  Joshua 173
Atkinson
  Mary 186
Attoway
  Thomas 16, 17, 154
Attwood
  Richard 77
Atway

Thomas 69
Atwood
    Richard 21, 32, 44,
        172
Aud
    Mary 26
    Thomas 26, 68
Aude
    Thomas 48, 59
Aunis
    Thomas 84
Austin
    Alice 187
    Ann 194
    Samuell 187, 194
    Thomas 24, 33

Badman
    Edward 102
Bagbie
    Samuell 93
Bagg
    Mary 176
    Thomas 176
Baggs
    Mary 166, 204
    Thomas 166, 174,
        204
Bagly
    Richard 80
Baily
    Richard 5, 13, 108,
        169
Bain
    John 119
Baine
    John 19
Bains
    Christopher 162
Baker
    Edward 81
    Elisabeth 21
    Isaac 94
    James 19, 205
    John 4, 12
    Maurice 181
    Morris 133
    Mrs. 90
    Roger 3
    William 91
Baldin
    Hester 104
Ball

Benjamin 31, 89,
    153, 193
Ed. 69
Edward 88, 103,
    120, 177
John 98
Martha 153
Micaell 88
Michaell 103, 120
Persilla 103, 177
Ballard
    Henry 191, 194
Ballowing
    Benjamin 93
Banes
    Christopher 92, 93,
        98, 170, 171
    Elisabeth 202
Banke
    Edward 97
Bankes
    Edward 90
Banks
    Nicholas 188, 196
Barber
    Cibilla 47
    Ed. 49
    Edward 17, 40, 47
    Luke 16
    Silbella 40
    Thomas 23, 26
Barcraft
    John 172
Barham
    William 138
Barker
    John 132, 142, 164
    Mary 132
    William 170
Barnard
    Sabina 110
    Thomas 110, 152
Barne
    William 69, 176
Barnes
    George 112
    John 112, 184
Barnett
    Elisabeth 187
    Thomas 87
    William 31, 48, 124
Barnwell
    Oliver 117
Baron

Thomas 23
Barracraft
Ed. 22
Barrett
John 91
Philip 68
Barron
Thomas 19
Bartlett
John 184
Sarah 184, 206
Barton
George 25, 58
Lewis 159, 161
Nathan 162
William 6, 9, 22,
23, 63, 80, 89,
91, 92, 127,
129, 148, 186,
205
Bartton
William 54
Bass
Charles 48, 156
Bassey
Joan 8, 11
Joane 41
Michael 8, 11
Michaell 41
Bateman
William 75
Batie
John 133, 146
Sarah 133, 146
Batson
Christopher 189
Edward 91, 98
Hannah 189
Battin
Margery 44
uncle 45
William 44
Bavington
John 64
Baxter
Edmond 160, 161
Edward 76, 199
Roger 53
Thomas 53, 115
Baxton
Francis 79
Mary 79
Bayly
Richard 167, 173,

184, 186, 189,
191
Bayne
John 74, 178
Beadle
Edward 41
Beadly
Charles 112
Beal
Ninian 16
Thomas 181
Beale
Ninian 64
Thomas 76, 172
Beall
Alexander 127
Ninian 25, 157
Beals
Ninion 90
Bean
John 19, 23
Beane
Ann 178
Elinor 44
John 45, 136, 145,
167, 178
Beanes
Christopher 176
Beans
Christopher 193
Beard
Andrew 98
Richard 123, 188,
206
Bearecroft
John 1, 8
Beauchamp
Edm. 29
James 171
Beaumont
Mary 70
Richard 70
Beavell
John 165
Beavens
William 28
Beavins
Rowland 162
Beck
Edward 186
Beckwith
Henry 195
Bedell
Henry 131

William 121, 166, 187
Birkhead
  Rebeckah 149
Biscoe
  John 56
Bishop
  Alce 73
  James 30, 113, 123, 131, 180
  John 30, 195
  Mary 195
  Roger 133, 146, 148
  William 112, 181
Bishopp
  Aaron 163
Biven
  Charles 92
  Thomas 91
Blackader
  Thomas 196
Blackiston
  Col. 43, 60
  Ebenezar 53
  Elisabeth 42, 154, 181
  Nehemiah 46, 131, 154, 181
Blackistone
  Mrs. 158
Blackwell
  Thomas 124, 136, 184, 205
Blackwood
  Phineas 8, 11
Bladen
  William 44, 82
Blagbourne
  Edward 91
Blagg
  Abraham 42, 43
Blaggs
  Abraham 42
Blake
  Jane 67
  Thomas 67, 152, 162, 201
  William 87
Blakiston
  Col. 29, 73
  Ebenezar 1
  Elisabeth 18
  Nehemiah 14, 16, 18
Bland

James 149
Thomas 72
Blandid
  John 151
Blaney
  David 148, 174
Blanford
  Thomas 90
Blay
  Ann 145, 176
  Anna 116
  Barbara 115
  Edward 14, 115, 145, 176, 184
Bleden
  William 27
Blinkhorne
  Robert 74, 90, 98
Blomfeild
  John 54
Bloyd
  Daniel 3
Boarman
  William 136, 157, 194, 204
Bodkin
  James 62
  Peter 31, 64, 78
Body
  Philip 168
  Sarah 168
Bond
  Peter 104
Bonham
  Ann 7
  Anne 10
  William 7, 10
Bonner
  Henry 22, 30, 37, 62, 73, 75, 80, 85, 107, 125, 137, 171, 180
Bonto
  George 169
Booger
  Roger 56
Booker
  John 32, 33, 164, 188
  Thomas 188
Boon
  John 196
Boone
  Humphrey 179

Humphry 191
Jane 188
John 42, 188
Boothby
  Ed. 68
  Edward 33, 34, 42,
    47, 64, 68, 105,
    123, 134, 146,
    159, 165, 169,
    170, 180
  Elisabeth 47
  Mr. 68
Boram
  John 188
Boseman
  William 78, 115,
    155
Bosewell
  Jane 164
Bosman
  Blandina 130
Bosswell
  Jane 32
  Robert 32
Bostick
  Thomas 7
Boston
  Henry 140, 148
Boswell
  Robert 164
Botty
  Lewis 21
Boucher
  John 7
Bouge
  John 21, 77
Boughton
  Richard 140, 157,
    164, 181, 182,
    189, 194
Boulay
  James 122, 131, 144
Bould
  Jane 38
  John 38, 47, 150
Bouldin
  William 115
Boulding
  William 64
Bouling
  James 188
Boulton
  Richard 121
Bourn

Samuell 86, 93
Bourne
  Ann 20
  Anne 34
  Madam 144
  Samuell 20, 34, 56,
    91, 92, 94, 97
  widow 122
Bouye
  John 21
Bovington
  John 190
Bowen
  Benjamin 169
  Jonas 147, 169,
    170, 180
  Richard 171
  Thomas 180
Bowin
  Jonas 134
  William 163
Bowld
  John 80
Bowlds
  John 11
Bowles
  John 14, 44
  Margery 44
  Thomas 5
Bowling
  James 45, 72
  Mary 45
Bowls
  Thomas 13
Boyan
  Jonas 170
Boyce
  Cornelius 159
  Elisabeth 159
Brabant
  William 21
Brace
  Elisabeth 174
  John 174
Bracher
  John 3
Brackhurst
  William 67
Braday
  John 35, 102
Brade
  Andrew 91
Bradley
  Charles 91

Baker 206
John 66, 105, 141
Judith 66, 70, 105,
   203
Mary 2, 8, 12
Robert 171
Roger 2, 8, 12
Samuell 102
Thomas 1, 18, 97,
   157, 158, 182,
   201, 202, 204
William 94
Brookes
John 25, 104
Mr. 19
Richard 90
Thomas 23
Brooks
Baker 24
Margaret 24
Roger 24
Browne
Ann 26
Col. 172
Daniell 201
David 41, 105, 131,
   149, 151
Ja. 151
James 2, 9, 24, 150
John 26, 74, 90,
   196
Mary 45
Michaell 149
Samuell 37, 41,
   106, 145, 201
Thomas 30, 33, 123,
   131, 180
William 98, 107
Browning
Anne 64, 156
Thomas 64, 156
Broxton
William 153
Brufe
Thomas 67
Bruff
Thomas 7, 10
Brufs
George 191, 194
Bryan
Daniell 173
Robert 196
Bryant
Daniell 117, 191,

   203
Bucher
Mr. 90
Bud
John 141
Buddno
Joshua 43
Bull
Thomas 98
Bullery
Ellenor 157
Francis 157
Bullet
Elisabeth 54
Bullett
Elisabeth 38
Bullock
John 2, 9, 16, 17,
   69
Bullwick
xx 96
Buras
John 157
Burchell
Adam 33, 34
Burd
John 90
Burdant
Ralph 43
Burden
Margrett 64
William 64, 101,
   190
Burford
Anne 3
Thomas 3
Burges
George 22, 103,
   124, 180
William 2, 14
Burgis
Capt. 87
Burke
Richard 90, 106
Burman
Ann 18
Anne 48
Robert 1, 18, 48,
   56, 60, 116, 145
Samuell 100
William 100, 112
Burnell
Thomas 21
Burnett

Richard 175
Cheverell
    John 76
Chew
    Ann 162
    Anne 83, 106
    John 197
    Jos. 5
    Joseph 13
    Margaret 5, 13
    Samuell 197, 198
    William 83
Chilcott
    Anthony 102
Childe
    Francis 39
Childs
    Mark 159
Chilton
    Humphrey 145
Chiney
    Eleanor 4, 12, 56
    Richard 4, 12, 56
Chipindale
    Christopher 20
Chirribub
    John 112
Chishire
    Richard 133
Chittam
    John 64, 79, 90,
        109, 127, 205
Chitten
    John 16
Christian
    Lawr. 7
    Thomas 7, 127
Christison
    Winlock 12
Clare
    Marke 179
Clark
    Abraham 153
    Gilbert 8
    Hannah 131
    John 3
    Philip 11, 73, 131,
        157
    Thomas 2, 8, 9
Clarke
    Abraham 21, 33, 81,
        91
    Benoni 196
    Daniell 70

Gilbert 25, 70, 168
Hanah 82
Hannah 50
James 80, 94, 111
Mary 196
Mr. 168
Philip 35, 41, 46,
    50, 54, 58, 59,
    71, 76, 81, 82,
    104, 118, 124,
    136, 145, 146,
    149, 172, 181,
    183
Richard 91, 152,
    158
Robert 23, 191
Thomas 23, 26, 74,
    83, 84, 101, 105
William 63, 116,
    133, 179, 192,
    205
Clauson
    Peter 156
Clawson
    Thomas 91
Clayton
    William 132, 148,
        174
Cleaford
    Grace 69
Clemens
    Thomas 187
Clements
    Thomas 36, 51, 140
Clift
    John 30
Clifton
    Hannah 55, 114
    Thomas 55, 114
Clouds
    Judith 109, 166
    Richard 8, 16, 17,
        25, 26, 32, 38,
        39, 69, 84, 109,
        148, 166, 199
Clyford
    Grace 142
Cob
    James 142
Cobb
    James 93
    Lydia 94, 95
Cobreth
    John 4

Cocke
  Guisbert 190
Cockey
  Sarah 200
  William 200
Cocknell
  Edward 98
Cocks
  William 51
Cockx
  Thomas 51
Colburne
  William 155
Cole
  Edward 23, 74, 84,
    198
  John 14
  Robert 84
  William 5, 13, 93
Coleburne
  William 155
Coleman
  Charles 94
  Stephen 100
Colier
  Robert 141
Collett
  John 41
Collier
  Fra. 89
  Franc. 19, 132
  Francis 3, 86, 87,
    89, 94, 145
  Giles 194
  Grace 194
  James 5, 13
  Mr. 18
  Sarah 3, 132, 145
  Thomas 19, 20, 23
Colliman
  Stephen 100
Collings
  Josias 205
  Patience 205
  Richard 113, 144
  Sarah 113, 144
Collingwood
  William 90
Collins
  Josias 63, 187
  Patience 187
  Thomas 6, 9
Collman
  Dennis 111

Colvert
  William 184
Comberford
  Garrett 206
Comegys
  Cornelius 8
Comigges
  Cornelius 121
  Rebecca 55
Compton
  Thomas 69
Conner
  Edward 151
Conoway
  John 91
Constable
  Henry 167, 179
  Katherine 179
  Samuell 98
  Thomas 90
Coode
  John 76, 152
Cooke
  Amos 6, 10
  Anne 35
  Thomas 35, 142,
    143, 154, 178,
    183
Cooksey
  Philip 189
  Samuell 76, 77, 81,
    120
  Sarah 189
Cooley
  John 205
Coolman
  Thomas 111
Cooper
  John 172
  Nicholas 24, 81,
    109, 128
  Patience 11, 60
  Robert 11, 60
  Roger 22, 103
  Sa. 29
  William 82, 159,
    165, 175, 199
Coosey
  Samuell 108
Copeland
  Samuell 89, 91, 92
Copley
  Ann 19
  Col. 19

Daft
    Anne 166
    Charles 135, 166,
        172, 199
Dakes
    Henry 31, 103, 177
    Persillia 31
Dale
    William 36
Damer
    Thomas 84
    Tomasine 172
Damett
    Hery 106
Dammer
    Thomas 69, 84, 172
    Thomasine 69, 84
Danman
    Cornelius 150
    Jane 150
Dant
    Thomas 136
Darbin
    Thomas 187, 201
Dardeen
    Stephen 148
Dare
    Nath. 152
    Nathaniell 61, 73,
        74, 76, 80, 91,
        105, 155
    William 154, 167
Darffe
    Anne 84
    Charles 84
Daring
    John 165
    Martha 165
Darke
    John 101
    Martha 101
Darnall
    Col. 182, 183, 203
    Henry 23, 88, 128,
        151, 158, 167
    John 198, 203
    Madam 182, 201
    Mary 23, 69, 158
Dash
    John 57, 108
Daugherty
    Nathaniel 10
    Nathaniell 5
David

Elisabeth 142
Jeremiah 142
Davies
    Ann 126
    Elisabeth 61
    Jermiah 61
    John 60, 81, 126
Davis
    Clement 85
    Clementius 182
    Elisabeth 118, 140,
        173
    Francis 4
    Henry 115, 191
    Jeremiah 142, 173
    John 6, 10, 30, 31,
        35, 51, 57, 71,
        92, 98, 103,
        140, 143, 166
    Philip 120
    Thomas 110
Daw
    Edward 90, 96, 98,
        118
    Mary 96, 99
    Nathan 96, 97, 99,
        118
Dawe
    Nathan 96
Dawking
    Joseph 151
Dawmer
    Thomas 16, 17
Dawsey
    James 90
Dawson
    (N) 54
    John 27, 28, 39,
        46, 50, 52, 53,
        66, 70, 71, 86,
        119, 126
    Mary 27, 28, 52, 71
    Ralph 27, 28, 39,
        46, 50, 52, 53,
        66, 70, 71, 86,
        119
    Sarah 27, 28, 52,
        71
    Thomas 133
Day
    Ed. 55
    Edward 29, 122, 128
    Jane 122, 128
    Robert 193

de la Grange
  Arnoldus 105
de Rochebrune
  Louis 192
Deane
  Sarah 126
  William 126
Deare
  Nathaniell 26, 42,
    61
Dearman
  John 141
Deavor
  Richard 201
Deavour
  Richard 22
Decosta
  Francis 81
  Frank 61
Deikes
  Henry 64
Delahay
  C. 174
  Thomas 36, 70, 71,
    113, 114, 199
Delehay
  Thomas 51
Demondidier
  Anthony 34
  Martha 34
Dennis
  Donnack 177
  Donnaugh 10
  Donnock 176
  Donnough 6, 56
  Edmond 73
Dent
  John 23, 108, 176
  Peter 78, 141, 163,
    195
  William 25, 33, 43,
    44, 47, 48, 57,
    73, 80, 90, 119,
    120, 121, 131,
    138, 140, 141,
    175, 186
Denton
  Henry 16, 17, 149,
    193
Denwood
  Levin 55
Deremple
  William 42
Dermont

Mary 186
Derumple
  James 19
  William 80, 92, 98,
    103, 182, 193,
    201
Devege
  Elisabeth 65
  John 65
Devegha
  John 159
Devine
  Elisabeth 87
  Henry 87, 90
Devins
  Henry 103
Devonport
  Humphrey 124
Devor
  Gilbert 90
Dew
  John 3
Deyson
  Elisabeth 34
  William 34, 159
Deyzar
  P. 42
Dicke
  James 91, 151
Dickinson
  Edward 91
Dickson
  Edward 153
Digges
  William 16
Dikinson
  Edward 68
Dillon
  Thomas 198
Dimond
  John 13
Dingley
  Henry 141
Dixon
  Ambrose 5, 10
  Elisabeth 12, 196
  Mary 5, 10
  Robert 105
  Thomas 38, 112, 155
  William 12, 28, 39,
    50, 54, 71, 86,
    196
Dobs
  John 200

Mary 200
Donellan
  Thomas 18
Donellon
  Thomas 28
Donnavan
  Daniell 19
  Mary 19
Donnelan
  Thomas 123, 177
Dorman
  John 152
  Judith 161
  Sellah 161
  Thomas 35
Dorrill
  Nicholas 77, 156
  Nichollas 101
Dorrington
  Ann 205
  Francis 127
  William 205
Dorsey
  Edward 4, 12, 67
  John 4, 12, 67,
    123, 133, 136,
    144, 153
  Joshua 4, 12, 67
Dorsone
  Thomas 75
Dossett
  John 48
Dossey
  William 195
Doude
  Izabella 66
Douglas
  Robert 112
Doulas
  Robert 34
Douse
  William 36
Dowglas
  Robert 66
Downes
  John 40, 53, 201
  Robert 24, 38, 81,
    109, 128
Doxey
  John 48
Doxie
  John 56
Doxy
  John 44

Doyne
  Robert 120, 181,
    199, 204
Doynes
  John 1
Drake
  Diana 78
  William 78, 111,
    128, 156
Draper
  John 35, 184
  Laurence 191
Drapper
  John 67
Drappier
  Laurence 187
Draysdaill
  Robert 161
Drifeild
  Ann 104
  Thomas 104
Drifield
  Thomas 63
Drinkwatter
  James 138
Druet
  Agnes 47
Drury
  Robert 39, 156
Dryden
  Henry 90
Dryfeild
  Anne 22
  Thomas 22
Dudley
  Richard 52
Dudlye
  Richard 52
Dudson
  Richard 178
Due
  John 56
Duglas
  Mary 58
  Robert 58
Duke
  James 99, 193
Duncan
  John 176
Duncon
  John 69
Dunderdale
  Margaret 7, 10
  William 7, 10, 37

Dunkan
    Elisabeth 190
    James 190
Dunkin
    James 27, 115
Dunwell
    Shute 94
Durdan
    Honor 5, 13
    John 5, 13
Durfft
    Charles 74
Durham
    John 134
    Richard 48
Duvall
    Elisabeth 137
    John 62, 85, 106,
      116, 118, 129,
      137
    Maren 62, 75
    Marren 85, 106,
      116, 117, 118,
      129, 136, 175
    Mary 85, 106
Dwyer
    Cornelius 51
    Hugh 51, 102
Dyemond
    John 5

Eager
    George 37, 200
Eagle
    Mary 126, 146
    Robert 63, 146
Eareckson
    Math. 126
    Mathew 40, 53
    Matt. 53
Earekson
    Mathew 147
Eareskson
    Mathew 115
Earle
    James 7, 10
    Mich. 188
    Michaell 179
    Thomas 117, 132,
      141, 142, 202
Ebden
    William 34
Eccleston

Hugh 35, 143, 149
Ecdleston
    Hugh 117
Edge
    Daniell 153
Edlen
    Richard 157, 175,
      200
Edlin
    Edward 115
    Richard 115
Edlo
    Joseph 90
Edloe
    Joseph 4, 18, 40,
      54, 58, 59, 122,
      146
Edlowes Choice
    xx 96
Edmonds
    Benjamin 153
    Elisabeth 5, 13
    Richard 5, 13, 41
Edmondson
    Archibald 144, 165
    James 28
    John 15, 18, 19,
      28, 36, 37, 39,
      43, 50, 51, 53,
      54, 64, 70, 71,
      82, 113, 123,
      139, 143, 157,
      159, 161, 177,
      179, 180, 183,
      184, 185, 188,
      189, 190, 204
    Mr. 87
    Robert 144, 165
Edmunds
    Elisabeth 14
Edwards
    Ann 97
    Anthony 46
    Edward 52
    John 8, 11, 17, 43,
      65, 94, 97, 177
    Joseph 31, 62, 82,
      84
    Mary 82, 84
    Moses 159
    William 4
Edwin
    William 126
Egion

Evins
    Ann 110
    Edward 164
    Obadia 110, 153
Ey
    (N) 121

Fairebrother
    John 187, 194
Fairfar
    Judith 161
    William 160, 161
Fall
    David 86
Farfar
    William 159
Farfare
    William 170
Fary
    Charles 153
    Francis 152
    Joseph 152, 162
    Mary 152, 153
    Robert 153
Fasitt
    William 19, 78
Fassett
    William 145, 153,
      155
Fassit
    William 131
Fassitt
    William 104, 141,
      155
Faulke
    Jane 39
    John 39
Fearnly
    Henry 87
Feast
    Elisabeth 111
    John 111
Feeddeman
    Richard 57
Fefe
    Jacob 113
Feild
    Edward 199
    William 171
Felps
    Walter 12
Fendall
    Capt. 45

Elisabeth 15
James 14, 15, 29,
  33, 37, 41, 42,
  61
John 15, 43
Jonas 44
Samuel 15
Samuell 29, 33, 40,
  42, 61, 62
Fenwick
    Richard 23, 55, 58
Fenwicke
    John 84, 90, 198
    Richard 84, 91
Fergason
    Jane 4
    William 4
Ferguson
    Jane 12
    William 12
Feris
    Charles 159
Ferneley
    Henry 95, 139, 202
Fernley
    Henry 87, 90, 203
Fernly
    Henry 54
Ferrey
    John 161
Ferron
    James 71
Ferry
    John 47, 154, 170
Fiddeman
    Richard 30
Fife
    Richard 90
Finch
    guy 3, 158
    Rebecca 3, 158
Finey
    Katherine 148, 206
    William 148, 206
Finney
    Katherine 167
    Lt. Col. 167
    Mary 167
    William 66, 174
Fish
    Ed. 174
    Edmond 166, 189
    Joan 174
    Joane 166, 189

Gautherine
    Mary 97, 99
    Mathew 99
    Matthew 97
Gauthering
    Mary 116
    Mathew 116
Gayne
    William 159
George
    Samson 39
Gerard
    Jus. 2
    Justinian 9
Gerrard
    Justinian 25, 157
    Thomas 178
Gibbs
    Edward 191
    Richard 79
Gibson
    Elisabeth 34, 41,
      146
    James 51, 102
    John 140, 148
    Martha 7
    Miles 34, 41, 43
    Robert 202
Gifford
    Henry 100, 154
Gift
    Christopher 150
Giles
    John 4, 12
    Mary 4, 12
Gill
    Hugh 22
    James 51, 102
    John 133
    Margarett 22
Gillett
    Walter 193
Gillmin
    Thomas 35
Gillmun
    Thomas 102
Gillum
    John 123
Gladstane
    Jo. 102
Glanrell
    William 171
Glovar
    John 140, 148

Godard
    Christian 161
    Elias 161
    John 198
    Peter 193
Godfrey
    George 157, 181
Godscrose
    John 48
Godsgrace
    John 91, 127
Godshall
    John 3, 54, 100,
      141, 194
Godward
    Christian 173
    Elias 173
Gofe
    Robert 123
Goffe
    Charles 71
Gold
    Barbara 19
Goldesborough
    Robert 168, 187
Goldsborough
    Robert 53, 137
Goldsmith
    George 33, 64
    John 109, 166
    Martha 14, 33
Gonge
    Anne 30
Gongo
    Faith 30, 103
Gongoe
    Faith 63
Goodard
    Peter 193
Goodfellow
    (N) 83, 106
Goodman
    Edmond 201
    Sarah 201
    William 63, 129
Goodson
    Christopher 2, 9
Goodt
    Richard 133
Goosey
    Samuell 89, 92
Goozey
    Jonathon 111
Gordon

Thomas 6, 10
Gore
  George 3
Gorley
  John 58
Gormack
  Judith 159
  Michaell 159
Gott
  Alice 137
  Richard 169
  Robert 75, 80, 137,
    146
Gough
  Charles 17
  Robert 51
  Stephen 54, 199
Gouldborough
  Robert 39
Gouldesborough
  Mr. 121, 176, 178
  R. 70, 131
  Robert 71, 124,
    131, 144, 147,
    155, 158, 165,
    173, 183, 186,
    188, 190, 196
Gouldsborough
  Robert 139
Gouldsmith
  George 123
Goulton
  James 83
Gourbe
  John 63
Gourley
  Barbare 164
  John 121, 164
Goversey
  John 100
Grafton
  Jonathon 14, 40
Graham
  Anne 50
  Robert 2, 11, 50
Grange
  Arnoldus de la 105
Graves
  Amey 94
  Dorathy 74, 164
  Elisabeth 79, 110
  Fran. 73
  James 73, 130, 152
  John 26, 30, 59, 68

Joshua 80, 164
Joshuah 74
William 79, 110
Gray
  Andrew 32, 35, 61
  John 5, 13, 107,
    108, 146, 177
  Michaell 135
  Miles 195
  Philadelphia 32
  Rachell 107, 146
Greare
  Benjamin 79, 110
  Joseph 79, 110, 142
Greares
  Benjamin 175
  Joseph 175
Green
  Edward 22, 163, 176
  Francis 9
  John 177
Greenbury
  Nicholas 192
Greene
  Anne 4
  Edward 15, 16, 169,
    190
  Francis 2
  Leonard 2, 9
  Thomas 4
Greenfeild
  Martha 158
  Mr. 20
  Thomas 1, 18, 19,
    20, 34, 64, 69,
    82, 83, 86, 87,
    88, 89, 90, 91,
    93, 94, 95, 97,
    98, 99, 122,
    133, 136, 144,
    146, 148, 151,
    158, 168, 175,
    176, 182, 185,
    204
Greengoe
  Mary 108
  William 108
Greenhalgh
  Capt. 46
Greenslade
  Orlanda 136
Greenwell
  James 45, 138
Greenwood

Samuel 154
Samuell 170
Gregory
Luke 37, 63, 116,
180
Gresham
John 150
Gresly
Samuell 87
Gressam
John 107
Griffin
Jane 202
Phillip 202
Thomas 2, 9, 54, 61
Griffith
Jenkin 5, 13
Griggs
John 56, 82, 84,
87, 88, 95, 96,
120
Grimshaw
Fredrick 28
Gringoe
William 89
Groom's Lott
xx 95
Groome's Lott
xx 95
Groome
Moses 134, 161
Samuell 42, 155
Grover
John 97, 193
Groves
William 22
Growin
Moses 160
Grundy
Debora 157
Deborah 57, 204
Judith 204
Robert 57, 70, 113,
124, 130, 157,
204
Grunwing
Thomas 26
Guibert
Joshua 15
Gumbrell
William 95
Gunbey
Francis 114
Gunby

Frances 141
Gunnell
Edward 170
George 106, 161,
170
Gunter
Tymothy 91
Guyat
John 22
Guyatt
John 38, 200
Guybert
Joseph 26
Joshua 108, 199
Guyn
John 112
Guyther
Owen 46, 56
Gwin
William 30, 140
Gwins
Richard 159
Gwither
Thomas 2, 9
Gwyther
Thomas 9
Gyatt
John 91

Hackett
Michaell 121
Hadaway
George 147, 201
Peter 155
Haddock
Benjamin 90
Thomas 54
Haggot
John 4, 12
Haimes
William 87, 91, 136
Haims
William 92
Haines
William 17
Hains
William 64
Hale
George 87
Hall
(N) 29
Alice 135
Benjamin 72, 75,

Hazelwood
  John 41
Hazledine
  Richard 196
Head
  William 22, 56, 79,
    88, 200
Heard
  John 171
  Susanna 171
  William 90
Heast
  Elisabeth 79
  John 79
Heath
  James 89, 202
  John 155
  Thomas 180
Heathcot
  John 156, 164
Heathcote
  Joseph 54, 68
Heather
  Mary 35, 102
  William 23, 26, 35,
    83, 102
Heathley
  Kath. 6
  Katharine 10
  William 6, 10
Hedge
  Thomas 41, 125
Hedger
  John 91, 149
  Richard 6, 9
Hedges
  William 171
Heigh
  James 22, 33, 193
Height
  James 149
Heley
  Clement 74, 105
  Darby 67
  Elisabeth 67
Heliard
  Ed. 136
Hellein
  David 73
  Susanna 73
Hellen
  David 90
Hellins
  John 73

Hely
  Clement 74, 84
Hempstead
  Elisabeth 160
Hemsley
  Charles 6, 9, 57
  Phillip 30
  William 132, 179,
    183
Hemsly
  Nich. 174
Hemslye
  William 121
Hen
  Richard 132
Henchman
  Nathaniell 169, 180
Henderson
  John 27
Hendrickson
  Mathew 41
  Mathew. 78
  Mathias 128
Hendry
  John 195
Henley
  Darby 151
Henly
  Ann 153
  Darby 153
  Robert 44
Hensley
  Roger 81
Herbert
  William 21, 25, 32,
    74, 112, 171
Herlock
  George 19
Herman
  August 161
  Caspares 39
  Casparus 60, 128
  Casparus Augustin
    193
  Thom. 118
Herron
  William 70
Hervy
  Thomas 112
Hewell
  Elisabeth 84
Hewes
  George 113
Hews

Robert 174
Hichock
  William 128
Hickes
  Thomas 35
Hickman
  Mary 202
  William 202
Hicks
  Thomas 149, 195
Hide
  Ezekiell 91
  Ruth 110, 175
Higdon
  John 75, 136
Higgens
  Beriah 43
Higgins
  Michaell 22, 200
Higgs
  Ann 39
  Christopher 166
  Henry 39, 165
  Thomas 185
Higham
  Elisabeth 109, 162
  Francis 109, 162,
    174, 176, 202
Highland
  Jane 137
  John 137
Higton
  John 183
Hill
  Clement 29, 49, 50,
    62, 167, 199
  John 134, 180
  Richard 78, 79, 85,
    107, 110, 115,
    144, 178, 187,
    191, 205
  Will. 117
  William 35, 134,
    149, 180
  Willmoth 115
  Wilmoth 78
Hillary
  Thomas 90, 104, 117
Hiller
  Michael 87
Hillery
  Thomas 31
Hilliard
  Edward 40

Hinckes
  John 43
Hinman
  (N) 27
Hinson
  Anne 40
  Charles 120
  John 28, 37, 40,
    158, 206
Hinton
  Thomas 69, 91, 92,
    116
Hitchcock
  William 204
Hobbs
  Robert 91
Hobkins
  Thomas 30
Hobs
  Robert 33
Hobson
  Benjamin 17
  Mr. 38
  Thomas 85
Hodges
  William 164, 197
Hodson
  Nicholas 77, 101
Holbrooke
  Thomas 141
Holden
  James 98
Holdsworth
  Isabell 88
  Isabella 54
  John 54, 88, 96, 98
  Rosamond 99
  Samuell 89, 95, 96,
    99
Holladay
  Thomas 90
Holland
  Frances 163
  Francis 5, 13
  John 26, 42, 118
  Nehemiah 163
  Otho 107, 144
  Richard 163
  Robert 55
  William 59, 60, 77,
    90, 102, 116,
    126, 152, 201,
    203
Hollands

John 91
Hollaway
 John 38
Holleadger
 Philip 127
Hollens
 Abraham 190
 Mary 190
Holles
 John 80
Hollet
 Jacob 63
Holliday
 Thomas 86, 93, 94,
  95, 96
Hollings
 John 91
Hollingsworth
 George 107
Hollins
 Abraham 186
 John 96, 98, 99
 Mr. 92
Hollinshead
 Joshua 90
Hollitt
 Jacob 116
Holloway
 John 3
 Richard 55
Hollyday
 Thomas 86, 87, 88
Holmes
 Archibald 114
Holms
 Sibilla 81
 William 81
Holsworth
 Elenor 177
 John 33, 34, 80,
  118, 125, 129,
  144
 Samuell 56, 177
Holton
 Jesse 28, 36
Homes
 Michaell 92
Honey
 Ann 17
 Nicholas 16, 17
Honsong
 John 149
Hony
 Henry 138

Hooke
 Jeremiah 173
 Roger 173
Hooker
 Thomas 192
Hooper
 George 35, 77, 142,
  164, 173
 Henry 94
 Maurice 192
 William 142, 164
Hopewell
 Agnes 88
 Ann 88
 Anne 84
 Elisabeth 32, 84,
  120
 Hugh 32, 84, 88,
  92, 119
 Mary 88
 Richard 88
 Susanna 88
Hopkins
 Clement 30, 126
 John 137
 S. 172
 Sall. 195
 Samuel 31, 64
 Samuell 27, 43, 55,
  64, 78, 101,
  105, 114, 130,
  131, 135, 141,
  155, 162, 163,
  168, 169, 176,
  177, 190, 194
 Thomas 19, 30, 126
 William 87
Hopper
 Robert 108, 125,
  182, 192, 194
Hopwell
 Elisabeth 62
 Hugh 62
Horne
 Richard 193
Horner
 Thomas 111
Horney
 Elisabeth 12
 Murty 12
Horny
 Jeffry 71
Horsey
 Nathaniell 31

Stephen 19, 135
Hoskins
  Laurence 24
  Phil. 100
  Philip 3, 185
  Phillip 38
Houlston
  Grace 27
Houlton
  Jesse 154
Houseing
  John 125
Houston
  Robert 27, 190
How
  Joseph 91
  Thomas 54, 80, 89,
    129
Howard
  Cornelius 136, 137
  Edmund 141
  Elenor 153, 201
  John 4, 12, 136,
    153, 184, 201
  Jos. 137
  Joseph 136
  Philip 107
  Samuell 123, 136
  William 91
Howe
  Thomas 92, 99, 162,
    174
  Ursula 117
Howell
  Elisabeth 139
  John 139, 168, 186,
    197
  Mary 7
  Nathaniell 7
Howes
  Thomas 96, 97
  William 4, 90, 95,
    97, 99, 117
Howse
  Ursula 74
  William 74
Howsin
  John 178
Howson
  John 139
Hubbard
  Richard 75
Hubbart
  Humphry 38, 46, 49

Richard 72
Simeon 142
Hubert
  Humphry 101
  Simon 69
Huchinson
  Francis 87
Huchison
  Joseph 58
Hudson
  Nicholas 144
Huett
  John 141
Hugh
  Abigall 111
  Charles 111
  Thomas 206
Hughes
  Thomas 90
Hughs
  Abigail 76
  Charles 76
Hughson
  John 197
Hull
  John 100
Hully
  Daniell 106
Hume
  James 109
  John 202, 204
  Sarah 109
Humes
  James 179
  John 91
  Sarah 179
Humphrys
  William 87
Hungford
  Nicholas 16
Hunt
  Benjamin 17, 32,
    35, 142, 173
  Jane 52, 72
  John 179
  William 86
  Wolfran 47, 49, 52,
    57, 59, 62, 67,
    72, 104, 118,
    206
Hunton
  (N) 139
  Mordica 139, 169,
    177

Hurle
  Capt. 52
Hurlock
  Edward 26, 33, 46,
    49, 87
  George 28
Hurson
  John 14
Hurst
  John 179, 194
Hurt
  John 164, 171, 197
Husband
  William 74, 135,
    136, 138, 149,
    166, 199
Husculah
  William 108, 176
Husey
  Thomas 47, 185
Hussee
  Hezkiah 119
Hussey
  Thomas 32, 39, 47,
    50, 69, 123, 178
Hutchings
  Francis 48
Hutchins
  Charles 41, 112
  Francis 89, 91, 93,
    96, 98
  Thomas 121
  William 91
Hutchison
  Thomas 71
  William 72, 187
Hyam
  Elisabeth 202
Hyde
  John 198
Hyhum
  Francis 89
Hykae
  Andrew 33
Hyland
  Jane 201
  John 201
Hynson
  Charles 40, 171
  John 1, 7

Imon
  Able 90

Impey
  Thomas 72, 157, 204
Inchbud
  William 140
Ingerson
  Daniell 120
  Seth 120
Inglish
  Edward 7, 45, 56
  Kath. 7
  William 7, 45, 56
Innes
  Cornelius 163
  William 163
Ireland
  Joseph 90
Isaac
  Edward 90
Isaack
  Edward 60
  Jane 60
Isaacks
  Edward 69
  Joseph 3
  Margaret 3
Isenonnger
  William 91
Island Neck
  xx 86
Isles
  Richard 3
Izgate
  Kalibb 30

Jackson
  Ezakell 202
  Ezekill 185, 190
  Isaack 147
  James 147, 187, 192
  John 68
  Ra. 70
  Ralph 70, 113, 130
  Samuell 6, 10
  Sarah 186
  Simeon 34, 68, 170
  William 188, 196
Jadwin
  Jeremiah 62
James
  Ann 129, 138, 145
  Anne 65, 120, 145
  Charles 39
  Ed. 53, 126

Edward 126, 147,
  156
John 65, 98, 111,
  120, 129, 138,
  145, 157
Jarbo
  John 17
Jarvis
  Humphrey 75
Jarvise
  Dina 110
  Robert 110, 153
Jeakins
  Jeremiah 77
Jeary
  Moses 54
Jefferis
  William 75
Jefferys
  William 187
Jeffris
  William 187
Jenkins
  Francis 155
  Jeremiah 106
  John 52, 99, 171
  Mrs. 94
  Richard 90, 94
Jenkinson
  William 6, 10
Jenkis
  John 96
Jervis
  Robert 91
Joanes
  Moses 141
Joce
  Thomas 126
Johns
  Richard 93, 144,
    162, 192, 198
  William 55
Johnson
  Ann 171
  Cornel. 6
  Cornelius 11, 102,
    112
  Edward 190
  George 91, 171
  Henry 47
  Jeremiah 91, 92, 93
  John 26, 92, 186
  Mark 5, 13
  Robert 101, 163

Samuel 19
Samuell 102
Stephen 201
Thomas 3, 73, 87,
  90
William 16, 18, 28,
  37, 54, 82, 93,
  123, 132, 143,
  161, 177, 204
Jones
  Anthony 114, 177
  Charles 88
  Christopher 20
  Diana 111, 156
  Ed. 76, 112, 128,
    144
  Edward 1, 67, 82,
    108, 125, 130,
    143, 167
  Evan 164, 189, 194
  George 89
  Hugh 89, 92, 160
  Humphrey 112
  Jane 112, 142
  Johanna 89
  Mary 128, 143, 177,
    204
  Mathew 177
  Morgan 14, 112,
    142, 171, 203
  Moses 100
  Nicholas 7
  Philip 133
  Richard 134, 179
  Robert 75, 135, 184
  Salomon 54, 61
  Thomas 19, 91, 150,
    161
  William 6, 7, 11,
    59, 61, 81, 101,
    102, 128, 165,
    166, 183, 189,
    197, 204
Jordain
  Charity 200
  John 183, 200
Joseph
  William 65, 117,
    142, 150, 151,
    178, 184, 191
Jowles
  Col. 93, 123
  H. 94
  Henry 23, 86, 87,

205

Killger
    Garratt 175
    Thomas 154
Kinard
    Richard 111
King
    (N) 124
    Elias 1, 40, 45,
        48, 53, 55, 56,
        60, 68, 87, 115,
        126, 147, 156,
        164, 171, 197,
        206
    John 19, 31, 78,
        103, 132, 179
    Jonathon 90
    Mr. 150
    Obadia 102
    Obadiah 67, 101,
        173
    Robert 31, 149, 179
    Walter 108
Kings
    Richard 82, 83, 146
Kingsale
    xx 204
Kingsbury
    Jonas 151
Kinimon
    Andrew 121
    John 121
Kinimont
    Ambrose 166
    Andrew 167
    John 133, 167
Kininmont
    Andrew 174
    John 174
Kinnard
    Richard 165
Kinnimont
    Ambros 167
Kinniston
    Thomas 186
Kinsley
    John 93
Kirk
    John 173
Kirke
    James 140
    John 36, 61, 68,
        119, 142
Kirker

George 90
Kirkland
    Robert 63
Kirtly
    Thomas 199
Kisby
    Paul 90
Kitly
    Humphrey 165
Knight
    John 63
Knighton
    Thomas 154
Knigton
    Thomas 126
Knowell
    John 98
Knowles
    Lawrence 57, 70,
        113
Knox
    James 82
Kukabert
    Ernesto 93

Lad's Desire
    xx 95
Ladd
    Ellon 95
    John 95
    Richard 95, 96, 99
Laddemore
    Edward 78, 196
Lademore
    Edward 77
Laftan
    Robert 100
Lamar
    Peter 91
Lamb
    Nicholas 203
Lambe
    Hanah 192
    Hannah 192
    Nicholas 192
Lambert
    John 25, 46, 120
Lambeth
    John 32, 141
Lampin
    Elisabeth 6, 10
    Thomas 6, 10
Lampton

Mackdannah
  Bryant 79
Mackdowell
  John 21, 22, 79,
    80, 118, 129,
    153
  Mary 153
Mackeel
  John 173
  William 173
Mackeell
  John 173
  Thomas 173
  William 173
Mackell
  Thomas 173
Mackenny
  Morris 102
Mackey
  Elisabeth 141
Macklen
  Daniell 190
  Margaret 190
Macklester
  James 131
  John 145, 153, 155
Mackmillian
  Peter 38
Macknitt
  John 31
Macubin
  John 4, 12
Madding
  William 139
Maddocks
  Cornelius 102
Maddox
  Alexander 163
  Jonas 78
  Lazarus 130
  Notley 199
Made
  Francis 133
Mading
  Dennis 133
  Mary 133
Madock
  Cornelius 63
Magdaniell
  Bryant 90
Magrother
  James 95
Magruder
  Samuell 152

Mahome
  Timothy 39
Mahoney
  Denis 51
Mahony
  Denis 104
  Timothy 198
Maine
  Robert 133, 136,
    137, 144
Makall
  David 112, 191
Makelfresh
  David 75
Makey
  John 130
  Martha 130
Maldin
  Francis 98
Male
  Mr. 121
Maneley
  Jefferey 96
Maning
  John 118
  Mr. 129
  Nath. 92
Mann
  Ed. 105
  Edward 19, 28, 29,
    36, 51, 59, 70,
    113, 121, 132,
    166, 196
  John 51, 114
  Lucy 196
Manners
  Lydia 45
Manning
  Edward 15
  John 88
  Nath. 92
Manninge
  John 90, 92
Mannyng
  John 95, 96
Mansfeild
  William 154
Manthorpe
  Samuel 18
Manthrop
  Samuell 48, 56, 60,
    145, 176
Marikin
  Hugh 63

Mark
   William 109
Marke
   John 183
Markham
   William 48
Marks
   Anne 79
   William 79, 205
Marriarty
   John 12
Marriorty
   John 4
Marriott
   John 107, 153
Marshall
   William 4, 12
Marsham's Rest
   xx 96
Marsham
   Richard 22, 24, 69,
     122, 128, 158
   Robert 202
Marston
   William 22, 39, 96
Martin
   (N) 125, 129
   Ed. 18
   Elisabeth 88
   Ja. 89, 174
   James 47
   John 96
   Lodwick 64, 170
   Michaell 24, 64
   William 54, 80, 88,
     89, 92, 129
Martyn
   (N) 144
   James 162
   William 129
Masey
   Nicholas 36
Mason
   Alice 103
   Edward 103
   Richard 164, 171,
     197
   Robert 9, 17, 25,
     108, 138, 149,
     158, 166, 172,
     174
   Thomas 6, 9, 56
Masse
   Philip 51

Massey
   Nicholas 36
   Samuell 43
Masson
   Edward 37, 203, 206
   Robert 40
Massy
   Philip 28
Mathews
   Roger 33, 37, 106
   William 30
Mathiason
   Mathias 165
Maulden
   Francis 90
Mauldin
   Francis 98
Mawman
   Thomas 66
Maxwell
   James 34, 65, 134,
     161
May
   Christopher 67
Maynard
   Hanah 31
   Hanna 174
   Hannah 206
   James 31, 206
   John 159, 160
Mead
   Frances 194
   Francis 75
Meade
   William 91
Meads
   William 4, 153
Meakes
   Francis 38
Mears
   William 192
Mecall
   George 50
   James 90, 98
Meceres
   William 90
Meconikin
   Alexander 53
   Allexander 115
   John 53, 200
   Mary 53
Medford
   Thomas 59, 62
Medkuff

Alderman 121
Medley
   Anne 1, 84
   William 1, 74, 84,
     166, 172
Meech
   Thomas 149, 172,
     181
Meekall
   George 131
Meeke
   Francis 61
Meekins
   Richard 69, 164
Meeks
   Sarah 7
   Walter 7
Meene
   Patrick 46
Meetch
   Thomas 149
Meillings
   Ed. 146
Mekall
   George 82
Melton
   William 73
Meradith
   Lewis 1
Merickan
   Hugh 167
Merickin
   Joshua 200
Merideth
   John 202
Meridith
   John 142
Meriken
   Joshua 187, 191
Merikin
   Jos. 63
Meriman
   Charles 170
Meriton
   John 75
Meritton
   John 144
Merriken
   Joshua 179
Metcalf
   Richard 148
Metcalfe
   Richard 166
Michew

William 68
Migdsley
   William 98
Milborn
   Mr. 121
Milburn
   Nicholas 166
Milburne
   Nicho. 196
   Nicholas 70, 113,
     114, 130, 133,
     143, 184, 185,
     206
Miles End
   xx 98
Miles
   Elisabeth 98
   Franc. 35, 57
   Frances 98
   Francis 49, 60, 71
   Frank 58
   John 98
   Mary 98
   Tobias 98, 119
Mileton
   Samuell 142
Mill Runn
   xx 98
Millar
   John 36, 51, 118
   Michaell 144, 171
Millbourne
   Nicholas 57
Millburn
   Nicholas 147
Miller
   David 27
   Dennis 130
   John 59, 62, 100,
     111, 165, 199
   Michaell 55, 60,
     115, 122, 131,
     147, 156
Milles
   Franc. 71
Millson
   Samuell 189
Millstead
   Edward 2
   Elisabeth 2
Milstead
   (N) 181, 186
   Edw. 65
   Edward 8, 47, 73

Elisabeth 8
Milsted
  (N) 124
Miney
  James 128
Ming
  Ed. 61
Minifre
  John 112
Minney
  James 22, 122
Minock
  Michaell 63
Mire
  May 140
Mires
  Christopher 140
Mishew
  William 111, 142,
    184
Mitchell
  Ann 6
  Anne 9
  Benjamin 21
  Hen. 93, 94
  Henry 3, 80, 96,
    98, 129
  Jeffris 155
  John 6, 9
  Thomas 25, 141
  William 95
Moldyn
  Franc. 71
Mollins
  Edward 54, 122
Montague
  William 71
Montgomery
  Hugh 3, 31, 73,
    122, 125, 126,
    138
  Katherine 178
Mony
  Robert 78
Moone
  Ra. 166
  Ralph 70, 114, 144,
    157, 174, 178,
    197
Mooney
  Rose 198
  Thomas 198
Moore
  Alexander 27, 28,

    69
  Bridgett 206
  Cilias 82
  Hugh 23, 63, 82
  James 33, 91, 103,
    158
  Margaret 3
  Mordecai 2, 13, 126
  Mordica 75, 125,
    129, 134, 138
  Mordicay 143, 146
  Ralph 143
  Sarah 27, 38, 69
  Ursula 2, 13
  William 3, 90
Moray
  Nicholas 107
More
  James 88
  John 155
  Thomas 206
Moreing
  John 128
Morgaine
  Elisabeth 166
Morgan
  Abraham 28, 39, 50,
    54, 71
  David 91
  Edward 2, 9, 51
  John 28
  William 109, 171
Moriat
  John 104
Morison
  William 28
Morreing
  John 109
  Mary 109
Morrey
  Garret 176
  Garrett 175
  Nicholas 125, 180
Morris
  Anne 170
  Elisabeth 142, 149
  Jenkin 6
  John 110, 142, 149,
    156, 165
  Thomas 5, 10, 163,
    170, 177
Morrison
  William 167, 168
Morry

Osborn
    Thomas 10
    William 37, 161
Osborne
    (N) 29
    Margarett 41, 42
    Martha 40
    Mary 123
    Samuell 184
    Thomas 5, 78
    William 34, 40, 41,
      42, 123
Osbourn
    Thomas 6
Osbourne
    Margaret 15
    Thomas 11
    William 15
Otridge
    John 40
Ottridge
    John 38, 40
Ouldham
    John 113
Owen
    Richard 61, 142
Owens
    Robert 30, 126
Owlas
    Robert 65, 160

Padgett
    John 89
    Thomas 79, 110
Pagan
    William 86, 89
Pain
    John 86, 87
Paine
    Jane 127
    John 36, 69
Painter
    John 32, 55
    Nicholas 2, 14
Palmer
    Dan. 169
    Daniel 26, 46
    Daniell 49, 170
    Nathaniell 152
    William 116
Pardo
    Jo. 92
Parish

Edward 47
Parker
    Andrew 34, 61, 115,
      143
    Elisabeth 126
    George 3, 73, 122,
      125, 126, 138,
      178
    Henry 89
    James 7
    John 194
    Judith 2, 14
    Katherine 178
    Mrs. 91
    Robert 66, 192
    Thomas 7, 120, 126,
      145, 176
    William 37, 48, 59,
      77, 87, 88, 91,
      93, 94, 98, 102,
      125, 138, 152,
      189
Parks
    John 100
Parney
    Mariel 105, 106
    Mick 106
    Mirriell 106
    Muriell 106
Parratt
    John 196
    William 196
Parrish
    Ed. 59, 118
    Edward 52, 57, 62,
      67, 72, 104, 206
    Mary 52, 72
Parrott
    Gabriell 66, 117,
      123, 134, 150,
      162, 168, 183,
      189, 200
Parsla
    Thomas 87
Parslo
    Thomas 73
Parslow
    Eleanor 20
    Eleoner 26
    Ellen 42
    Thomas 20, 26, 42,
      91, 93, 94, 97,
      177
Parson

Pettybone
  John 4
  Thomas 4
Peverell
  Daniel 37, 41
Phelps
  Walter 4, 108
Pheppard
  Capt. 168
  Peter 4
Philipps
  Daniel 91
Philips
  James 146
Phillips
  James 33, 34, 169,
    170
Phippard
  Peter 58
Pierson
  John 61
Pile
  Jos. 15
  Joseph 8
  Thomas 6
Piles
  Joseph 85, 205
  Thomas 10
Pindar
  Edward 35, 36, 117,
    127, 185
  Sarah 36, 61, 117,
    127, 185
Pinder
  Henry 110, 203
Pindle
  James 56
Piner
  Thomas 14, 178
Pinher
  James 111
Pinner
  Thomas 176
Pinnock
  Martha 3
Pitcher
  Emanuell 21, 44,
    48, 56, 166
  Jane 20, 21, 44
  Manuell 20
Pitt
  John 183, 196
  Phillip 61
Pitts

John 114
Phillip 36, 61
Plaised
  Elisabeth 43
  Elisha 43
Plaissed
  John 43
Plaisted
  Elisabeth 43
  Elisha 64
  John 43
  Licia 43
  Lisha 43
Plater
  (N) 168
  Ann 181, 199
  George 13, 15, 32,
    48, 49, 50, 59,
    62, 65, 68, 82,
    90, 94, 120,
    124, 151, 181,
    199, 204
Playne
  Kath. 7
Ploumer
  Elisabeth 80
  Thomas 80, 129
Plowden
  George 3
Polk
  John 155
Pollard
  Edward 70, 124,
    130, 196
  John 131
  Martha 70
  Richard 91
Ponds
  Grisl 57
Poole
  Edward 101, 173
  John 27
  Martha 27, 130
Pope
  John 55, 135, 184
Porten
  Paul 42
Porter
  Elisabeth 169
  Hugh 177
  James 77
  William 169
Portwood
  Elisabeth 2, 9

John 2, 9
Pottel
    Francis 5
Pottell
    Francis 13
    Mary 5, 13
Poulter
    Henry 26, 38, 199
    Mary 16
Powell
    Charles 35, 61,
        101, 117, 127
    Cornelius 171
    Elisabeth 171, 177
    Gabriell 114
    John 66, 90, 103,
        135, 162, 163,
        177, 182, 191
    Mary 105
    Thomas 186
    Walter 163
    William 22, 37, 63,
        163
Power
    Bridgett 197
    John 57, 197
Prance
    Morgan 2, 9
Prater
    Jonathon 90
Pratt
    George 67
    Henry 120
Preene
    Jacob 146
Preston
    Samuell 90
Price
    Andrew 188, 197
    Jane 190
    John 52, 123
    Mordica 133, 169
    Richard 33, 48
    Thomas 189, 202
Prichett
    Hann 142
    William 61, 142
Pride
    Benjamin 129
Prior
    Margarett 111
    Thomas 111
Prise
    Edward 190

Jane 190
Procter
    Rachell 107, 123
    Robert 123, 136,
        137
Prous
    George 195
    Mary 195
Prouse
    George 195
    Mary 195
Pryer
    Thomas 127
Pryor
    Margarett 192
    Thomas 192
Pue
    Ann 26
    Thomas 2, 9, 24, 26
Purie
    Edward 132
Purnall
    Richard 122
Purnell
    John 55, 163, 177
    Richard 22
    Thomas 39, 55, 91,
        98, 105, 163
    William 140
Pursell
    John 51, 52
Pursinah
    Arthur 183
Pye
    Ann 185
    Col. 185, 191
    Edward 1, 2, 8, 12,
        144, 172, 178,
        184
Pyner
    Thomas 126

Quan
    John 196
Quatermus
    Jane 75
    John 75, 202
Quillam
    Thomas 162
Quinney
    Sutton 14

Rabetts
  William 192
Rablin
  John 69
Racke
  Richard 103
Rackliffe
  Charles 168
  Elisabeth 169
  Rackliffe Charles
    169
Raddon
  Henry 68, 119
Radford
  John 90
Radiagh
  Jane 20
  Michaell 20, 21,
    32, 44
Rallinges
  Edward 156
Rallings
  John 65
Ramiger
  Samuell 175
Ramsey
  Bartholomew 7, 10
Randolph
  (N) 72
  Edward 18, 46
Raullings
  Jane 153
  Richard 153
Raven
  Luke 160, 170
Rawlens
  Paul 149
Rawlings
  Daniell 192
  John 101, 111, 115,
    118, 141, 164,
    173, 174, 176,
    180, 184, 191,
    195
  Richard 202
Rawlins
  John 67, 105
Ray
  Alexander 133
  John 107, 167
Raye
  Alexander 167
Raylon
  Sarah 46, 81

William 46, 47, 81
Raynolds
  Thomas 185
Read
  Amy 182
  Henry 60, 78
  James 187
  John 26, 49, 97,
    182, 191
  Perthenia 60
  Robert 98
  Walter 135
  William 26, 49
Reade
  John 132
  William 46
Realy
  Michaell 135
Reccinkles
  James 98
Red
  Bethania 54
  Henry 54
Redd
  William 57
Redgrave
  Abraham 156, 165
  Margaret 156
  Mary 165
Ree
  Thomas 188
Reed
  Henry 132, 143
  John 90
  Parthenia 143
  Robert 90
  William 90
Reeves
  Edward 5, 13
  Jane 175
  Mary 5, 13, 14
  Ubgatt 175
Regon
  James 189, 194
  Joane 189
Rennalls
  George 54
Renolls
  George 84
Reston
  Thomas 160
Revell
  Randall 19
Reyley

Salter
    John 121, 166, 174,
       183
Samon
    Thomas 21
Samson
    Richard 134, 161
Samway
    Jonathon 174
Samwes
    Jonathon 149
    Mary 149
Sander
    Edward 112
    William 128
Sanderline
    John 91
Sanders
    Edward 167
    James 22, 75, 85,
       117, 129
    John 135
    Mathew 194
    Richard 52
    William 111, 127
Santee
    Christopher 196
Sapcoate
    Abraham 140, 182
Sargeant
    Damares 47
    John 140
    William 47
Sarson
    Edward 49
Sawell
    Ignatius 143
    Peter 193
Sayle
    Clement 173
Saywell
    James 36, 132
Scarborough
    Mathew 55
    Mr. 174, 206
Scarbrough
    Mathew 31, 163, 195
    Walter 163
Scholdfield
    Henry 163
Scholfeild
    Grace 190
Scholfield
    Henry 163

Scidmore
    Ed. 53
Scoot
    William 197
Scoott
    William 188
Scot
    Cuthbert 11
    Thomas 11
Scott
    Edward 166
    James 30, 168
    John 41, 63, 80,
      91, 118, 125,
      129, 144, 182,
      201, 202
    Sarah 41
    Thomas 8
    William 30, 133,
      168
Scrivener
    Benjamin 15, 25,
      107
Scrivner
    Benjamin 13
Scrukin
    Mathew 158
Scutt
    John 187, 192
    Katherine 187, 192
Scuty
    Bryan 199
Seager
    Charles 16
Seales
    Clement 123
Sealous
    Mary 164
    Stephen 164, 173
Seatam
    Elisabeth 121
Seaton
    Elisabeth 132
    Joseph 132
Seaward
    Josias 191
Seawell
    Timothy 16
Seawick
    John 12
    Susanna 12
Sedgewick
    James 6, 9
Sedgweek

James 113
Sedgwick
  Ann 110, 171
  James 113
  Thomas 37, 97, 110,
    143, 171
Sedwick
  Thomas 93
Sedwicks
  Thomas 90
Seeling
  George 98
Seemes
  Anthony 124
  Fortue 82
  Marmaduke 82
Segar
  Charles 17
Selby
  Daniell 190
  Edward 4, 12, 107,
    150
  Mary 190
  Parker 177, 190
  Thomas 190, 195
Seley
  George 96, 97
Sellman
  John 191
Selous
  Mary 173
Sempill
  Joseph 37
  Mary 37
Sequence
  John 156, 196
Sergeant
  (N) 186
  Damarias 181
  Damaris 65, 73
  John 140, 148
  William 24, 65, 73,
    181
Sergent
  (N) 124
Serjant
  Mr. 148
Serjeant
  Damaras 8
  Damoras 2
  William 2, 8
Seserson
  Isaac 132
Seth

Jacob 140
Settle
  William 87
Sewall
  Jane 172
  Maj. 120, 172
  Nicholas 3, 62,
    144, 178, 184,
    191
Seward
  Josias 130
Sewell
  Jane 130
  Thomas 130
Sewick
  John 4
  Susanna 4
Shaderin
  Jeremiah 139
Shainton
  William 32
Shanahan
  William 51
Shankland
  William 190
Sharadine
  Daniell 91
Sharp
  William 12, 36, 39,
    50, 71, 185,
    188, 204, 205
Sharpe
  William 28, 54
Shaw
  Christopher 159,
    160
  Ralph 157, 181, 194
  William 4
Sheirendine
  Jeremiah 91
Sheirtliffe
  William 136
Shenton
  William 164
Shepard
  Robert 193
Shephard
  Richard 91
Shepherd
  Charles 24
  Francis 67
  Richard 92
Sheppard
  Charles 47

Sheridan
  Jeremiah 171
Sheriden
  Jeremiah 80, 110,
    111
Sheridin
  Daniel 4
Sheridon
  Jeremiah 109
Sherindine
  Jeremiah 92, 93
Sherwood
  Daniell 52, 126
  Hugh 70, 105, 203
Sheul
  Owen 90
Shinton
  William 69
Shirley
  Richard 21
Shirly
  Richard 84
Shirtley
  William 172
Shirtly
  William 135
Shittle
  William 90, 98
Short
  Ann 202
  George 19, 23, 145,
    178
  John 79, 103, 104,
    119, 202
Shrigley
  John 116
Sickes
  Thomas 62
Sickmore
  Samuell 160
Sides
  Alice 113
  John 113, 154
  Peter 113, 154
Sikes
  Thomas 59
Sikmore
  Samuell 160
Silvester
  James 140, 157
Simes
  Anthony 72, 75
Simmons
  Joseph 135

Simms
  Alexander 156
Simons
  Daniell 98
  William 91
Simpers
  Thomas 39
Simpson
  Anne 116
  Jeremiah 116
  Jeremias 93
  John 93
  Thomas 93
Sims
  Anthony 157
Simson
  Ann 93
  William 147, 155,
    201
Sincler
  William 68
Skeddmore
  Richard 67
Skidmore
  Ed. 101
  Edward 39, 40, 78,
    100
  Joseph 40
  Michaell 40
  Nicholas 75, 80
  Samuell 40
Skillington
  Thomas 161, 162
Skilton
  John 65
Skinner
  Ann 157, 158
  Clarke 142
  Robert 158, 159,
    193, 200
Skipper
  James 172
  Jane 16, 81, 172
  John 16, 81
Skippers
  John 91, 94
Skrigley
  John 57
Slade
  Anne 3
  William 65
Sladen
  William 147
Slany

John 91
Sutton
  John 61, 117
  Thomas 139
  William 133, 134,
    165, 181
Swaine
  John 188, 195
  Mary 195
Swallow
  John 132, 140
Swallwell
  John 143
Swan
  Edward 119, 182
  Mary 119, 182
Swann
  James 2, 9, 24
Sweales
  Francis 48
Sweatnam
  Edward 8, 60, 120
Swelling
  William 52
Swetnam
  Edward 126
Swift
  Margarett 48, 116
  Michaell 48, 116
Swinstire
  John 201
Syley
  John 51
Symons
  John 167
Sympson
  Thomas 39

Tafft
  Thomas 181
Taft
  Thomas 157
Tailer
  William 194
Tailler
  Magdlen 194
  William 194
Talbot
  Elisabeth 16
Talbott
  Elisabeth 17
Tall
  Phillip 36

Talley
  John 53
Taman
  John 193
Tanehill
  Andrew 119, 202
Taney
  Michaell 95, 142,
    143, 197, 198,
    203
  Mr. 97
  Thomas 48, 110,
    111, 139, 142,
    148, 202
Tanman
  John 91
Tant
  John 199
Tanyhill
  Andrew 4
Tarfer
  William 170
Tarr
  Elisabeth 135
  John 135
Tasker
  Mr. 97
  Thomas 1, 18, 19,
    20, 52, 88, 89,
    91, 93, 94, 95,
    96, 97, 98, 99,
    152
Tauney
  Thomas 79
Taunhill
  Andrew 103
Taunt
  John 17, 49, 54, 64
Tawney
  Michaell 91, 93
Taylard
  William 19, 59, 65,
    108, 121, 130,
    131, 206
Tayler
  John 155
Taylor
  Abraham 40
  Edward 191
  Gilbert 162, 195
  Henry 31, 40, 45,
    89, 92, 104
  Hope 176
  Jacob 197

Joseph 28
Rowland 134
Thornburgh
Ann 169
Rowland 169
Thornbury
Rouland 160
Thorowgood
Francis 27, 163
Thurston
David 159
Martha 159
Thomas 106, 145,
201
Tibbals
John 28
Tickpenny
John 92
Tilby
Charles 107
Tilden
Charles 14, 38,
156, 178
Tiley
John 166
Tilghman
Richard 188
Tillotson
John 197
Tilton
Humphry 120
Tinsly
Thomas 90
Tipton
Ed. 57
Edward 1
Toas
Daniel 71
Thomas 51
Tolly
Roger 59, 61
Tolye
John 28
Tomkins
William 114, 163
Tomlin
Samuell 155
Tompson
John 27
Richard 112
Tong
John 2, 9
Tonnard
Andrew 35, 70, 113

Thomas 35
Toope
William 36
Topping
Thomas 90
Torner
Thomas 108
Totershill
Laurence 64
Toullson
Joseph 147
Toulson
Andrew 60, 115, 201
Sarah 60, 115
Towe
Robert 51, 102
Towell
Thomas 19, 23
Towers
Jonathon 114, 164
Margaret 164
Margarett 114
Tracy
Charles 91
Treuant
Robert 158
Trew
John 156, 178, 200
William 156, 200
Trotter
William 115
Trotton
Roger 8, 11
Troughton
Elisabeth 184
Roger 184
True
John 171
William 171
Trueman
Henry 87, 110, 142,
202, 203
Jane 142, 202
Mary 57, 157
Truman
Henry 87, 127, 138
Jane 127
William 158
Trumell
Mich. 53
Michaell 53
Tucker
Dorathy 116
Seaborne 116

Bazill 145
Elisabeth 45, 172
Humphrey 70, 99,
    119, 130, 178
Humphry 8, 12, 25,
    45
Ignatius 85
John 85
Margery 100, 119
Marjery 130
Notley 100, 178,
    181, 203
Nuteley 119
Rebecka 84
Thomas 84, 181, 203
William 45, 49, 64,
    172
Warwicke
    William 194
Wasker
    John 93
Waters
    Christopher 182
    John 191
    Joseph 90
    Penellope 191
Watkin
    Samuell 151
Watkins
    Alice 31, 124
    Ann 19, 138, 140,
        148, 197
    Anne 150
    Francis 170
    James 41, 84
    Mary 170
    Peter 140, 148, 197
    Richard 138
    Samuell 19, 43, 49,
        50, 54, 65, 82,
        123, 146, 150,
        151, 157, 161,
        167, 168, 186,
        200
Watkinson
    Cornelius 90
Wats
    Peter 132
Watson
    Jane 50
    John 11, 21, 32,
        44, 46, 48, 50,
        131
Wattermore

John 105
Watters
    John 137, 146
    Thomas 30, 69, 81
Watts
    Charles 26, 59, 62,
        81
    Elisabeth 62, 81
    James 99
    Peter 113, 132, 138
    William 52, 62,
        114, 121, 138
Wattson
    John 21, 127
Waughob
    Thomas 2, 9, 11
Waughop
    Thomas 49, 50
Wayman
    L. 137
    Leon. 137
    Leonard 66, 107,
        151, 192, 194
    R. 70
Weathers
    Samuell 159
Webb
    (N) 44
    John 101, 114, 195
    Robert 67
    Thomas 7
    William 156, 164,
        197
Webster
    John 111, 127, 134
Welch
    John 107, 122, 151
    Richard 191
    Silvester 107, 122,
        151
    Thomas 51
    William 7, 10
Welham
    Thomas 77, 83
Wellden
    Henry 147
Weller
    Richard 95, 97, 99
Wells
    Benjamin 169
    Catherine 166
    George 169
    Haniball 35
    John 40, 53, 60

105, 117, 145,
152, 165
Whitton
(N) 145
Ann 39
Richard 39, 120,
129, 138, 145,
157
Thomas 65, 101,
129, 138, 154,
175, 196
Whitworth
Sydrock 206
Syrack 184
Whrightson
John 159
Wickers
Thomas 34
Wickham
Nathaniell 152
Sabena 152
Wicks
Joseph 1, 14, 206
Wigget
Joseph 36
Wiggett
Joseph 36, 51, 114
Wight
John 148
Wild
Robert 6, 9, 56
Wilde
Abraham 107
Wilder
John 25, 119, 178
Wilkinson
William 92, 96,
135, 170
Wilkison
William 169
Willham
Thomas 7
Williams
Baruch 90, 93
Baruck 31, 104, 117
Benjamin 66, 103,
107, 116, 126,
138, 151
Charles 195
Edith 66
Edward 36, 101,
114, 173
Elisabeth 54, 81
Hugh 149

Isaac 110
Isaack 79, 149, 175
Jacob 88
John 27
Joseph 66, 103,
116, 126, 138
Joseph John 47
Peter 191
Richard 27
Robert 50
Samuell 40
Thomas 54, 81
William 31, 52, 89,
90, 92
Williamson
Christopher 120
Samuell 47, 49
Willimott
John 90
Willin
Alice 6, 10
Thomas 6, 10, 56
Willis
John 61
Philip 176
Phillip 79
Willisey
Philip 79
Willkinson
John 194
William 64, 201
Willman
John 147
Willmer
Lambert 156
Simon 156
Willmott
Joane 170
John 95
Robert 134
Willoughby
William 101
Willson
Alexander 75, 113
Anne 122
Elisabeth 37, 116,
180
Ephraim 78, 169
Giles 120, 138
James 101
John 37, 116, 180
Joseph 122, 181,
193, 203
Mary 101, 167

Roger 36, 68, 119
Woollman
  Henry 140
Worgan
  Mary 105
  Sarah 104
  William 25, 104,
    115
Workman
  Anthony 53
Worley
  John 148
Worrell
  William 106
Worthington
  John 133, 134, 179,
    192, 203
  Samuell 78
Wosly
  Samuell 67
Wouldhave
  William 78
Wridson
  John 111
Wright
  Ann 202
  John 80, 100, 154,
    202
Wrightson
  Mary 113
Wriothesly
  Henry 26, 68, 76,
    85, 106, 153
Wroth
  James 184
Wyott
  Philip 143
Wythinton
  Thomas 21

Yarsly
  Mary 87
Yates
  Rebeccah 44
  Robert 18, 24, 25,
    44, 80
Yeackly
  Michaell 93
Yearsley
  Thomas 49, 58
Yearsly
  Thomas 35, 71
Yeats

Capt. 87
Yeovell
  Thomas 174
Yerberry
  Thomas 7
Yerbery
  Elisabeth 7
Yokley
  Mich. 155
Yong
  Samuell 5
  Thomas 6, 9
Yonger
  John 7
Yore
  James 11, 15, 18,
    60
Yorke
  Elisabeth 160
  Mary 160
  William 160
Youell
  Thomas 120
Young
  Arthur 89
  Athur 192
  Elisabeth 136, 167,
    183, 204
  George 31, 79, 119
  Jacob 196
  Samuell 22, 69, 75,
    85, 107, 117,
    129
  Thomas 28
Younge
  George 89
Younger
  John 10, 56
  Samuell 13
Yovell
  Sarah 166, 200
  Thomas 166, 200

INDEX OF EQUITY CASES

www.ingramcontent.com/pod-product-compliance
Lightning Source LLC
Chambersburg PA
CBHW061005280326
41935CB00009B/835